EDITED BY

Patricia J. Kolb

Social Work Practice

with Ethnically and Racially Diverse

Nursing Home Residents and Their Families

COLUMBIA UNIVERSITY PRESS

NEW YORK

Columbia University Press
Publishers Since 1893
New York   Chichester, West Sussex
Copyright © 2007 Columbia University Press
All rights reserved

Library of Congress Cataloging-in-Publication Data

Social work practice with ethnically and racially diverse nursing home residents and their
    families / edited by Patricia J. Kolb.
        p. cm.
    ISBN-13: 978-0-231-12532-1 (alk. paper)
    ISBN-13: 978-0-231-12533-8 (pbk: alk. paper)
    1. Social service—United States.   2. Nursing home patients—Services for—United
States.   3. Minorities—Services for—United States.   I. Kolb, Patricia J.
    HV91.S6257   2007
    36216—dc22

                                                                                2006102257

Columbia University Press books are printed on permanent
    and durable acid-free paper.
Printed in the United States of America
c 10 9 8 7 6 5 4 3 2 1
p 10 9 8 7 6 5 4 3 2 1

Social Work Practice
with Ethnically and Racially Diverse
Nursing Home Residents and Their Families

For Social Workers who strive to achieve cultural competence

In memory of George and Mary Jane Kolb & Cristina and Mario Torchio

Contents

Acknowledgments

It is with great pleasure that I acknowledge the contributions of people who have made the writing and publication of this book possible. This book would not exist if the contributors had not been willing to expend a great deal of time and effort over many years sharing their professional, academic, and personal knowledge. I have learned from each contributor and know that this book will be useful to people in many disciplines who work with older adults and their families in nursing homes and other settings.

I am grateful to the staff at Columbia University Press for understanding that this book is necessary and important, and appreciate the support that I have received from the editorial staff. The feedback provided from the individuals who reviewed this book has been very important.

I am grateful to Lehman College administration, faculty and staff in the Department of Sociology and Social Work, and to colleagues and staff in other departments who make this college a fine professional environment in which to work. Professor Norma Phillips, Director of the Social Work Program, and Professor Madeline Moran, Chairperson of the Sociology and Social Work Department, have been very supportive to me and understand the importance of gerontology in today's society. I am privileged to deepen my understanding of people and of human diversity daily as I interact with the wonderfully diverse student body at this college.

Finally, I appreciate the contributions of my relatives the Kolbs, Torchios, Jochers, and all the members of their extended families who have helped me to learn and think deeply about culture in relation to myself and others. My understanding of myself and others has been deepened by far too many people to mention here, but especially by Dr. Stanford M. Lyman, Dr. Bernice Berk, Ms. Blanche Polovetz, Ms. Anna Capell, and Ms. Enriqueta Thomas.

I am grateful to my son, Anthony Torchio, for his patience while I was working on this book, his confidence in my ability to accomplish this project, and his understanding of why it is important.

Contributors

MARIA CUADRADO, M.S.W., PH.D was born in Bayamón, Puerto Rico, and migrated to New York City as a child. She received her B.A. from Hunter College of the City University of New York and subsequently served in Ecuador with the Peace Corps. Dr. Cuadrado earned her M.S.W. at Fordham University and a Ph.D. in Urban Education from Fordham. She was Director of Social Services at a nursing home in Brooklyn for ten years and a Deputy Director at the New York City Department for the Aging. Her current position is at the Institute for Puerto Rican/Hispanic Elderly, where she oversees the agency's senior services.

MOLLY EVERETT DAVIS, M.S.W., ED.D. is an Associate Professor in the Social Work Department at George Mason University. She received her M.S.W. from Tulane University and Ed.D. from Florida State University. She has an extensive background in practice and research in gerontological social work. Dr. Davis is an expert trainer for the Gero Education Center funded by the Council on Social Work Education and John A. Hartford Foundation, and has experience as a nursing home ombudsman. She engages in research, writing, and training in gerontology and intergenerational practice.

PRISCILLA DAY, M.S.W., ED.D. is a full professor at the University of Minnesota at Duluth, where she has taught in the Department of Social Work since 1993. She received her M.S.W. from the University of Minnesota at Duluth and Ed.D. from the University of Minnesota Leadership Academy. Dr. Day is an enrolled member of the Leech Lake Band of Ojibwe and returns to her home reservation often for ceremonies and family events. Her areas of teaching and research include American Indian family preservation and cultural competence. She is the Director of the Center for Regional and Tribal Child Welfare Studies at the University of Minnesota at Duluth.

ROSEMARIE AMATO HOFSTEIN, L.M.S.W. received her M.S.W. from Fordham University with a concentration in Geriatrics and Health. She is Director of Social Services at a nursing home in New York City and has been a practicing social worker in long-term care for more than twenty years. She is experienced in hospice care and certified in palliative care, and has led support groups for the Alzheimer's Association. She has provided supervision for baccalaureate and master's degree social work students for more than twelve years.

SUK-YOUNG KANG, M.S., PH.D. is an Assistant Professor at the Arizona State University College of Public Programs School of Social Work. He received his M.S. and Ph.D. degrees from the Columbia University School of Social Work, and his B.S.W. from Seoul National University, Korea. Prior to beginning doctoral studies, he was the Program Coordinator of home-based case management at the Korean American Senior Center in Chicago. His research interests include family caregiver strain, community-based social work for frail Korean and Chinese elders, and self-care strategies among elders, and he is a faculty scholar in the John A. Hartford Foundation Geriatric Social Work Faculty Scholars Program.

PATRICIA KOLB, M.S.S.A., M.A., PH.D. is an Associate Professor in the B.A. and M.S.W. programs in social work at Lehman College of the City University of New York. She received her M.S.S.A. degree in social work from Case Western Reserve University and M.A. and Ph.D. degrees in sociology from the New School for Social Research. Dr. Kolb has more than twenty-five years of direct practice experience in gerontological social work and has worked in community programs and a nursing home. Her research and writing interests include race, ethnicity, and nursing home placement; nursing home social services; gerontological theories; and student interest in careers in gerontological social work. Her previous book was *Caring for Our Elders: Multicultural Experiences with Nursing Home Placement*.

SU-JEONG PARK, M.S. received her graduate degree in social work from the Columbia University School of Social Work and B.A. from Pusan National University in Korea. She is a social work doctoral student in the Hunter College program at the City University of New York Graduate Center. She is Director of Social Work at a nursing home in New York City and has more than ten years of gerontological social work experience in long-term care. Her professional interests include Asian American elders in long-term care, aging policy, mental health, minority aging issues, social support and quality-of-life issues among elders. She has developed and implemented culturally appropriate interventions, programs, and in-service staff training pertaining to Asian American nursing home residents.

TAZUKO SHIBUSAWA, PH.D., LCSW is an Associate Professor at the New York University School of Social Work. She received her M.S.W. and Ph.D. from the University of California, Los Angeles. Dr. Shibusawa's research is in the area of aging among vulnerable populations, including Asian immigrant elders, drug-involved elders, and older victims of partner abuse. Her clinical experiences include Director of Social Services at a Japanese nursing home in California; psychiatric social worker for the Los Angeles County Department of Mental Health, and co-director of Counseling International in Tokyo, Japan.

YVETTE SOLIS-LONGORIA, M.S.W. received her B.S.W. from Texas State University and M.S.W. from Our Lady of the Lake University. She has worked for many years in gerontological social work, including work as a Licensed Clinical Social Worker at a nursing home in San Antonio, Texas, and has actively participated in professional organizations.

RHODA KITCHING WONG, M.S.W., L.C.S.W.-R. works at a New York State psychiatric hospital serving multicultural populations. She has worked for more than twelve years in health and mental health social services since completing her graduate degree at the University of Alabama. She worked for several years in nursing homes and continues to participate and engage in study of culturally sensitive programs serving Chinese-speaking older adults, mental health consumers, and their caregivers. Her women's empowerment and grassroots organizing work in Hong Kong and New York City created a foundation for her social work interests. She especially thanks Dr. Kolb for the opportunity to write this chapter that reflects Ms. Wong's experiences and knowledge from working with Chinese-speaking older adults and for Dr. Kolb's editorial assistance.

Social Work Practice
with Ethnically and Racially Diverse
Nursing Home Residents and Their Families

Introduction

Patricia J. Kolb

The primary goal of this book is to provide social work practitioners with information about the histories, traditions, and contemporary experiences of older adults and their families from diverse ethnic and racial groups in the United States, and to present culturally appropriate ways to work with nursing home residents and their families. Included in the book are groups that have not used nursing homes in large numbers in the past but may need to do so in the future because of certain social changes: increased life expectancy; a growing number of women, the traditional caregivers in many cultures, working outside the home; and higher divorce rates resulting in large numbers of women having to work outside the home or take on additional employment for financial reasons (Kolb 2003). The continuing lack of adequate institutional supports outside the family is another factor preventing older adults from remaining in their own homes or living in the homes of relatives for longer periods (Kolb 2003).

The contributors to this volume provide specific demographic information about people belonging to the populations they are discussing, as well as a wealth of historical, cultural, and practice information essential to understanding and providing services to older adults and their families. The book offers a comprehensive, focused examination of cultural phenomena and their relevance to culturally competent social work practice and practice approaches. Many of the topics explored in each chapter are similar, but each addresses specific experiences of members of the racial or ethnic group being discussed.

Older adults and their families—across groups—share experiences, both past and present. For example, relatives in diverse ethnic, nationality, and racial groups share a history of providing assistance to older relatives, and many families continue to do so as needed. Similarly, older adults in many groups provide intergenerational assistance to relatives. For all the groups examined in these chapters, attitudes, values, and behaviors pertaining to intergenerational relationships have been shaped by historical experiences, including victimization resulting from the prejudiced attitudes and discriminatory behaviors of others, and some of these experiences are similar in different groups.

The need for culturally competent gerontological social work practice is highlighted by demographic realities in the United States documented by census data. In 2004 the U.S. Census Bureau American Community Survey found that the population in this country was approximately 285.7 million, and 12 percent was estimated to be age sixty-five or older (U.S. Census Bureau 2004). Within the U.S., 12 percent of the population identified themselves as black or African American; 1 percent as American Indian and Alaska Native; 4 percent as Asian; 14 percent as Hispanic/Latino; less than .5 percent as Native Hawaiian and Other Pacific Islander; and 67 percent as white non-Hispanic. There were also people who reported more than one racial ancestry or named an ancestry outside the above categories (U.S. Census Bureau 2004).

There are approximately seventeen thousand Medicare and Medicaid certified nursing homes nationwide with more than 1.6 million beds (Administration on Aging 2005). Addressed in these chapters are life experiences, past and present, of older adults in nursing homes who are African American, American Indian, Chinese American, Italian American, Japanese American, Korean American, Mexican American, or Puerto Rican, all with diverse histories, heritages, and cultural practices. This book is only one part of each reader's journey toward cultural competence, but, for many, it will be an important part of their personal and professional journeys. The experiences of people belonging to different ethnic and racial groups are obviously quite diverse; these chapters provide important insights but do not replace the objective assessment of each individual with whom you work as a social worker.

This book has been written by social workers for social workers and other service providers, as the contributors believe that gerontological services must be provided in culturally competent ways in order to achieve the very best services. Cultural attributes, such as language, traditions, norms, values, and sanctions, are influential in shaping the experiences of nursing home residents and their relatives and friends. Although there are both long-term and short-term stays in nursing homes, and some nursing home residents are younger, a great many nursing home residents have experienced physical or cognitive debilitation and increased dependence as older adults, and cultural differences create variations in how these changes are experienced and addressed. Distinct personality and situational variables also contribute to unique experiences. The authors touch upon all these areas in presenting information they consider important in understanding and providing services to older adults and their families from different ethnic and racial groups.

Relatively little has been written about the characteristics, needs, and experiences of racially and ethnically diverse nursing home residents and their families and the requirements for appropriate social work practice among residents from diverse cultures. This volume, along with my previous book, *Caring for Our Elders: Multicultural Experiences with Nursing Home Placement* (2003), is intended to help meet the need for more information on this subject.

McGoldrick, Giordano, and Garcia-Preto (2005) suggest that dimensions of culture include ethnicity, gender, socioeconomic status, geography, race, religion, and politics. Information about these is presented in this book, but cultural competence or cultural sensitivity is not limited to learning about specific dimensions of culture, as these scholars are well aware. To understand the complex factors that have contributed over lifetimes to the perspectives of nursing home residents and their families, Bonder, Martin, and Miracle's (2001) concept of "culture emergent" is useful, as it reflects the multiple influences shaping human experiences in which "culture emerges in interaction of transient circumstances and traditional patterns of behavior" (p. 36), and the idea of "culture emergent" reflects the approaches of the contributors to this book.

According to Bonder, Martin, and Miracle (2001), the idea of culture emergent results in five suppositions that are useful in professional practice: (1) culture is learned and is transmitted from one generation to another; (2) culture is localized in the sense that it is "created through specific interactions with specific individuals. Each person draws meaningful elements from these interactions and shares them with some but not all individuals within society"; (3) cultural patterns emerge from repetitions of behavior and talk, and these patterns establish the "normal and customary explanations that structure social interactions"; (4) culture is evaluative, including values reflected in individual behaviors and existing as a central component of cultures, and reflects shared beliefs that facilitate social interaction; and (5) "culture has continuity, with change. In general, cultural identity is stable, but one's cultural knowledge changes over the life course as one encounters new objects, situations, and ideas in the personal environment" (p. 36). Significantly, they note that these experiences contribute to the uniqueness of the individual.

When social workers address clients' experiences related to nursing home placement, it is important to remain cognizant of the strengths of older people and their families, and to be aware that some of their strengths are derived from their cultural backgrounds. Also important to remember is that "family" should be regarded broadly and can include people who are not related biologically or through marriage. Bonder, Martin, and Miracle (2001) note that, "although the popular perception is that elders change little, the reality is that they must be masters of adaptability to adapt to the alterations in their physical, cognitive, and social environments. Their values and patterns give them a structure within which to manage these changes" (p. 36). The information provided in this book is consistent with these authors' recommendation that service providers try to understand the influence of culture on daily life and on the construction of the current illness or disability. They ask: "How does culture affect the client's social networks, mobility requirements, demands on auditory abilities, and general sense of well-being? What beliefs does the individual have about his or her current health situation and the place of older adults in the society? And, perhaps most important, what matters to the person?" (p. 36).

Knowing that some factual knowledge is vital and that it is important to acknowledge the centrality of culture and to encourage positive attitudes, Bonder, Martin, and Miracle also propose that an ethnographic approach to cultural competency based on anthropological methods provides a strategy of "learning how to ask" (p. 39). It is imperative that social workers and other service providers ask residents and their relatives for help in understanding their clients' value systems.

The information in this book should also increase readers' self-awareness regarding ethnicity and race, which, for many reasons, can be difficult to develop in the United States. One factor is that, at the same time that this nation speaks an ethos of freedom and equality, millions of its citizens are treated as if they are less deserving of privilege, and every day are subjected to prejudice and discrimination, overtly and covertly. As social workers, we need to acknowledge that members of all the groups discussed in this book have been victims of prejudice and discrimination and that this is a vital factor in the personal and collective histories of our nation.

We need to accept and fulfill our professional and personal responsibilities to develop self-awareness regarding gaps in our knowledge, and also address our prejudices and the biases of others. In recognition of the importance of confronting our own lack of knowledge and understanding, the field of social work and many other professions have established standards for cultural competence, but achieving this is easier said than done.

We know that children are often socialized into prejudiced beliefs that they do not question until they are adults and that some people never question their beliefs at all. As I was reading the chapter by Priscilla A. Day about American Indians, I was reminded of growing up in a small Midwestern town. I do not remember knowing any American Indians when I was a child but realize now that perhaps American Indians were "invisible" to me at the time, outside my consciousness as a white child in a community where few people were not white. My friends and I would accuse one another, in anger, of being an "Indian giver." To us, without question, an "Indian giver" was someone who gave something to you and then took it back. Were we meant to believe, as children, that American Indians had been given a lot and then unfairly wanted it back? Were we to believe that they deserved nothing? Yes, that was the precise message. How absurd this is to me now, when, as an adult, I recognize the shared humanity of all people and the damage such phrases can cause. Now I understand how much, in fact, has been taken from American Indians and how little they have been given in return. American Indians were the first to inhabit this nation, but today they comprise only 1 percent of the population. We, as social workers, must unlearn prejudices of all types by educating ourselves about the realities of past and present experiences of people belonging to diverse groups. Oppressor and oppressed are complementary roles, both part of the same picture, and, to be fully aware of the experiences of people who are oppressed, we must be open to learning about the objective realities of oppression in the U.S. and about the oppressors as well as the oppressed.

The authors of the chapters in this book are social workers who were invited to contribute to this book because of their personal and professional knowledge of older adults in the racial or ethnic group about which they have written. As I spoke with social workers about my intention to be editor of a book on this subject, I was quite aware when I had found the right people to write the chapters. They understood the critically important nature of this subject. They had thought about the importance of cultural competence a great deal and integrated culturally competent practices into their work. Some had taken the initiative to provide in-service training to interdisciplinary staff in nursing homes, formally or informally. When I told them that I would like for them to write about what they consider most important for social workers to know about the racial or ethnic group about which they would be writing, especially if the reader knew nothing about the group, they understood exactly what I was asking and why this is important, and this is exactly what they have done.

REFERENCES

Administration on Aging (2005). Administration on Aging Internet Information Notes: Nursing Homes. http://AOAMAIN/prof/notes/docs/nursinghomes.%5Fhomes.doc. Retrieved May 8, 2006,

Bonder, B., Martin, L., & Miracle, A. (2001). Achieving cultural competence: The challenge for clients and healthcare workers in a multicultural society. *Generations* 25 (1), 35–42.

Kolb, P. (2003). *Caring for our elders: Multicultural experiences with nursing home placement.* New York: Columbia University Press.

McGoldrick, M., Giordano, J., & García-Preto, N. (Eds.) (2005). *Ethnicity and Family Therapy.* New York: Guilford.

U.S. Census Bureau (2004). *Census 2004 American Community Survey: Population and Housing Narrative Profile.* Washington, D.C.: U.S. Government Printing Office. http://fact finder.census.gov/servlet/NPTable? Retrieved May 8, 2006.

1

African American Elders

Molly Davis

Mrs. Brown, a ninety-six-year-old black female, was admitted to a nursing home by her eighty-seven-year-old cousin. Mrs. Brown had been living in a family home in an area that many years earlier had been a strong middle-class neighborhood in the black community. For the last twenty years the neighborhood had deteriorated significantly, becoming a residence for thieves and drug addicts. Mrs. Brown's home had been broken into several times prior to her installation of a burglar alarm system. Mrs. Greer, her cousin, received a call from the police after responding to a false alarm from Mrs. Brown's house. Upon noticing a large sore on her leg that appeared to be infected, they insisted that Mrs. Brown contact a relative or someone who could provide assistance in getting medical care. The police then brought Mrs. Brown to Mrs. Greer's home, who, after one look at the disheveled and partially confused woman, knew that she could no longer live alone. Mrs. Brown was a proud and private woman. Mrs. Greer had talked to Mrs. Brown often on the phone when the latter had lived alone, but she had not been to her home because of her limited driving ability. Mrs. Greer, realizing that she was unable to care for Mrs. Brown herself, began to make calls to try to have her admitted into a nursing home facility.

Mrs. Brown was admitted to a nursing home in a nearby community so that Mrs. Greer could drive the short distance to visit her. The nursing home was fairly new but had not been well maintained. Ninety-eight percent of its residents were black, and 96 percent were Medicaid recipients. The administrator and the top staff were Caucasian, and most of the aides and nursing staff were black.

Mrs. Brown was severely in need of nursing care to address the open wound on her leg. Mrs. Greer, the only known relative in the city, was glad to have found an available bed for her cousin. Mrs. Brown had been a public school teacher for forty years. She held a Master's degree from Syracuse University at a time when most blacks could not even attend college. She was articulate and intelligent even at age ninety-six. Mrs. Greer recognized that the other residents of the nursing home were clearly from a lower socioeconomic level. In fact, Mrs. Brown was the only private-pay resident in the facility.

Nursing staff were able to provide medical assistance to deal with the wound on Mrs. Brown's leg. Mrs. Greer visited her at least once a week. She was never happy with the care Mrs. Brown received. She was particularly irritated when the nice robes, slippers, and clothes that she brought for her cousin disappeared. She often complained to the staff that Mrs. Brown was wearing mismatched clothes that did not belong to her. Frequently she found her sitting in a wheel chair with her wig on backward. Mrs. Greer always brought these matters to the attention of the nursing staff. Once the staff realized that Mrs. Greer usually visited on a specific day of the week, she would arrive to find Mrs. Brown nicely dressed with her hair combed. If she varied the day of her visit, however, Mrs. Brown would be in a disheveled condition.

As Mrs. Brown's mental condition began to deteriorate, injuries began to appear. First she had an unexplained cut on her arm and then a broken ankle that no one could explain. The Adult Protective Services worker simply checked to see if the injury was documented through the proper forms. No further investigation occurred. Poor nursing care became more common in the case of Mrs. Brown. One day she just stopped eating. Upon checking into the nursing home Mrs. Brown had signed a form indicating that she wanted no extraordinary efforts to keep her alive. She died after a week of starvation.

MRS. LEONA MAE FREEMAN

Mrs. Freeman, a seventy-four-year-old black woman, was admitted to a nursing home from the hospital after having broken her hip from a fall at home. She is the mother of three sons and a daughter. Two of her children live in the local area, and two live in other states. Upon admission, staff noticed that Mrs. Freeman was rather non-communicative. Belinda, her daughter, kept telling her mother that she would be all right in the nursing home, but Mrs. Freeman seemed to ignore her. When she was brought to her room, Mrs. Freeman was introduced to her roommate, an eighty-two-year-old Caucasian woman named Mrs. Ali Smith. Mrs. Smith attempted to befriend Mrs. Freeman by letting her know that she had never lived with a "Negro" before but that she imagined it would be an "interesting experience." She did not mean to offend Mrs. Freeman, but Mrs. Freeman made no response. Her children left the facility on the first day of admission and indicated that they would be frequent visitors. They assured Mrs. Freeman that when her hip healed, she should be able to return home.

The social worker noticed that Mrs. Freeman was very quiet. When asked a question, she would respond politely, simply saying "yes maam" or "no maam." She often sat by the window, quietly staring out. The social worker noted that after a month and a half had passed Mrs. Freeman had no visits from her children. Several of her church members had come to visit, but Mrs. Freeman instructed the staff to tell them that she was asleep. The social worker became increasingly concerned that Mrs. Freeman was clinically depressed. She thought that Mrs. Freeman should probably see a psychiatrist and be given medication to elevate her mood.

One day, as a black nursing aide was making the bed, Mrs. Freeman quietly said, "I am so ashamed and humiliated." When the aide asked her what she meant, Mrs. Freeman explained that in her day when parents are put into a nursing home and not cared for by their own children, it is a disgrace. The aide assured her that many people are placed in nursing homes by their relatives because they need the medical and nursing attention that the home can provide. Mrs. Freeman answered that a nursing home is a place to die. She believed that the doctor had confided to her children that she is terminally ill and will die. When the aide tried to assure her that she is not terminally ill, Mrs. Freeman grabbed the aide's hand and began to sob. The aide tried to comfort Mrs. Freeman and then decided that she should tell the social worker what had happened. When she did, the social worker could not understand why Mrs. Freeman would not talk to her but would talk to the aide.

MRS. MISSY ANDERSON

Missy Anderson, a 108-year-old African American woman, has been in a nursing home for only two years, despite her age. She had been able to live in her own home with the support of a niece. Although over a hundred, her only medical complaint is arthritis. Every Sunday a van picks her up at the nursing home to take her to church. She can walk with the support of a walker and uses a wheel chair when necessary. Mrs. Anderson credits her long life to her faith and to her efforts to follow the tenets of a former Sunday school teacher who told her to "be kind to everyone."

Mrs. Anderson, born just before the turn of the century, was one of fifteen children. Her grandmother had been a slave, and Mrs. Anderson had heard many stories about the hardships of slave life. Her room in the nursing home was bright and filled with many pictures congratulating her for her longevity. Although she often uses a wheel chair herself, she assists her roommate who is unable to walk without the wheel chair. Mrs. Anderson has resigned herself to living out her days in the nursing home, but if she is allowed to continue to attend church and participate in the services, she believes she can tolerate the nursing home.

INTRODUCTION

The case studies of Mrs. Brown, Mrs. Freeman, and Mrs. Anderson represent a composite of the many facets of the African American experience in a nursing home. Mrs. Brown, a highly intelligent, independent woman finds herself with no other option than nursing home care. After living a life of achievement and self-sufficiency, her adjustment to the nursing home is very much impacted by the downward trajectory that has forced her into long-term care. She ends up in a nursing home which is poorly funded because of low Medicaid reimbursement rates in her state, and the expenses of a large proportion of the residents are paid for by Medicaid. These homes are sometimes referred to as "lower-tier" nursing homes (Mor et al. 2004). In this lower-tier home, Mrs. Brown is living with individuals whose life experiences have been totally unlike hers.

Mrs. Freeman also exemplifies a common experience of African American adults seventy years of age and older. A fall and a broken hip have resulted in an outcome that Mrs. Freeman has feared and resisted most of her life. There is shame and humiliation associated with her children being unable to take care of her. Her lifeways developed in her early years teach a tradition of filial piety by which children take care of their parents' needs.

Mrs. Anderson is resilient as a 108-year-old African American woman who "has seen it all." She is resigned to living in the nursing home until she dies. She has a cheerful, bright room and a bulletin board recognizing her many years of life. She is happiest about being able to attend church every Sunday. Her faith is a driving force in her life and being able to participate in church services is vital to her adaptation to the nursing home.

Historically, nursing homes were relatively uncommon resources for African American elderly. If assistance was required, families were expected to take care of their own relatives. It was not uncommon that shame was associated with having to spend time in an "old folks' home." Rural communities often had no such facility. The shame and humiliation that Mrs. Freeman experienced because of her family's lack of involvement is often experienced by African Americans in nursing homes. Her attitude about family responsibility is indicative of many from her generation and cohort. Family involvement is strongly connected to life satisfaction in African American older adults (Johnson, Reimer, & Schwiebert 2000). Her family's lack of involvement provides a clue to Mrs. Freeman's despair, a sentiment often reflected in such statements as "I would rather die than have to go to a nursing home."

Mrs. Anderson's case demonstrates the power of spirituality in shaping the perspective of older African Americans who find themselves in a nursing home. Mrs. Anderson's positive attitude and ability to connect to staff in the facility has led to her receiving very responsive care. Her pleasant personality and inclination to be kind to those who provide her care has been a positive influence. Her ability to continue to attend church and connect with her spiritual roots has served as a major factor in her resilience since her admission to the nursing home.

Factors such as traumatic precipitating conditions leading to nursing home placement, negative perceptions about nursing homes, and the ability to maintain spirituality are core issues for African American elders in nursing homes. They are rooted in the African American experience in this country. Such factors mold and shape the response of the African American older adult to nursing home placement.

Nursing homes are still predominantly composed of white residents (Mor et al. 2004), and a number of researchers have documented the wide racial and socioeconomic disparities that exist within nursing homes in the United States. African Americans are four times more likely than white Americans to end up in poorly funded, understaffed nursing homes that often provide substandard care (Mor et al. 2004). Mor et al. (2004) found that nursing home care as it exists in the United States is a two-tier system. They estimate that approximately 40 percent of African Americans in nursing homes live in low-tier facilities, which are characterized by limited budgets, an overrepresentation of Medicaid recipients, less well trained staff, and frequent financial or managerial problems.

The combination of traumatic precipitating conditions that necessitate African American elderly going into a nursing home of lower quality can lead to stressful experiences for the resident. African American elders tend to use familial support and assistance more than formal support services. Taylor (1985) identified a hierarchy of preference of African American elderly for support. His ranking indicates that spouses, followed by adult children, were most frequently preferred as sources of support, and formal services were the least preferred. The historical reticence of older African Americans toward receiving care outside the family context and mistrust of health institutions makes it clear that there are many potential issues facing black nursing home residents.

AFRICAN AMERICAN HISTORY: INTERGENERATIONAL TRANSMISSION

Culture represents the traditions, rituals, customs, and ways of living of a people, and these lifeways are transmitted across generations. They help to stabilize family lives and provide a historical map of the family's trajectory over time. Many of the patterns observed in people today who are sixty-five and older derive from lifeways passed down through generations. A brief review of some of the elements of the history of African Americans in this country provides clear links to many of the beliefs, patterns, and lifeways that can be observed in contemporary African American elderly. With each succeeding generation, some lifeways, or the context for the development of the lifeways, are lost, without oral and written histories having been preserved.

AFRICAN AMERICAN ANCESTRY

African Americans are a diverse group of people of mixed ethnicity, culture, lifeways, and traditions. They possess a unique background when compared to members of other minority groups in the United States. Members of many ethnic groups have immigrated to this country, but the historical heritage of African Americans is not based on immigration. They comprise the only group that was forcefully taken from their country of origin and brought to this country. The slave trade brought the ancestors of African Americans from West and Central Africa to serve as a workforce within this country.

As with any ethnic group, African Americans have been impacted by historical factors and the events that shape their history and ways of life. African Americans came to British colonial America as early as 1619 and, as slaves, were treated harshly and considered less than human. Concerted efforts were made to destroy the development of family relations and family life so as to reduce the complications that would arise from the eventual selling of family members to support the slave master's economic goals. Education was also discouraged out of fear that educated slaves would rebel which would ultimately lead to the demise of the slave system.

ROLES OF OLDER ADULTS

Although African cultures supported reverence and respect for older members of the village, the institution of slavery had no such philosophy. In a culture where one is valued by the amount of work and procreation that can be sustained, older African Americans were in jeopardy. They had little value from an economic perspective and usually found themselves working until they died. This pattern varied somewhat, as some slave masters dealt with older, disabled adult slaves paternally, much as one would treat a young child or an old dog. Some older slaves were set free when they were no longer of use to the slave master, although this was not common (Blassingame 1977).

The role of the older slave within the slave community was often to protect the collective memory of the family; the older the slave, the less likely he or she would be sold, although some older slaves were sold if efforts were made to hide their age (Hurmence 1984). The older slave provided the oral history of family members who had been sold or had died, a valued role in the slave community, as families hoped one day to be reunited with sons, daughters, uncles, aunts, and cousins in freedom.

Many older African Americans today still assume this role within the family, although the mobility of the family and changing values of the young may lead to the loss of this role in the future. There is a growing interest among some African Americans to preserve their history and genealogy. Since African American family information was not historically recorded in deeds such as birth and death records in public institutions, many families rely on older members of the family as well as bibles, cemetery markers, and other similar sources of information. Without efforts to preserve a family's heritage, an older person's death may close the door to important family information.

LEGACIES OF INSTITUTIONAL RACISM

The institution of slavery was more than the brain child of a few evil men; it represented an institutional strategy toward African Americans endorsed by mainstream society. As an institutional expression of sentiment toward the African American, it sent a harsh message about American society. Slaves learned early on that you cannot trust "the system." The laws and policies of this country were supportive of the humiliation, degradation, even killing of African American slaves.

This mistrust of institutional systems and the perpetuation of institutional racism persist to this day, particularly in older African Americans who have lived through segregation, racial discrimination, bigotry, and violence toward blacks. African American slaves learned that the institutional systems of the U.S. did not have the slave's best interest at heart, and many African American elders have maintained this attitude and belief about oppression and institutions in our country. These beliefs have not only been maintained because of oral traditions being handed down; they exist because of the personal experiences of many African American elders seeking to confront the social welfare system of this society.

YEAR 2005

Two teenaged boys were riding in the automobile with their 90-year-old grandmother. As they drove down the street, their grandmother remarked about a particular community where only "colored people live." The two boys couldn't believe what they heard. Did you say "colored"? Their granny calmly said, "Yes, that's what we call black people."

YEAR 1937

Marster and old Miss Julia was mighty strict, but they was good to us. Colored folks on some of the other plantations wasn't so lucky. Some of them had overseers, mean, cruel men.

(Slave narrative, Betty Cofer, interviewed in 1937 at age 84, born 1853 into slavery)

(*Hermence 2001*)

These excerpts, spoken many years apart, show how some terms have been passed down through generations. The term "colored" used in slavery still has some usage among older African Americans. These vestiges of slavery are still evident in African American lifeways.

FAMILY LIFE: A DERIVATIVE OF PATTERNS IN SLAVERY

There is much debate about slave life and its impact on the lives of African American elderly. It is clear that some form of family life survived slavery. This family life tended to be characterized by family fragmentation owing to the constant threat of separation by the slave owner. The slave was thought of as property, and so slave owners did not recognize that slaves had a "family life" apart from the continual efforts to "breed" more slaves for work (Schwartz 2000). The slave family often did not live together; the male slave could be owned by a slave master on a different plantation. The central bond of the slave child was with the mother, and this was often referred to as a "uterine society." This pattern has continued even after slavery, since the most common work for former slaves was domestic work usually done by women, and men were more often unable to find work.

Getting married and having a family was a joke in the days of slavery, as the main thing in allowing any form of matrimony among the slaves was to raise more slaves in the same sense and for the same purpose as stock raisers raise horses and mules, that is, for work. A woman who could produce fast was in great demand and would bring a good price on the auction block. Children were sold from their mothers and the father was not considered in any way as a family part.

(Slave narrative, Thomas Hall, age 81)

(*Hermence 2001*)

African American elderly women still serve as the "uterine" of many families. Their ability to outlive the males of the family and the greater representation of women in nursing homes has important implications for the maintenance of cohesion in residents' family relationships.

Old disabled slaves were sometimes perceived as a problem and sometimes as serving useful roles. The treatment of old, frail slaves ranged from concern and care to extreme neglect and indifference (Genovese 1974). Some slaves were sold as they got older. It was reported that young slaves were expected to show respect toward older slaves (Douglass 1855), and it was not uncommon for the slave community to share their meager resources with the old. Often, in return, the older slave would serve as a midwife or care for ill slaves using folk medicine (Smith 1881). African American families still exhibit this relationship pattern.

Despite the hardships of slavery, many slaves lived to an old age. This has been explained by a "survival of the fittest" perspective on longevity and also by the idea of the "crossover phenomenon" (Manton, Poss, & Wing 1979). A slave's transit from Africa to the Americas was difficult, and many did not survive the passage. Those who did probably represented the hardiest and most resilient. A slave's life was also difficult, and many did not survive the harsh treatment and hard work from sunrise to sunset. Those who did survive likely represented the strongest, thus producing individuals who were capable of living a long time. This crossover phenomenon is still apparent today. Although life expectancy for African Americans is less than for white Americans, many blacks live to be quite elderly. As we saw above, Mrs. Missy Anderson is 108 years old, and she is not the oldest person in her nursing home. The secret of her long life, she told a local reporter in an interview, was eating vegetables and treating everyone kindly.

THE CIVIL WAR

The Civil War sent a clear message to African American slaves that the slave owner's ill regard and negative sentiment toward blacks was shared by society at large. The willingness of the South to wage war against the North rather than free the slaves was a significant comment on justice in America. Those who held power in the economic, political, and social systems of the South were poised to fight and die rather than offer freedom to the slave. This may have been the first recognition of institutional patterns of discrimination by the larger society.

This perspective that American society is unjust has contributed to concerns on the part of older African Americans that the system cannot be trusted. Not only did the slave master not have the slave's best interest at heart, but the larger economic, political, and social systems were also suspect.

A UNIFIED EFFORT TO SEEK JUSTICE: THE CIVIL RIGHTS MOVEMENT

The Civil Rights movement of the late 1950s and 1960s overtly challenged the economic, political, and social systems of the country in response to perceived injustice. Although limited covert attempts were made to defy the institution of slavery, the Civil Rights movement was a unified effort to seek justice. African American blacks were united in their desire for equal opportunity and respect. Young and old across generations sought equality and the right to vote. Older African Americans were supportive of the young, although they had more tolerance of the societal status quo. A separate and unequal black community had developed in cities and rural areas throughout the country, and African Americans felt nurtured and respected within these communities, even though venturing outside them meant discrimination, injustice, even danger.

Distrust of the larger societal systems led to the development of informal and formal systems within the black community. Many of these black structures were diminished with the passage of civil rights legislation promoting integration. One institution that has been impacted but still remains largely segregated is the black church.

INFORMAL AND FORMAL SYSTEMS WITHIN THE AFRICAN AMERICAN COMMUNITY: CHURCH AND ADVOCACY LIFE

The church was the first political action system to advocate for equality for African Americans. Even during slavery, when there was no strong black institutional church, the gatherings of slaves in the field, unknown to the slave master, began to solidify a diverse group of individuals from different tribes and villages.

Over time, the church has served less and less as a source of material support for older African Americans (Bowles et al. 2000). As governmental social welfare systems began to develop, African American elderly and their families tended to make use of these systems, although they are still underutilized by African Americans. The role of the church should not be downplayed, however. Smith (1981) described religion as vital to the mental health and survival of many African Americans. Prayer and faith often help African American elderly to overcome the obstacles of oppression and discrimination and may prove helpful in coping with life in a nursing home. Friends and church members are of great importance to older African Americans (Fried & Mehrotra 1998). The church supplements the services provided by family and also gives meaning to their lives.

Mrs. Missy Anderson is satisfied with her life in the nursing home. Although she would like to live at home, at least she is able to go to Sunday school and church every Sunday. This allows her to continue a pattern she has maintained since childhood. Attending church brings stability to her life and helps her to cope with living in a nursing home. When she cannot attend church because the van broke down and there is no one to pick her up, she feels badly. Her faith is the foundation of her life. She is referred to as the "mother" of the church, and everyone expects her to be there. "To be recognized and appreciated by the church after a lifetime as a maid in a white folks' home is very important."

African American elderly are likely to be religious and to be involved in religious organizations (Taylor & Chatters 1991). The more frequent the church attendance, the more likely the elder person will receive aid or informal assistance from the church (Chatters & Taylor 1989).

The black church provides a means for elderly African Americans to achieve status and recognition. Cook and Wiley (2000) described the black church as a place where African Americans could escape the rejection imposed by society and find acceptance and status. Older members are highly regarded within the church, and women are often called "mothers" of the church although no designation of "fathers" is common for older men. These individuals are often given special recognition during church celebrations, and for many African Americans who spent their lives working as servants, janitors, maids, and in other low-paying service jobs, status within the church is important. Because of poor education, discrimination, and lack of opportunity, holding a church office is often the only opportunity for real status and respect. Religious and spiritual practices often provide healthy alternatives for dealing with life's problems (Brooks & Haskins 2004). To the extent that contact with the church or other religious institutions can be maintained for African American nursing home residents, great value will be gained. It is also important for social workers to understand that although many African Americans have a long history of affiliation with Protestant or Catholic congregations, some have strong spiritual beliefs but are not affiliated with a formal religious organization, and others do not have a strong sense of spirituality or a formal religious affiliation in later adulthood. African American older adults represent a varied group, and much of this diversity is the result of cohort factors; that is, experiences depend on the age of the older person, the person's historical life events, and the role of the church and religion in early life. As the baby boomers enter old age, there will be significant differences compared to previous cohorts.

WHO ARE THE AFRICAN AMERICAN ELDERLY?

Older African Americans are often characterized by intense family kinship bonds, strong faith, spirituality and religiosity, and a greater commitment to vote than the young (Taylor & Chatters 1991). They are a diverse group representing a variety of demographic characteristics.

Since 1970 the number of African Americans aged sixty-five and older has steadily grown, and older African Americans represent the largest population of this age among racial and ethnic minority groups. According to the U.S. Census Bureau, in 2000 almost three million African Americans aged sixty-five and older lived in the United States, and more than thirty-five million individuals, or 8 percent of the U.S. population, identified themselves as black, Negro, or African American. Even though Hispanics have become the largest minority group overall, the number of African Americans who are sixty-five years of age and older will continue to exceed the number of Hispanics in this age group. The difference is the result of the continuing migration of younger Puerto Ricans to the mainland and the immigration of young people who are of other Hispanic nationalities. Immigration patterns often involve younger individuals migrating to the U.S. and older adults remaining in the country of origin, a factor contributing to immigrant African American populations having more individuals who are young and of working age than older immigrants. Although Latinos now outnumber African Americans, there continues to be a greater number of older adults in the African American population.

EDUCATION

Forty-four percent of African Americans aged sixty-five and older have a high school diploma or a more advanced degree (Administration on Aging 1996). The oldest among this group are more likely to have only a few years of education because of the historically segregated nature of education in this country.

Mrs. Missy Anderson, age 108, remembers her childhood and early school years. She always liked school. She remembers crying when her parents told her that she would have to stop going to school because they needed the children to help on the farm. There was plenty of work from sunrise to sunset, and her family needed all the help they could find. Families had a lot of children during that time because the children were workers, and the more, the better. Missy recalls that she cried for days because she wanted to go to school.

The low educational levels often found among elderly African Americans must be understood from a historical perspective. Discrimination, lack of equal opportunity, and oppression characterize the life history of many elderly African Americans (Jackson 1980). The U.S. educational system has been marked historically by its concerted efforts to deny blacks an education, and this practice has continued until today. Nevertheless literacy rates for African Americans are expected to increase with each successive generation of black elderly as more opportunities become available (Jackson & Chatters 1993). Although many older African Americans completed few years of school, they still value education and instill in their children and grandchildren the need for one.

Although it is not uncommon for elderly African Americans to have completed only elementary school, many of these individuals have learned to read and, as a way to compensate, are very adaptive in life skills. The recorded educational level of an older black person should never be the standard by which to assess their capabilities. It is also true that there are African American elders who have achieved a high educational level.

Mrs. Brown sat in her chair in the social area of the nursing home, longing to have a conversation with someone. She looked around at the residents who were of African American heritage. A quick conversation with most of them would clearly reveal that their interests did not match her own. She thought about the Master's degree she earned from Rutgers University, the many trips she had taken to Europe and other exciting places, and she wondered how she ended up in a nursing home.

SOCIOECONOMIC STATUS

The poverty rate for African Americans who are sixty-five and older is more than twice that of all older people (23.9 percent vs. 10.4 percent) (U.S. Census Bureau 2003). It is estimated that, excluding Social Security benefits, the portion of African Americans aged sixty-five and older that is below the poverty line would increase from 23.9 percent to 58.2 percent. African Americans, compared to whites, experience more chronic diseases, more acute illnesses and hospitalizations, and an increased incidence of Alzheimer's disease and other forms of dementia in their old age. These conditions, coupled with poverty, decrease the life expectancy of many older African Americans (Taylor and Lockery 1995).

There has been little change in the poverty rate for African Americans in the last twenty years. In 1990, 34 percent of black elderly were living below the poverty line (Tacuber 1992). Poverty can be predicted based on living arrangements, as black elders who live alone have higher rates of poverty. Elderly black women tend to have lower income levels and a higher incidence of poverty than elderly black men. The combined effects of low socioeconomic status, gender, and age create triple jeopardy (Jackson 1988). The older the African American, the more likely he or she is poor and with little education, and this situation exists particularly among those in the South (Siegel 1993).

LIFE EXPECTANCY AND HEALTH

Life expectancy among African Americans presents some interesting trends. When life expectancy is calculated at birth, African Americans tend to have a shorter life span. When African Americans live to be sixty-five or older, however, their life expectancy may exceed that of whites. For example, African American women had a life expectancy of 74.7 in 1997, but life expectancy for African American women at age 85 was 6.7 years longer, placing it at 91.7 years (Kramerow et al. 1999). This is an example of the "crossover phenomenon" that occurs in contemporary times.

Similar to the crossover phenomenon that may have existed during slavery, the current phenomenon is also based on the idea that African Americans have a lower life expectancy because of discrimination, poverty, increased health risks, and other factors that negatively impinge on the lives of racial and ethnic minorities in the United States. Death rates for African Americans are higher than many other racial and ethnic groups (Harris 2001). The crossover effect suggests that if individuals survive the major challenges posed by their increased risks as African Americans, then they are likely to live a long time.

The leading causes of death for African Americans aged sixty-five and older are heart disease, cancer, and stroke, followed by diabetes and pneumonia or influenza. The death rate for all cancers is higher among African Americans than among whites (Sahyoun et al. 2001). Numerous studies have shown that hypertension, coronary artery disease, and stroke are major health hazards for older African American adults. These conditions are chronic and impact the lifestyles of individuals, although a number of people with these diseases live many years. Cancer affects the lives of African Americans disproportionately, since age-adjusted comparisons for all types of cancer indicate that African Americans are 19 percent more likely to die from this disease than are whites (U.S. Department of Health and Human Services 2005). African American men have a 50 percent higher death rate from prostate cancer than white men, and the death rate for African American women from breast cancer is 33 percent higher than for white women, although the disease is diagnosed 24.5 percent more frequently in white women (U.S. Department of Health and Human Services 2005). Glaucoma is six to eight times more common in African American elderly than in whites, and there is also a greater risk that blindness will occur; further, blindness associated with cataracts that have not undergone surgery is also common in African American elders (Richardson 1996). Because of poverty and the lack of access to health care, among other factors, African American elderly often do not receive preventive care, resulting in many diseases going untreated at a late stage. The need for early intervention with African American elderly is clear, but there are many obstacles to achieving this.

A study assessing rates of dementia in several ethnic groups indicated that Hispanics had the highest rates of dementia, followed closely by African Americans (Gurland, Wilder, and Coleton 1997). Although Alzheimer's disease is more commonly diagnosed in whites, vascular dementia is more common in African American elders (Yeo, Gallagher-Thompson, & Lieberman 1996).

RETIREMENT

The work history and life experiences of the black elderly have a significant impact on retirement patterns (Gibson 1993). African Americans represent 11 percent of the labor force but receive 18 percent of the Social Security disability benefits, and 47 percent of African Americans who receive these benefits are recipients of disability or survivor's benefits and not retirement benefits (Social Security Administration 2000).

Although African American elderly tend to have worked most of their lives, their Social Security benefit formula often provides minimal income during old age. This may be the result of underemployment during most of their lives or the failure of their employers, such as domestic home owners, to pay into Social Security programs. Many African American elders were paid in cash daily or weekly. These practices have led many African Americans to live in poverty in their old age. An estimated 24 percent of African Americans who receive Social Security live in poverty, and 40 percent of African Americans identify Social Security as their only source of retirement income (Social Security Administration 2004). Eighty percent of African Americans over the age of sixty-five have no income from private pensions and annuities (Social Security Administration 2000), and generally African Americans and Hispanics have higher disability rates and lower lifetime earnings and therefore are more dependent upon Social Security and the assistance of an informal network of family and friends (Administration on Aging 2000).

LEGAL SYSTEM

The legal system, because it is an institutional system, is mistrusted by many African American elders. Many legal functions within the African American community are traditionally handled informally. A large number of children were adopted within the community with no legal representative involved, and thus wills and statements reflecting wishes for the dissolution of inheritance were also informally handled within the family.

It is widely recognized within the African American community that the justice system provides little justice for African Americans. Elderly African Americans have had a lifetime of opportunities to become familiar with the inequities of the law. Because of a lack of awareness and involvement with the legal system, African American elderly can be extremely disadvantaged in court proceedings and need guidance from advocates.

POLITICAL PARTICIPATION

Older African Americans are far more likely to vote than younger African Americans (Robinson 1990), perhaps because they have a greater respect for their right to vote because they had been denied the opportunity. Income, education, and church attendance are predictors of voting behavior, and church attendees are more likely to participate in the political process (Taylor and Thorton 1992).

AFRICAN AMERICANS AND NURSING
HOME PLACEMENT: DEMOGRAPHICS

A review of nursing home demographics reveals that the nursing home population is primarily white, and women make up almost two-thirds of the population (Moody 2000). African Americans are four times more likely than their white counterparts to reside in substandard nursing homes (Mor et al. 2004), and nursing home demographics are impacted by racial disparities in the provision of health care. African Americans are less likely to receive a range of medical options when they become ill (Chen et al. 2001) and are more likely to receive Medicaid to fund nursing home care. The quality of care received by African Americans in nursing homes is less than that of whites because of the dependence of the former on Medicaid and the likelihood that these facilities will be considered lower-tier facilities (Mor et al. 2004). Further, these facilities are characterized by inadequate staffing levels, frequent changes in ownership, financial mismanagement, and the fact that they are more likely to be cited for health-related deficiencies (Mor et al. 2004).

FAMILY CAREGIVING

The long tradition of a culture of caring persists within the African American community, and it is based not only on blood ties but on a different sense of community. It may result from vestiges of ties that existed in African villages or may have been reflected in the slave quarters of the plantation when it was obvious that slaves could not count on the master's benevolence in times of need. The family support system has been critical to the survival of the black community, and African Americans often rely heavily on family members as a primary source of support (Dilworth-Anderson, Williams, & Gibson 2002). These cultural values are passed on to each successive generation.

Strong bonds of attachment enable an ongoing exchange of support, which is facilitated by open communication. This process is commonly observed in the African American community. Family members provide material support to meet the needs of elderly family members, and in return the older person provides counsel in resolving family issues and serves as the core on which the family network remains connected.

Underutilization of formal services is a well-established fact for African Americans (Cagney and Agree 1999). African American families prefer caregiving at home when feasible. This preference is based on a culture that supports informal care, a culture that believes one should take care of one's own family and distrusts formal care-giving organizations. It is important to note that organizational and institutional barriers discourage families from trying to negotiate the system to obtain services for loved ones.

Caregiving of elderly African Americans often reflects the utilization of coping strategies that may not be highly regarded within formal organizations. Reliance upon folk medicine, faith, and prayer may be seen in a negative light, although a number of research studies suggest that faith plays a positive role (Peterson 1990). Both formal and informal support is vital to the African American elderly resident of a nursing home.

INTERGENERATIONAL CONFLICT

Although there has been a long-standing history of reliance upon the family system to support older African Americans, each new generation introduces certain changes. The term "cohort" represents a shared historical and life context of a group of people born during the same period. Cohorts of people not only share the experience of certain life events, but they also develop specific lifeways as a result of these experiences. For example, it is well established that many individuals who lived during the Great Depression of the 1930s have similar lifeways. These are often characterized by frugality, a distrust of banks, and a greater propensity to save money. In comparing the cohort of older adults who lived during the Depression to baby boomers nearing old age, significant differences in lifeways are obvious.

Intergenerational conflict is manifested not only in generational cohort differences. Family relationships have a history and change over time. This history within families often crosses generations and may also lead to intergenerational conflict. The term "filial crisis" refers to parent-child conflicts which began in adolescence and often continue into later life. The underlying concept is that long-term, complex family problems and unresolved conflicts that influence family relations can impact the treatment of older persons (Godkin, Wolf, & Pillemer 1989).

African American families are not immune to this dynamic just because of their culture of intergenerational caring. Many family members no longer have a firm conviction that it is their responsibility to take care of older adults. Although some may feel this responsibility more strongly than others, we cannot assume that there is a consensus. The following case study illustrates how a long-standing conflict between a mother and daughter affects the mother's ultimate admission to a nursing home.

Jean and her mother were always in conflict. Mrs. Brown felt that Jean was the only one of her children who gave her problems. She continually compared Jean to her siblings. Jean and her mother would only see each other once a year, and eventually they would argue. When Mrs. Brown could no longer live alone and needed nursing home care, Jean was the only sibling living in the same town. Although she visited her mother during the first week of her stay in the nursing home, the staff witnessed an argument between the two. Jean has not returned for the last three months.

Intergenerational conflict is often manifested in the refusal of children to visit and respond to the needs of an elderly parent in a nursing home. Nursing home staff are called upon to provide extra assistance to residents who rarely have visits from family members, even though they may live nearby.

Many African American families do not have strong attachments for a variety of reasons. These families have been impacted by the same forces that adversely affect the dominant culture, for example, violence, trauma, substance abuse, and dysfunctional familial patterns. An increasing number of divorces, extended families, and cohabiting couples also create fragmentation and significantly enlarge the family network, sometimes beyond the family's ability to sustain contact and maintain relationships. Further, corporate patterns of work increase the geographic distances between family members. It is not uncommon for younger family members to have little or no contact with older family members. These detached relationships ultimately impact the older adult when assistance or support is required.

HEALTH ISSUES AND NURSING HOME CARE

Older African Americans often suffer chronic health problems because of the lack of preventive health care. Instead of seeking medical care, many African American elders have traditionally employed their knowledge of folk medicine techniques to care for themselves and their families at home (Baer & Merrill 1981), and this practice continues today. Medical visits often only occur long after it is clear that a folk remedy is not working. These attitudes about treating illnesses are intergenerational and are reinforced through their frequent use by many family members.

Many African American elders have a "matter of fact" attitude about illness. They are often less likely to seek health care early and more likely to rate their health as poor (Adams and Jackson 2000). The mere fact that the older adult has survived into old age is viewed with gratitude. Nursing home residents have limited ability to access and apply folk remedies and may demonstrate displeasure with their medical treatment, often suggesting certain "more effective" folkways. Although this is questionable, their belief may persist and result in noncompliance with their treatment. Such noncompliance may also reflect their historic distrust of the system.

In the past African American elderly often used the nursing home for rehabilitation. Traditionally, lower rates of nursing home care were associated with home caregiving, Medicaid discrimination, and the lack of available beds at the federal/state rate (Mavundla 1996). More recently, however, the pattern of nursing home utilization by African Americans has changed. Nursing home utilization is currently equal to or greater than that of White Americans (National Center for Health Statistics 1999).

It is widely recognized that a patient's race and sex may influence medical treatment and recommendations for care (Schulman et al. 1999). In the Tuskegee project, for example, African Americans were used for experiments without their consent, even though patients were harmed by these practices (Thomas & Quinn 2000). They have traditionally received different treatment than whites and different access to health care. In sum, the African American community has a history of medical mistreatment and health care exploitation which results in distrust of the health care system and anxiety and fear when interacting with its services (Randall 1996).

Medical staff within the nursing home must be vigilant to diagnose changing medical conditions. The tolerance of African American elderly for symptoms that are often called "old-age related" and the failure to identify early pain or other symptoms may lead to undiagnosed conditions. For example, sometimes the early stage of skin sores is overlooked because of their dark skin pigmentation (Richardson 1996). Arthritis is also commonly tolerated among African American older adults.

As with all nursing home patients, most elderly African Americans enter nursing homes because they are unable to function owing to severe illness. The nursing home should be a place where individuals can access supportive care, but in the lower-tier nursing homes where African Americans frequently reside, this supportive care is least available. Too few wheelchairs, difficulty accessing products for incontinence, missing walkers, and a host of other conditions often work against the care of the older person in such a nursing home. Insufficient staffing and access to medical personnel make the experience in the nursing home inadequate to support good health care for the resident.

Every effort should be made to develop an ongoing relationship with medical personnel. Listening and asking appropriate questions will provide information necessary to understand the resident's condition and provide correct treatment. The increased reliance upon care outside the family has resulted in a greater number of African American elderly considering nursing home care as an option.

MENTAL HEALTH

Traditionally, African American elderly do not seek mental health treatment, as mental illness is associated with elements of taboo. A number of studies, however, offer another clue as to why African American elders do not seek mental health care. Many African American elderly experienced segregated health care and social services systems when they were younger, and these systems were often of poor quality. The attitudes and stereotypes held by the service providers made the experience unpleasant at best. Sue, Fujino, and Hu (1991) replicated a study completed twenty years earlier regarding whether changes had occurred in mental health services that had sought to become more culturally responsive. They concluded that services for African Americans had not improved, and, to remedy the situation, they suggested "ethnic matching," that is, linking African American clients to African American therapists for mental health therapy.

A common mental health disorder of nursing home residents is depression. According to Thomas and Sillin (1972), in the past many psychiatrists believed that African American elderly did not suffer depression because of their increased tolerance for oppression and the fact that they were able to survive and function during a lifetime of negative life events. If loss was at the core of depression, then because African Americans had less to lose, depression would be less of a problem. This rationale does not fit the facts because there is a strong connection between depression, disability, morbidity, and mortality (Harralson et al. 2002). It is not uncommon that nursing home residents suffer from a number of these conditions.

African Americans often view symptoms of dementia as indicators of mental illness. Failure to diagnose depression, as well as other disorders, in African American elderly residents is often linked to stereotypical thinking (Williams 1986). Are African Americans "happy go lucky" under all circumstances? The answer is an emphatic no. This erroneous thinking has led to misdiagnosis and the suffering of residents who could have benefited from receiving proper medication and treatment. Nursing aides may be the most accurate source of information in diagnosing depression in African American elderly. In one study, nurses tended to over report depression among residents, whereas social workers underreported depression (Teresik 2002). These results indicate a clear need for training in the identification and diagnosis of depression in African American elderly.

African American rates of dementia and Alzheimer's disease are higher than those of whites. Greene et al. (2002) reported that first-degree relatives of African Americans with Alzheimer's disease had a higher cumulative risk of dementia than do those of whites with Alzheimer's disease, and other research suggests that the number of African Americans at risk for dementia will increase by more than 200 percent by 2030 (Borson and Katon 1995). These data suggest that more needs to be understood about African American risk for various forms of dementia, and nursing homes must prepare to meet the needs of a growing population of older African Americans with dementia.

CARE RECEIVING

In order to understand African Americans' perception of institutional care, one must understand certain factors regarding African American cohorts. For African Americans born before 1935, the nursing home in their youth was referred to as an "old folks' home." It was a facility that existed in most communities and was usually reserved for frail older adults and those with no family. They saw the facility in a negative light, and no one who had a family wanted to go there. Residing in such a facility meant that no family was available to help.

The norm within most families, as noted above, was that children should take care of their older family members, and the long tradition of valuing elders may have a foundation in the faith and religious teachings of African Americans (Moody 1996). The majority of older African Americans adhered to the belief that families were to take care of their older adult family members and viewed institutional care as necessary only when the family could not perform the function. Shame was associated with the recognition that family members would not provide care for a member.

In the early twentieth century elderly African Americans were largely cared for by their families, and institutional care was viewed as an extension of a system that was unresponsive to the needs of African Americans. Indeed, both the private and public systems failed to meet the needs of black families (Axinn & Herman 1997). Exchanges with institutional systems were marked by mistreatment, racism, and the inability to have needs met, and, for African Americans, distrust of institutional systems and extreme discomfort were byproducts of these experiences. Office workers were often rude and disparaging to African Americans seeking services, and the latter were often served in substandard segregated spaces with little regard for personal privacy.

The nursing home is often seen as simply another biased institution, and so African American residents frequently dread placement in a nursing home. Many negative messages about these facilities are passed across generations. "Institutional racism" is a term that refers to patterns within societal structures that create discriminatory and oppressive policies and practices (Specter 2000), and these consistent patterns, sometimes beginning with the very first contact with an agency, have sent a message that receiving services comes with a price.

COPING STYLES

When African Americans contact social service agencies, and many avoid doing so altogether, they tend to be taciturn, are often reluctant to ask questions, and are usually compliant with agents despite the conditions. The early life experiences that provided the genesis of these behaviors continue to impact their interactions with social service agencies.

USE OF RESTRAINTS

The use of restraints is a controversial issue within long-term care facilities, with continuing debate about when they may be necessary (Mavundla 1996). These discussions are related to ensuring that residents of nursing home facilities are not subjected to cruel and harsh treatment. Overuse of restraints commonly occurs in lower-tier nursing homes. These facilities, as noted above, tend to have an overrepresentation of African American residents who are Medicaid recipients. As such, African Americans elderly are more often subjected to the use of restraints (Mor et al. 2004).

FOOD PREFERENCES

An issue of importance to nursing home residents of all ethnic backgrounds is the compatibility of foods with lifelong preferences. Food is an important aspect of social life and is usually involved in meaningful social interactions. The food preferences of African American older adults are linked to their lifestyles, cultural lifeways, and economic status. It is not uncommon for older African Americans to have strong preferences for vegetables. Growing a garden is not only good exercise, but for poor people it is a primary way to produce food at relatively low cost in rural communities. Turnips, mustard, and collard greens, kale, green beans, peas and corn, along with cornbread, were often the core of a meal, with meat, which was usually chicken, reserved for special occasions. In southern rural areas chickens, pigs, and cattle were raised and slaughtered for the family.

For African American residents of nursing homes, food is an important way to maintain their familiar lifeways. Although health conditions may preclude eating certain foods, vegetables, for example, are usually acceptable for most diets. One useful strategy in providing foods more familiar to African Americans is to consult African American staff who may be working in the kitchen; these staffers might then work with the dietician to recommend "soul food" for black residents. Black nurses or nursing assistants may also be able to share favorite recipes that are more familiar to African American residents. Simple strategies can help facilitate the adaptation of African American residents.

BATHING AND PERSONAL CARE

The history of racism and discrimination reveals a deep and abiding disrespect for African Americans, which was translated into behaviors designed to humiliate them. As a result, it is critical to African American nursing home residents that they are shown respect and dignity and are treated as worthy individuals. This respect must be demonstrated through appropriate communication and behavior. Particularly when engaging in private activities, such as bathing or providing personal care to residents, it is essential that staff members find ways to demonstrate respect and allow as much privacy as possible, taking all measures not to violate the resident's dignity. One should always take care to address the person appropriately, for example, "Mrs. Brown, I am about to assist you with your bath; would you like me to help you get into the tub?" and "Mrs. Brown, it is time for you to return to your room; are you comfortable?"

Bathing and personal care are private activities that often become less private in the nursing home setting. Being touched or handled in private ways and having others see what has always been unseen except by the resident or close family is a violation of dignity. Although this kind of treatment may be necessary in the care of the resident, it is important for staff to find ways to demonstrate respect and to allow as much privacy as is possible.

Although the staff is going through routine procedures, asking and informing the resident gives the person an element of control and makes the individual feel respected. Simple actions such as knocking on a door before entering and asking the resident's preferences are important gestures. The issue of respect is generally more important to African American elderly than to white residents.

INTERACTION WITH OTHER RESIDENTS

Older African Americans may be somewhat uncomfortable in social settings in the nursing home that involve interactions with whites or members of other ethnic groups. This discomfort may be temporary, based on the resident's limited opportunities to regularly interact with whites. Many nursing homes of lower-tier status house mostly Medicaid recipients and hence there is less diversity in these nursing homes.

African American residents are mindful of the times when interactions between the races were minimal, and interactions that did exist were often not based on equality. African American residents, when speaking to a white resident, may use the term "Maam" or "Sir." This is not in deference to age but may be linked to a perceived difference in status. Each resident has developed lifeways based on his or her individual lifetime experiences. Although these ways of life may not be relevant in the nursing home setting, social workers need to be aware that these perceptions exist. African American residents can learn to interact comfortably in the nursing home setting, but it may take time.

Older white residents in the nursing home setting may have the reverse experience. Because of their life experiences, they may refer to a male African American resident as "boy." They may even use terms such as "colored" or "nigger," if that is their frame of reference. These negative behaviors must be consistently confronted and corrected within the nursing home setting. Usually they are more problematic among white residents since the behaviors of African Americans tend to be more deferential.

Usually, through the process of adaptation, interactions between African Americans and residents of other ethnic groups will become more natural and appropriate. People with biased language, stereotypes, and attitudes developed from past experiences should be encouraged to change.

COMMUNICATION AND INTERACTION

Language provides a picture of the life experiences of African American elderly. It reveals historical context, education, and mental status, and when language is transmitted across cohorts, it is not uncommon that meaning is lost or distorted. There is a duality to the language of African American elderly, as certain terms are only expressed in the presence of other African Americans.

Missy remembers: "When I was a little girl, people were not embalmed when they died. They were placed on a cooling board and often remained at home for family visitation."

When Missy recounts this story, it is important to ask for clarification, for example, "What is a cooling board?" This is an example of language that has historical meaning, which may not be understood by people who did not live during a specific time. Even the language used to describe elderly African Americans may need to be validated with the resident or relative. For instance, it may not be uncommon to call an elderly African American either "colored," "black," "African American," "Negro," and so on. All these terms have been used appropriately at different times. When an elderly person uses a term that is no longer commonly used to refer to African Americans, a discussion should take place to determine how the term was used at an earlier time. Working with older African Americans might require staff to learn unfamiliar terms that are only understood by the resident. Open communication is vital. Most important, listening provides significant clues to understanding many issues, including major decisions.

INTERACTION BETWEEN STAFF, RESIDENTS, AND RELATIVES

As previously discussed, working with African American residents and their families requires understanding their perceptions and distrust of social institutions. It is essential for staff to demonstrate respect toward the resident and family members, and encourage openness, so that the latter can have input in decisions regarding the resident. If staff members demonstrate prejudicial behavior toward African American clients and their families, this may well engender anger, resentment, and charges of discrimination. Open discussion between staff and family is crucial to achieve understanding and reconciliation. African American residents may often fear unfair or abusive treatment, and some families believe that being vigilant is the only way to avoid these behaviors. When staff observes families being hyper-vigilant with regard to the resident, it is important to have a discussion in an open climate to try to understand the family's concerns. Generalized fears having little to do with specific care issues in the nursing home may surface, and families must be allowed to share these concerns and encouraged to work with staff to achieve mutually satisfactory solutions.

Effective interaction between staff and African American elderly in nursing homes depends critically on the staff demonstrating respect for the residents. According to Moody (1996, 13–18), there are ten elements of dignity:

Self-respect versus Shame
Honor versus Humiliation
Decorum versus Inappropriate Behavior
Privacy versus Exposure
Power versus Vulnerability
Equality versus Favoritism
Adulthood versus Infantilization
Ego Integrity versus Despair
Individuation versus Objectification
Autonomy versus Dependence

Understanding these polarities will enhance the ability of staff to demonstrate dignity and respect to African American residents in nursing homes. Having experienced powerlessness and the indignity of racism and oppression, the issue of respect is especially important for African American residents.

RECREATIONAL ACTIVITIES

Many older African American residents have different perspectives about recreation. Most may have led a life of hard work and little leisure and may be unfamiliar with the basic recreational activities in nursing homes. Ping pong, shuffle board, and bridge may be unfamiliar activities to African American elders. They often spend leisure time watching the "stories" (soap operas), and quilting, gardening, and knitting may have been activities vital to meeting family needs and yet frequently considered recreational. Dancing and music are common recreational activities among African American residents. Nursing home staff should be open to discussing recreational activities with residents and be flexible in their responses.

END-OF-LIFE CARE

Older African Americans often utilize their spiritual beliefs to shape their perception of death and their preferences for end-of-life care (Wykle and Segal 1991). They commonly have little fear of death and are more fearful about the circumstances of death. A general desire is to be able to die a "good death," that is, one free of suffering and long illness, and one that does not drain the family's financial resources. Many older African Americans do not want to be a burden to their family regarding end-of-life care.

The response to death depends on the age of death. African Americans tend to use the Bible as a standard for defining long life, and death at an old age, sometimes defined as seventy or older, is accepted as natural and normal. The place of death is also important, and most older African Americans would prefer to die at home with friends and family. It is not uncommon that final wishes involve being able to go home, even if the individual is in a nursing home.

Older African Americans do not utilize hospice care to a significant degree. Only 8 percent of hospice patients are African American compared to 83 percent who are white patients (Crawley, Bolden, and Washington 2000). Underutilization of hospice care is the result of several factors. First, many do not know that hospice care is available. Physicians must make referrals for hospice care, and lack of awareness often results in patients not taking advantage of this resource. Second, hospice care represents the involvement of another system outside the family, and older African Americans prefer to be cared for by family caregivers.

African Americans are more likely than whites to prefer life-prolonging measures in the treatment of terminal illnesses (Hopp and Duffy 2000). This pattern may be related to a distrust of institutional systems; there is a lingering concern that, if given the opportunity, those in the dominant society would take advantage of people who are poor and members of minority groups. Denial of critical medical treatment is a fear expressed by many older African Americans. African American elderly are usually not supportive of euthanasia or assisted suicide. Death is viewed as a transition often preceded by pain and suffering, and the common belief is that if one can endure the suffering, there will be relief through death at the proper time. This is an integration of traditional spiritual beliefs.

Older African Americans often believe that doctors exercise more authority and control over their medical treatment than they do. There is little awareness of patients' rights, and the elderly person may believe that medical staff is withholding certain medical information in an effort to protect or shelter (Caralis et al. 1993). This kind of thinking shows little awareness of the responsibility of medical staff to fully inform the patient, and a belief also exists that doctors can "force" elders into a nursing home and not allow them to live alone. This type of paternalistic perspective is common among African American elders, and social workers and other hospital staff should provide education about competent decision making and the rights of patients.

Many African American elders believe in end-of-life planning. Funerals are important statements about worth and value, and it is also considered important to leave an inheritance to family members. Although this planning is not unusual, it is often done informally. Instructions may be written in the family Bible, and usually one or more family members are informed about the wishes of the older person.

African Americans are less likely to complete living wills and other forms of advanced directives, such as "do not resuscitate" (DNR) orders (Hopp and Duffy 2000), and differ from European Americans both in their unwillingness to complete advance directives and their attitudes about life-sustaining treatment (Garrett 1993). A study by Blackhall et al. (1995) found that when faced with a diagnosis of terminal illness African American elderly favored a patient-centered model of decision making rather than a family-centered model. The patient-autonomy model suggests that African American elderly seek to make decisions about their own care, although they may heavily consider family wishes in this process. This result suggests that medical staff should ask patients whether they want to involve their families in decision making about their care or whether they prefer the family simply to be provided the information. Assumptions about family involvement may lead to lack of regard for the patient's decision-making preferences.

CONCLUSION

The history of the experiences of African Americans in the U.S. has brought about the development of unique lifeways and perspectives in individuals and families. Older African Americans embody the results of discrimination, oppression, and mistreatment, and yet the resilience and ability to overcome that is demonstrated by generations who have survived. The nursing home setting has unique and increasing opportunities to develop effective strategies to serve the needs of African American residents. Effective care of African Americans in the nursing home or other service settings must reflect an understanding of the history and contribution of a people who were displaced from another culture. African American older adults today are a composite of all those who have gone before, developing unique and characteristic perspectives and patterns of behavior. The story of older African Americans is a mosaic of triumph and tragedy, risk and resilience, and, most of all, transition and empowerment.

REFERENCES

Adams, V. H., & Jackson, J. (2000). The contribution of hope to the quality of life among aging African Americans, 1980–1992. *International Journal of Aging and Human Development* 50 (4), 279–295.

Administration on Aging (1996). *Aging into the 21st century*. Washington, D.C.: Department of Health and Human Services, Administration on Aging.

Administration on Aging. (2000). The many faces of aging: Resources to effectively serve minority older persons. http://www.aoa.gov/minorityaccess/default.html. Washington, D.C.: U.S. Department of Health and Human Services.

Administration on Aging (2000). *Facts and figures: Statistics on minority aging in the U.S.* Washington, D.C.: Department of Health and Human Services, Administration on Aging. http://www.aoa.dhhs.gov/prof/statistics/minority_aging/facts_minority_aging.asp.

Axinn, J., & Herman, L. (1997). *Social welfare: A history of the American response to need*. White Plains, N.Y.: Longman.

Bach, P. B., Cramer, L. D., & Warren, J. L. (1999). Racial differences in the treatment of early stage lung cancer. *New England Journal of Medicine* 341, 1198–1205

Baer, R. D., & Merrill, S. (1981). Toward a typology of Black sectarianism as a response to racial stratification. *Anthropology Quarterly* 54, 1–14.

Billingsley, A. (1996). *Climbing Jacob's ladder.* New York: Simon and Schuster.

Blackhall, L. J., Murphy, G., Murphy, S., Frank, G., Micheal , V., & Azen, S. (1995). *Ethnicity and attitudes toward patient autonomy.* Los Angeles: Department of Medicine, Pacific Center for Health Policy and Ethics, University of Southern California.

Blassingame, J. (1977). *Slave testimony.* Baton Rouge: Louisiana State University Press.

Borson, W., & Katon, W. (1995). Differential clinical characteristics of older Black and White nursing home residents. *American Journal of Geriatric Psychiatry* 3, 229–238.

Bowles, J., Brooks, T., Hayes-Reams, B., Butts, P., Myers, T., Allen, H., & Kingston, W. (2000). Frailty, family and church support among urban African American elderly. *Journal of Health Care for the Poor and Underserved* 11 (1), 87–99.

Brooks, L., & Haskins, D. G. (2004). Counseling and psychotherapy with African American clients." In T. Smith (Ed.), *Practicing Multiculturalism,* pp. 1–29. Boston, Mass.: Allyn and Bacon.

Cagney, K. A., & Agree, E. M. (1999). Racial difference in skilled nursing care and home health use: The mediating effects of family structure and social class. *Journal of Gerontology: Social Sciences* 54B, S223–S236.

Caralis, P., Davis, B., Wright, I., & Marcia, E.(1993). The influence of ethnicity and race on attitudes toward advance directives, life prolonging treatments and euthanasia. *Journal of Clinical Ethics* 4, 155–165.

Chatters, L. M., & Taylor, R. J. (1989) Age differences in religious participation among Black adults. *Journal of Gerontology: Social Sciences* 44, S183–189.

Chen, J., Radford, M.J., Wang, Y., & Kreamhoilz, H. M. Racial differences in the use of cardiac catheterization after acute myocardial infarction. *New England Journal of Medicine* 344, 1443–1449.

Coke, M. (1992). Correlates of life satisfaction among elderly African Americans. *Journal of Gerontology* 47 (5), 316–320.

Cook, D. A., & Wiley, C.Y. (2000). Psychotherapy with members of the African American churches and spiritual traditions. In P. S. Richards and A. E. Bergin (Eds.), *Handbook of Psychotherapy and Religious Diversity,* pp. 369–396. Washington D.C.: American Psychological Association.

Crawley, I., Payne, R., Bolden, J., Payne, T., Washington, P., & Williams, S. (2000). The initiative to improve palliative and end of life care in the African American community. *Journal of the American Medical Association* 284, 2518–2521.

Dilworth-Anderson, P., Williams, I. C., & Gibson, B. (2002). Issues of race, ethnicity and culture in caregiving research: A twenty-year review (1980–2000). *The Gerontologist* 42, 237–272.

Douglass, F. (1855). *My bondage and my freedom.* New York: Miller, Orton, and Mulligan.

Fabricatore, A. N., Handai, P. J., & Fenzel, L. M. (2000). Personal spirituality as a moderator of the relationship between stressors and subjective well-being. *Journal of Psychology and Theology* 28 (3), 221–228.

Farley, R., & Allen, W. (1987). *The color line and the quality of life in America.* New York: Russell Sage.

Fried, S. B., and Mehrotra, C. M. (1998). *Aging and diversity: An active learning experience.* Washington, D.C.: Taylor and Francis.

Garrett, J. M. (1993). Life-sustaining treatments during terminal illness: Who wants what? *Journal of General Internal Medicine* 8, 361, 363.

Genovese, E. D. (1974). *Roll Jordan roll: The world the slaves made.* New York: Basic Books.

Gibson, R. C. (1993). The Black American retirement experience. In J. S. Jackson, L. M. Chatters, and R. J. Taylor (Eds), *Aging in Black America*, pp. 277–297. Newbury Park, Calif.: Sage.

Godkin, M. A., Wolf, R. S., & Pillemer, K. A. (1989). A case comparison analysis of elder abuse and neglect. *International Journal of Aging and Human Development* 28, 207–225.

Green, R. C., Cupples, L. A., Go, R., Benke, K. S., Edeki, T., Griffith, P. A., Williams, M., Hipps, Y., Graff-Radford, N., Bachman, D., & Farrrer, L. A. (2002). MIRAGE Study Group. Risk of dementia among white and African American relatives of patients with Alzheimer's disease. *JAMA* 287 (3), 329–336.

Green, R. C., Cupples, L. A., Kurz, A., Auerbach, S., Rodney, G. Sadovnick, D., Duara, R., Kukull, W., Chui, H., Edeki, T., Griffith, P., Freedland, R., & Bachman, D. (2003). Depression as a risk factor for Alzheimer's disease: The mirage study. *Archives of Neurology* 60, 753–759.

Gurland, B., Wilder, D., & Coleton, M. I. (1997). Differences in rates of dementia between ethno-racial groups. In L. G. Martin and B. Soldo (Eds.), *Racial and ethnic difference in the health of older Americans*, pp. 233–269. Washington, D.C.: National Academy Press.

Harralson, R., Tracela, M., Regenberg, A., Kallen, M., TenHave, T., Parmlee, P., & Johnson, J. (2002.) Similarities and differences in depression among Black and White nursing home residents. *American Journal of Geriatric Psychiatry* 10, 175–184.

Harris, M. I. (2001) Racial and ethnic differences in health care access and health outcomes for adults with type 2 diabetes. *Diabetes Care* 24 (3), 454–459.

Hopp, F. P., and Duffy, S. (2000). Racial variations in end of life care. *Journal of the American Geriatric Society* 49, 658–663.

Hurmence, B. (1984). *My folks don't want me to talk about slavery*. Winston-Salem, S.C.: John Blair.

Jackson, J. J. (1980). *Minority aging*. Belmont, Calif.: Wadsworth.

Jackson, J. S. (Ed.). (1988). *The Black American elderly*. New York: Springer.

Jackson, J. S., Chatters, L., & Taylor, R. J. (1993). *Aging in Black America*. Newbury Park, Calif.: Sage.

Johnson, R., Reimer, T., & Schwiebert, V. (2000). Residential references and eldercare: Some African American elders' views. *Journal of Multicultural Nursing* 6, 14–20.

Johnson, R. A., Schwiebert, V., & Rosenmann, P. (1994). Factors influencing nursing home placement decision. *Clinical Nursing Research* 3 (3), 269–281.

Kramerow, E., Lentzner, H., Rooks, R., Weeks, J., & Saydah, S. (1999). *Health and aging chartbook*. Hyattsville, Md.: National Center for Health Statistics.

Levin, J. S., & Chatters, L. M. (1998). Religion, health and psychological well-being in older adults. *Journal of Aging and Health* 10 (4), 504–531.

Manton, K. G., Poss, S. S., & Wing, S. (1979). The Black/White mortality crossover: Investigation from the perspective of the components of aging. *The Gerontologist* 19 (3), 291–300.

Manton, K. G., & Stallard, E. (1997). Health and disability differences among racial and ethnic groups. In L. G. Martin and B. Soldo (Eds.), *Racial and ethnic differences in the health of older Americans*, pp. 43–105. Washington, D.C.: National Academy Press.

Mavundla, T. R. (1996). Factors leading to Black elderly persons' decisions to seek institutional care in a home in the Eastern Cape. *Curationis* 19 (3), 47–50.

McCallion, J., Janiciki, M., Grant-Griffin, L., & McCallion, P. (1997). Exploring the impact of culture and acculturation on older families for persons with developmental disabilities. *Family Relations* 46, 347–357.

McKinney, E. A., & Williams, M. (Eds.) (1990). *Black aged: Understanding diversity and service needs*. Newbury Park, Calif.: Sage.

Moody, H. R. (1996). Why dignity in old age matters. *Journal of Gerontological Social Work* 29, 13–38.

Moody, H. R. (2000). Nursing home statistics. American Health Care Association. http://www.efmoody.com/longterm/nursing/statistics.html.

Mor, V., et al. (2004). Driven to tiers: Socioeconomic and racial disparities in the quality of nursing home care. *Milbank Quarterly* 82 (2), 8202–8210.

National Caucus and Center on Black Aged. Aging Resources, August, 2005. http://www.ncba-aged.org.

National Center for Health Statistics. (1999). http://www.cdc.gov, Health Disparities.

Perry, C. M., & Johnson, C. L. (1994). Families and support networks among African American oldest old. *International Journal of Aging and Human Development* 38 (1), 41–50.

Peterson, J. (1990) Age of wisdom: Elderly Black women in family and church. In Jay Sokolovsky (Ed.), *The cultural context of aging*, pp. 213–228. New York: Bergin and Garvey.

Randall, V. R. (1996). Slavery, segregation and racism: Trusting the health care system ain't always easy! An African American perspective on bioethics. *St. Louis University Publications Law Review* 15,191–235.

Richardson, J. (1996). *Aging and health: Black American elders*. SGEC Working Paper #4. Stanford, Calif.: Stanford Geriatric Education Center.

Robinson Brown, D. (1990). The Black elderly: Implications for the family. In M. S. Harper (Ed.), *Minority aging: Essential curricula content for selected health and allied health professions*. Health, Resources and Services Administration, Department of Health and Human Services DHHS, Publication No. HRS (PDV904). Washington, D.C.: U.S. Government Printing Office.

Sahyoun, N. R., Lentzner, H., Hoyert, D., & Robinson, K. N. (2001). Trends in causes of death among the elderly. In *Trends in Health and Aging*, at http://www.nchs.gov.

Schulman , K. A., Berlin, J. A., Harless, W., Kerner, J. F., & Sistrunk, S. (1999). The effect of race and sex on physicians' recommendations for cardiac catheterization. *New England Journal of Medicine* 340 (8), 618–625.

Schwartz, M. J. (2000). *Born in bondage: Growing up enslaved in the antebellum South*. Cambridge, Mass.: Harvard University Press.

Siegel, J. (1993). *A generation of change: A profile of America's older population*. New York: Russell Sage.

Smith, A. (1981). Religion and mental health among Blacks. *Journal of Religion and Health* 20, 264–287.

Smith J. L. (1881). *Autobiography of James L. Smith*. Norwich, Conn.: Press of the Bulletin Company.

Social Security Administration (2000). Income of Population 55 or Older.

Social Security Administration (2004). http://www.ssa.gov/policy/statistics.

Spector, R. E. (2000). *Cultural diversity in health and illness*. Upper Saddle River, N.J.: Prentice Hall Health.

Sue, D. S., Fujino, D. C., & Hu, L. (1991). Community mental health services for ethnic minority groups: A test of the cultural responsiveness hypothesis. *Journal of Consulting and Clinical Psychology* 59, 533–540

Tacuber, C. (1992). *Sixty-five plus in America*. U.S. Census Bureau, *Current Population Reports*, Special Studies 23–178. Washington, D.C.: U.S. Census Bureau.

Taylor, R. (1985). The extended family as a source of support to elderly Blacks. *The Gerontologist* 25 (5), 488–495.

Taylor, R., & Lockery, S. (1995). Socioeconomic status of older Black Americans: Education, income, poverty, political participation and religious involvement. *African American Research Perspectives* 2 (1), 1–6.

Taylor, R. J., & Chatters, L. M. (1991). Religious life of Black Americans. In J. S. Jackson (Ed.), *Life in Black America,* pp.105–123. Newbury Park, Calif.: Sage.

Taylor, R. J., & Chatters, L. M. (1991). Non-organizational religious participation among elderly Black adults. *Journal of Gerontology* 46 (4), 210–217.

Taylor, R. J., & Thorton, M. D. (1992). Demographic and religious correlates of voting behavior among older Black Americans. In J. S. Jackson, I. M. Chatters, & R. J. Taylor (Eds.), *Aging in Black America.* Newbury Park, Calif.: Sage.

Teresik, J., Abrams, R. (2002). Influence of cognitive impairment, illness, gender and African American status on psychiatric ratings and staff recognition of depression. *American Journal of Geriatric Psychiatry* 10, 506–514.

Thomas, A., and Sillin, S. (1972). *Racism and psychiatry.* New York: Brunner-Mazel.

Thomas, S., & Quinn, S. (2000). Public health then and now: The Tuskegee Syphilis Study, 1932 to 1972. In E. Stoller & R. Gibson (Eds.), *Worlds of difference: Inequality in the aging experience,* pp. 290–291. Thousand Oaks, Calif..: Pine Forge.

U.S. Census Bureau (2000). Population Finder. http://www.census.gov/population/www/index.html.

U.S. Census Bureau (2001). *Poverty in the U.S.* 60–219, Fed Doc 01-401.Washington, D.C.: U.S. Census Bureau.

U.S. Census Bureau (2003). *Current population survey.* AARP Public Policy Initiative.

U.S. Department of Health and Human Services (2005). *Closing the health gap: Cancer.* http://www.healthgap.omhrc.gov/cancer.htm.

Williams, D. H. (1986). The epidemiology of mental illness in Afro-Americans. *Hospital and Community Psychiatry* 37 (1), 42–49.

Wykle, M., & Segal, M. (1991). A comparison of Black and White family caregivers' experience with dementia. *Journal of the National Black Nurses Association* 5, 29–41.

Yeo, G., Gallagher-Thompson, D., & Lieberman, M. (1996). Variations in dementia characteristics by ethnic category. In G. Yeo and D. Gallagher-Thompson (Eds.), *Ethnicity and dementia,* pp. 195–208. Washington, D.C.: Taylor and Francis.

RESOURCES

Organizations and Websites

African American Almanac. http://www.toptags.com/aama/docs/jcraw.htm.

African American Elderly. http://www.questia.com/library/sociology.

African American Gerontology Websites. http://www.questia.com/library/pm.qust?a = oand d = 5001757088.

African American Studies: MetaSites. http://libwww.syr.edu/research/internet/african_american/metasites.html.

African American Web Connection. http://www.aawc.com/aawco.html.

Aging and Diversity Web Links. http://www.aging.unc.edu/cad/links.html.

Alzheimers Association, Diversity Toolbox. http://www.alz.org/Resources/Diversity/overview.
    asp.
American Society on Aging- African American Elderly. http://www.asaging.org.
Black/African American Senior References. http://www.blackrefer.com/black_seniors.html.
Care of Dying: Supportive Care of the Dying. http://www.careofdying/org/NEWS/0502NEWS.
    ASP.
Center on Ethnic and Minority Aging. http://www.cema-infro.net/links.html.
Closing the Health Gap. http://www.healthgap.omhrc.gov.
Gero-Edu website (selections). http://www.gero-edu.org.
National Caucus and Center on Black Aged. http://www.ncba-aged.org.
National Citizen's Coalition for Nursing Home Reform. http://www.nccnhr.org.
National Family Caregivers Association. http://www.nfcacares.org.
Portrait of Older Minorities. http://research.aarp.org/general/portminjo.
Resource Centers for Minority Aging Research. http://www.rcmar.ucla.edu.
Stanford Geriatric Education Center. http://sgec.stanford.edu/resources/res.htm.

Readings

Brangman, S. A. (1995). African American elders: Implications for health care providers, *Clinics of Geriatric Medicine* 11 (1), 15–23.

Damon-Rodriguez, J. (1998). Respecting ethnic elders. *Journal of Gerontological Social Work* 29 (2/3), 53–72.

McIntosh, B. R., & Danigelis, N. L. (1995). Race, gender and the relevance of productive activity for elders' affect. *Journals of Gerontology, Series B.: Psychological Sciences and Social Sciences* 50B, S229-S239.

Ruiz, D. S. (2004). *Amazing grace.* Westport, Conn.: Praeger.

2

American Indian Elders

Priscilla A. Day

Mrs. Ruth Jones is a ninety-three-year-old American Indian (Anishinaabe) woman with some chronic health problems related to aging. She lived independently but in close proximity to her seventy-year-old daughter on an American Indian reservation in northern Minnesota where she was born and lived all her life. Mrs. Jones started to exhibit behaviors that indicated it was becoming dangerous for her to continue to live by herself. For example, one day she left wild rice cooking on the stove and when she woke up from a nap she smelled smoke and tried to hurry to the stove but she fell down striking her head. Luckily she was able to get to the phone to call her daughter, but the incident convinced her family that she could no longer live alone.

Her daughter lived about a half-mile away so Mrs. Jones moved in with her daughter where she lived for the next six months. During this time she continued to fall occasionally and eventually ended up using a wheelchair most of the time. She was able to transfer herself to and from her wheel chair, which was important, as her daughter had her own health problems; the daughter needed to use oxygen so she was not able to assist her mother very much. They both received limited services from the reservation such as medication management, meals on wheels, and transportation to the local Indian Health Service Clinic twenty-five miles away.

This arrangement seemed to be working out, but then the daughter became seriously ill and required hospitalization. Mrs. Jones then went to live in another community, 150 miles from the reservation in an urban area with her forty-seven-year old granddaughter and her family. Her health continued to slowly decline. During the winter she developed pneumonia, and fell and broke her hip. After hospitalization and rehab it was decided that the best plan was to admit Mrs. Jones into a nursing home for long-term care, as her granddaughter and the granddaughter's husband worked full-time. Prior to breaking her hip, Mrs. Jones had diabetes, congestive heart failure, and pulmonary disease requiring the use of oxygen, but she had been able to assist when she needed to be moved. After her fall she did not regain the ability to walk or transfer herself, so she now needed assistance twenty-four hours a day.

What factors will affect her adjustment in the nursing home? Besides the usual assessment of physical, cognitive, and social abilities, what cultural considerations should the social worker take into account? What role can the social worker play to assist in this adjustment?

INTRODUCTION

American Indians, Native Americans, Alaska Natives, Indigenous peoples, and hundreds of different tribal names all refer to the groups of peoples who originated on the American continents. The National Congress of American Indians and the National Tribal Chairman's Association in 1977 issued a joint resolution stating that "in the absence of specific tribal designations, the preferred reference to people indigenous to North American is American Indian and/or Alaska Native (U.S. Department of Health and Human Services 1999). This is also the "official" term used by the Indian Health Service, the U.S. Census Bureau, and in treaty language, and is the most common way in which indigenous people in the U.S. refer to themselves (Seideman et al. 1996). How these groups prefer to be addressed varies by region, but, for the purposes of this chapter, the term "American Indian" will be used.

It is impossible to provide an in-depth understanding of a culture in the context of a chapter or even a book. People of all cultures are complex and have been affected by various forces in their lives. It is important not to stereotype or to make overgeneralizations. There are more than five hundred distinct American Indian tribal cultures in the United States, with languages, customs, and beliefs unique to each (Jervis, Jackson, Manson 2002; Indian Health Service 2001a). Therefore, as you read this chapter, keep in mind that everything written here is a generalization across tribal cultures. Much of what is written tends to be true for many American Indian people but should not be used as the definitive answer when working with American Indian elders and their families. Instead, view the information provided as a good starting place along with the recommendations at the end of the chapter. A wonderful aspect of working with people is the dynamic nature of relationships. If one approaches one's work with American Indian elders with genuine interest and sincerity, with some general information and a willingness to learn, most American Indians will respond positively.

This chapter provides a historical and contemporary context to those who work with American Indian elders. It is hoped that by gaining an increased understanding of both the history and contemporary realities of American Indians, you will be able to respond in a respectful manner to assist these elders to live well to the end of their days.

HISTORICAL OVERVIEW

There are various academic theories about where North American Indians "came from," but the tribal groups themselves believe in the oral histories passed down through generations. Most of these stories describe the groups as having originated on this continent. These stories of origin are too extensive and varied to describe here. One can learn more by contacting local tribal groups that can relate the stories written about their people. Many American Indian elders may not want these stories to be written down but will share them with you in certain settings and in certain seasons.

The history of American Indians is, unfortunately, similar across the Americas. Although the general public has a sense of this history, most people do not know the extent or specifics of the policies of exploitation and annihilation that many American Indian elders lived through. These policies and practices continue to have enormous consequences for the American Indian population throughout the country. It is therefore critical that social workers and other providers of health and human services understand and address these influences.

The clash between cultures began with first contact in the 1400s. Whereas the native groups lived in harmony and balance with nature, recognizing that survival depended on this harmonious philosophy, non-natives who came to this continent believed in domination over nature and other "inferior" cultures (Peacock & Wisuri 2002; White Shield 2001). The estimated population of indigenous peoples on this continent at first contact varies, with ten million as a conservative estimate. Mass numbers died from disease, especially smallpox (Cook 2001; Indian Health Service 2001a; U.S. Department of Health and Human Services 1999; Zinn 2003), which was often deliberately introduced to natives through "gifts" of blankets (Red Horse et al. 2000). Some researchers have estimated that 90–99 percent of the American Indian population died as a result of contact with Europeans (Brucker & Perry 1998; Stiffarm & Lane 1992; U.S. Department of Health and Human Services 1999).

The U.S. policies toward American Indians were designed to forever destroy the cultures, languages, religions, and other practices of tribes across the nation. The impact of these policies is still felt today (Weaver & Yellow Horse Brave Heart 1999; Red Horse et al. 2000; Struthers & Lowe 2003). One example was the Allotment Act of 1887 through which land occupied by American Indians was divided into individual tracts. Some were "given" to

American Indian individuals, but most of the land was opened up for white homesteaders. American Indians did not practice or understand individual land ownership. Consequently millions of additional acreage was lost through fraud and failure to pay taxes (Peacock & Wisuri 2002; U.S. Department of Health and Human Services 1999). This was especially heinous, as land was considered sacred to tribal people and not to be "owned." Many American Indian elders who lived through this era may have life stories illustrating their struggle to hold onto traditional lands. Living through these kinds of traumas created distrust of government and those in positions of authority. Chronic stress from these traumas has been found to impact the health and well-being of tribal peoples (Mason 2001; Struthers & Lowe 2003; Yellow Horse Brave Heart 1999). It is important for providers to know about this history and understand its impact on American Indian elders.

AMERICAN INDIAN SOVEREIGNTY

American Indians are unique as a minority because of the sovereign status of tribes. Tribes have a "government to government" relationship directly with the federal government that dates back to treaties and has been reinforced by executive orders and court cases (Indian Health Service 2001b). American Indian tribes, as sovereign governments, entered into treaties with the federal government outlining tribal ownership of land through reservations and a tribal governmental land base within the U.S. Because of the treaties, the American Indians trust that the U.S. government will honor its obligation to adhere to the contents of the treaties and "represent the best interests of tribes and their members" (Poupart et al. 2000, p. 23). Tribes are thus able to engage in economic (gaming), social (tribal human services, housing, schools), legal (tribal law enforcement and courts) and other activities of a sovereign nation (ibid.). It is important for health and human service providers to understand this unique designation when working with American Indian elders and their families. This legal status provides dual citizenship to American Indians who are enrolled members of a tribe. Enrolled tribal members are citizens and are able to participate in the rights and privileges of their tribe as well as their rights and privileges as U.S. citizens.

AMERICAN INDIAN BOARDING SCHOOLS

One of the most devastating federal policies directed toward American Indians is referred to as the "boarding school era." Although written accounts document the formation of these schools as early as the 1600s, residential boarding schools for American Indians really flourished after the passage of the Indian Civilization Act in 1824. This act "provided federal funding for the formal schooling of Indians" (Peacock & Wisuri 2002, p. 80). Its sole purpose was to remove Indian children from their families and communities and to replace tribal culture, language, and religion with mainstream culture (Cleary & Peacock 1998; Struthers & Lowe 2003; U.S. Department of Health and Human Services 1999). Many American Indian elders were placed in boarding schools, often at very young ages. Some remained there until they were eighteen or nineteen years old. Usually, they were sent to a school a long distance away from their families, ensuring that they would have no contact with their family or tribal community. This practice was not only destructive to individual children and families but to entire tribal cultures (Red Horse et al. 2000; Struthers & Lowe 2003; U.S. Department of Health and Human Services 1999).

The history of boarding schools has received little publicity among people in mainstream American society, even though it is one of the most defining historical events for American Indians. It is important to remember that developmentally children tend to internalize this kind of trauma, blaming themselves rather than the adults who inflicted the trauma. Cultural values, beliefs, and traditions held by today's American Indian elders were greatly influenced by many of the policies and practices of the federal government toward American Indians. The historical impact of boarding schools is especially significant to American Indian elders, many of whom where sent or forced to attend boarding schools. It was common for children four or five years of age to be sent to government- or mission-run boarding schools where they were forced to give up all they had known. It is estimated that during the 1930s and 1940s, half of all American Indians attended boarding schools (U.S. Department of Health and Human Services 1999). Today these individuals would be in their seventies, eighties, and nineties.

Once in a boarding school, the children were often treated in harsh, institutional ways. Many boarding schools were fashioned after the military: young children had their hair cut short, a sign of mourning in many tribal cultures; they were literally scrubbed down; they were not allowed to speak their native language; they were forced to follow a regimented schedule; and they lived in dormitories. The boys wore military-type uniforms, and the girls had to wear dresses. Their days were divided between academic studies, much of which stressed a "civilized" lifestyle while criticizing native ways of life, and instruction in technical skills. The boys were taught skills such as farming and carpentry, and the girls were taught housekeeping or cooking skills (Lowe 1996; Poupart et al. 2000).

The personal histories of many American Indian elders have surfaced in recent years (Weaver & Yellow Horse Brave Heart 1999). Today American Indian elders are beginning to share their boarding school stories in an effort to help people understand their experiences and how it affected them. They share their pain and trauma and talk about how the policies of assimilation and boarding schools have affected generations of Indian families (Red Horse et al. 2000; U.S. Department of Health and Human Services 1999).

One elder spoke of being taken from her family when she was five years old and placed in a government-run boarding school. She only knew her native language, but she and the other children were slapped if they spoke anything but English. She claimed to have been "lucky" to have had her aunt, who was nine, with her to help her learn English and instruct her on how to behave in an institutional environment. She remembered seeing one little girl beaten until she was black and blue "on her back so no one could tell" (Carnahan 2003). Many other American Indian elders experienced both physical and sexual abuse while in boarding schools (Weaver & Yellow Horse Brave Heart 1999).

Sadly, these experiences were commonplace for many American Indian elders when they were children (Yellow Horse Brave Heart 2001). Most American Indian elders never speak of these experiences but have been deeply affected by them. The elder who recounted the above story did so for the first time when she was ninety-six years old. Living in a nursing home may bring back repressed memories and feelings of sadness or anger. Knowledge of the boarding school era may help providers understand the context of some behaviors so that they can respond compassionately.

DEMOGRAPHICS

Throughout the years, because of war, smallpox and other diseases, and oppressive actions by the U.S. government and military, the American Indian population was reduced to less than a quarter of a million people by 1900 (Indian Health Service 2001b). Today American Indian populations have grown to approximately 4.1 million people, or about 1.5 percent of the total population (U.S. Census Bureau 2001). The rapidly growing American Indian population is diverse and lives throughout the U.S. and Canada. Although American Indians are small in number, it is almost certain that health professionals today will work with an American Indian patient (Brucker & Perry 1998). Approximately half of all Indians live on reservations or trust lands, and the other half live in urban areas (Brucker & Perry 1998; Lowe & Struthers 2001; Redford 2002).

The Indian Health Service Current Population (1997–99) survey found that, compared to the general population, American Indians have bigger families, little or no health insurance, and low median incomes (Benson 2002; Redford 2002; Trujillo 2000). The poverty level for American Indians is three times higher than for the general population (http://infor.his.gov/ Indian Health Service 2001a), with 32 percent of the population living below the poverty line. From 1990 to 2001 the American Indian/Alaska Native population grew by 26 percent (Garrett 2002). Thirty percent of American Indians over twenty-five years of age who reside on reservations do not have high school diplomas (Indian Health Service 2001a). Overall American Indians are economically poor, and this poverty affects their health outcomes as they have limited resources and lack of access to health care (Benson 2002; Redford 2002).

American Indian elders are more often located in rural areas (Garrett 2002), whereas younger family members have moved to urban areas for employment. This is not to say that American Indian elders do not live in urban areas. The federal government's relocation program during the 1950s promoted urban dwelling by offering American Indians incentives to move to large urban areas across the country (Forquera 2002; Peacock & Wisuri 2002). Many American Indians moved to urban centers at that time and never returned to reservations. There are now many American Indians who have never lived or even been to their home reservation (Forquera 2002; Seideman et al. 1996). Although this lessened cultural ties for some families, it also inadvertently created pan-traditional Indian communities in urban areas that are composed of many tribal groups that support one another and share indigenous worldviews and practices. Elders living in an urban setting may be less able to count on extended family support as they age, and so they are more likely to enter nursing homes (Forquera 2002; Smith 1993).

ROLE OF CULTURE

The Administration on Aging (2002, p. 8) defines culture as "the shared values, traditions, norms, customs, arts, history, folklore, and institutions of a group of people." It is important for practitioners to see American Indian culture as a resource and a strength. Understanding culture helps us to place people, behaviors, and a worldview in context while avoiding stereotypes and our own biases. Once we do that, we can make decisions about the most effective ways to interact as practitioners with members of another culture (ibid.).

The degree to which American Indian elders and their family members practice traditional culture varies greatly. This continuum has been refer-enced in different ways throughout the literature on American Indians. It is often described as the level of a person's acculturation, that is, the extent to which a person of color participates in mainstream values and behaviors rather than those of the person's cultural group (Locke 1992; Lum 1996; Dubray & Sanders 1999). The cultural continuum is not always linear but sometimes occurs in spirals. For example, Mrs. Jones, of our case study, grew up speaking her traditional language, Ojibwe, as her first language until the age of five when she was sent to a boarding school. Up to that time she was knowledgeable about her tribal language and cultural traditions. Once at boarding school, however, English and Christianity replaced Ojibwe and her traditional native religion. Of course, it is very difficult to replace one's cultural worldview entirely, and so Mrs. Jones, like most American Indian elders, respects traditional practices and sees the world through an indigenous lens with regard to values and norms of behavior. This tends to be true whether or not the elder actively practices traditional ways of behaving. The cultural continuum ranges from those who practice primarily traditional American Indian ways to those who are virtually non-practicing. The midpoint is someone who is said to be "bi-cultural," able to walk in both worlds (Locke 1992; Lum 1996; Dubray & Sanders 1999).

Mrs. Jones, like most American Indian elders, falls somewhere in the middle of this continuum. She speaks and understands her language but does not actively participate in traditional cultural practices. She considers herself a Catholic. On the other hand, some American Indian elders speak only their traditional language and are totally immersed in their traditions. Members of this group would find living in a nursing home most uncomfortable, especially a non-Indian nursing home. Non-practicing or acculturated American Indian elders may have the easiest cultural adjustment. Providers that understand the role culture plays in adjustment will be more successful in working with American Indian elders and their families (Dubray & Sanders 1999). The adjustment made by Mrs. Jones and others like her is greatly affected by the involvement of family and extended family. The latter is very important to American Indians and may include not only immediate family members but also more distantly related relatives (Red Horse 1997; Joe & Malach 1992; Brucker & Perry 1998). Because Mrs. Jones's granddaughter lives close to the nursing home, she will likely continue to play an important role in her grandmother's transition to the nursing home.

Some tribal groups consider clan members to be extended family, and it is not unusual to be adopted culturally. Unless providers understand not only the role of families but also the extent of family systems, there may be misunderstandings. Trying to work collaboratively with the family, as well as with the elders, is critical (Red Horse 1997; Brucker & Perry 1998; Dubray & Sanders 1999). In the case example, family was the first option explored by Mrs. Jones. Research has consistently found that American Indian elders expect to be cared for within their families whenever feasible (Henderson 2002; Redford 2002). When Mrs. Jones needed assistance, she initially went to live with her daughter. When this option was no longer available because of her daughter's ill health, her granddaughter was able to provide care even though this required Mrs. Jones to move away from the reservation to an urban area. Mrs. Jones entered the nursing home only when her level of care became more than what her granddaughter's family could reasonably provide. Even though home care is preferred by most native people, the changes in family structure and the growing American Indian elder population has created an increased need for residential long-term care (Benson 2002; Henderson 2002; Redford 2002).

AMERICAN INDIAN IDENTITY

American Indians as a group have tended to want to retain their identity in spite of the enormous pressures to assimilate (Dubray & Sanders 1999; Garrett & Garrett 1994). This is evidenced through the maintenance of their culture, language, and worldview in spite of the many efforts to eradicate American Indian culture and practices. In urban areas multiple tribal groups maintain indigenous worldviews through community gatherings, tribal schools, and tribal social services (housing, group homes for adolescents, chemical dependency programs, shelters, etc.). These community gatherings and organizations provide opportunities to maintain tribal identity, often across multiple tribal groups. On reservations these activities tend to be focused on the main tribal group rather than on many tribal cultures.

At a community gathering in Minneapolis, Minnesota, an Ojibwe elder talked about how American Indians are unique because, when we look at the world, we "look through the eyes of our elders." His example was that seeing an old tree or a rock painting that has existed for generations might evoke strong feelings (Kinew 2003), and these feeling may be identical to those of our ancestors when they came upon the same tree or rock painting. A similar outlook is described in the book *Ojibwe Waasa Inaabidaa—We Look in All Directions*. The authors of this book describe the teachings of living in harmony with the natural world and the "collective nature of things" as an "essential part of our ways of being" (Peacock & Wisuri 2002, p. 45). One of the authors goes on to talk about returning to the ancestral home of his father and grandparents. He walked up a path and sat on a bench that looked over Lake Superior:

> I sat on a bench my ancestor had built many, many years ago, and I was overcome with a sense of awe and wonderment at the collective spirit of that place. . . . I could feel the spirits of my father and great-grandparents sitting on the bench with me that day, and it was as though I saw the world with the same sense of wonder that children, like my granddaughters, see the world with. The past, present, and future, all were a part of the collective spirit of that place. (p. 45)

This "collective consciousness," or awareness on a subconscious level, can also explain the historic trauma that many American Indians feel. Not only do the elders deal with the traumas they may have experienced firsthand, but they also experience the upset that their ancestors felt during the time of great upheaval in native cultures across this country (de Graaf 2001). Duran (2001) describes this as a wounding of the soul in which the spirit is injured. Although this extreme awareness of one's ancestry can be a burden, it also has allowed tribal cultures to persevere against great odds. The capacity of American Indians to endure against the powerful forces of assimilation is based on the survival of their culture, and oral tradition is at the heart of Indian culture (Weaver & Yellow Horse Brave Heart 1999).

STATUS OF ELDERS

The role and status of American Indian elders within their families and communities is well documented (Henderson 2002; Red Horse et al. 2000). American Indian children are taught from an early age to respect and care for their elders (Dubray & Sanders 1999). Because of the strong role that elders play in the family and community fabric, most American Indian elders are cared for within the context of their families. Currently one of four American Indians is a caregiver for a family member or friend (Administration on Aging 2002).

Unlike most non-Indian elders, American Indian elders are expected to assume "increased kinship responsibilities" as they age (Red Horse 1997, p. 245). "Elders are 'libraries' of Indian knowledge, history, and tradition. Their wisdom is a source of strength in Indian communities" (Poupart et al. 2000, p. 33). American Indian elders, both on reservations and in urban areas, play a significant role in both family life and the continuance of culture within the tribal group (Henderson 2002; Red Horse 1997). Providers should respect this role when working with American Indian elders and their families (Clarke, Zales, & Sacco 1982; Anderson & Stewart 1983; Joe & Malach 1992; Dubray and Sanders 1999).

HEALTH

While inactivity and a change in diet has occurred throughout American culture, policies of extermination greatly impacted the healthier traditional foods and activities of American Indians (Peacock & Wisuri 2002). American Indians, compared to other groups, have poor health outcomes (Dubray 1992, 1993; Dubray & Sanders 1999; Redford 2002) which has been attributed to reservation life, the boarding school experience, and the overall disruption of the American Indian way of life (Struthers & Lowe 2003). Traditional native diets have generally been replaced by foods high in fat, starch, and carbohydrates. The survival of American Indians at one time required a great deal of activity, but this changed with the move to reservations. Along with a more sedentary lifestyle, traditional games and sports were replaced with inactivity, and all this affected their physical health (Cook 1998).

American Indians have high rates of alcoholism, diabetes, and heart disease (Dubray & Sanders 1999; Yellow Horse Brave Heart 1999), all of which lead to debilitating conditions and greater levels of chronic disability. These illnesses can result in the need for nursing home care (Benson 2002; Bernard, Lampley-Dallas, & Smith 1997; Jervis, Jackson, & Manson 2002; Redford 2002). Not surprisingly American Indians have high rates of mortality in comparison with the general population. Alcoholism is 740 percent higher; tuberculosis, 500 percent higher; diabetes, 390 percent higher; and injuries, 340 percent higher (Indian Health Service 2001b). According to the Administration on Aging (2002, p. 13), American Indians are 50 percent more likely to have congestive heart failure; 44 percent more likely to have asthma; and 18 percent more likely to have a stroke. These health issues are at crisis levels and often result in the need for long-term care for American Indian elders. "Elders are again the forgotten people when it comes to overall health care that has been promised to our Native Americans" (Smith 1993, p. 50).

Life expectancy for American Indians has improved significantly since the 1950s but is still below that for the general population: 71.1 years for American Indians compared to 78.9 years for whites (Administration on Aging 2002, p. 13). It is predicted that the percentage of American Indian elders over age sixty-five will grow significantly between 1990 and 2030 (Administration on Aging 2002, p. 13). Even though the health status of American Indians has improved somewhat since the 1950s, American Indians continue to lag behind in educational attainment, have high rates of unemployment, and have the poorest health outcomes of any group in the United States (Indian Health Service 2001b).

HEALTH AND SPIRITUALITY

For American Indians, spirituality is incorporated into everything (Red Horse 1997; Dubray & Sanders 1999). Spirituality is "the essence of our being, which permeates our living and infuses our ongoing awareness of who and what we are, our purpose in being, and our inner resources, and shapes our life journey" (Burkhardt & Nagai Jacobson 2000, p. 91).

American Indians throughout the country share a common belief that when things are in balance everything else will be okay. In regions of the Midwest and Canada, the Anishinaabe people live where they have lived for centuries. They believe that living a good life means living in connection and harmony in a spiritual way with everything and everyone around you—"mino-bimaadiziwin"—the good life (Peacock & Wisuri 2002, p. 91). This means being ever aware of the seasons and participating in traditional rituals and ceremonies.

This holistic perspective—that mind, body, and spirit are linked—has implications for working with American Indian elders. Because the American Indian worldview connects everything with the natural world and with spirituality, there is a belief about the interconnectedness of all things, including physical, spiritual, and psychological health (Joe & Malach 1992; Dubray & Sanders 1999; Lowe & Struthers 2001). "In the time of our greatest need, we call upon the Creator and the spirits of our ancestors, our parents, our grandparents, and our aunties and uncles who have passed before us to give us solace, to be with us, to help us, and to guide us in making important decisions" (Peacock & Wisuri 2002, p. 98). The concept of "illness" is often thought of as being out of balance and may require a ceremony or ritual to restore that balance (Brucker & Perry 1998; Dubray & Sanders 1999; Yellow Horse Brave Heart 2001). American Indians have always known that spirituality is important for maintaining and restoring both physical and mental health (Duran 2001; Mehl-Medora 1999; Meisenhelder & Chandler 2000).

In addition to spiritual interventions, plants are often used in healing in various ways, for example, drinking a medicinal tea. Plants may also be used in ceremonies or to purify or clear sickness or death from a person or space. Traditional practices may be unfamiliar to the professional but appropriate within the context of one's culture (Crowe 1997; Duran 2001; Dubray & Sanders 1999). According to Garwick (2000, p. 6), "families who used native healing practices want healthcare professionals to know about and respect herbal remedies, healing ceremonies, and traditional healers." This can often present problems in nursing homes, since staff may be unaware of these practices or such remedies may not be allowed or may be seen as invalid forms of treatment. Because of the oppression they experienced regarding their traditional religion, many native people will not discuss ceremonies or practices with non-natives (Peacock & Wisuri 2002), and this makes it difficult for elders in mainstream nursing homes to utilize these ceremonies and practices to restore their balance.

MENTAL HEALTH

American Indian researchers have studied the devastating impact of federal policy on American Indians. Intergenerational post-traumatic stress has been found to be related to boarding schools and other oppressive practices (Duran & Duran 1996; Dubray & Sanders 1999; Red Horse et al. 2000). This trauma can be carried through generations.

Indian children were also removed in massive numbers from their homes through placement in foster care and adoptive homes. The Bureau of Indian Affairs partnered with the Child Welfare League of America in 1957 to develop the Indian Adoption Project. It is estimated that, through these practices, 25–35 percent of all Indian children ended up being cared for outside their homes (Red Horse et. al. 2000). In 1978 the Indian Child Welfare Act was passed in an effort to reduce the number of children being taken from their families, communities, and culture (Seideman et al. 1996). Many of today's American Indian elders and their families were either victims of boarding schools or of the child welfare system.

In recent years a new term, "historic trauma," has been used to describe this cultural devastation. The term refers to "cumulative wounding across generations as well as during one's life span. For native people, the legacy of genocide includes distortions of indigenous identity, self-concept, and values. The process of colonization and varying degrees of assimilation into the dominant cultural value system have resulted in altered states of an Indian sense of self" (Weaver & Yellow Horse Brave Heart 1999, p. 22). The impact has long been documented by reports of high rates of alcoholism, depression, and early death among tribal peoples. Only within the last ten years has the genesis of these behaviors been explored in depth, on both the individual and community levels.

"Collective trauma unfolds as an omnipresent, community-wide phenomenon, while individual trauma unfolds as a personal psychological phenomenon unrelated to a collective common experience" (Red Horse et al. 2000, p. 14). Today American Indians still suffer high rates of alcoholism, mental health issues, and violence. This connection between historical trauma and contemporary individual and community health is critical for understanding what is happening today with American Indians (Duran & Duran 1996; Cleary & Peacock 2002). This is especially relevant to American Indian elders, many of whom experienced these traumas directly.

Policies of termination forced traditional religion, language, and culture to go underground in an effort to keep practices alive. As a result, the number of American Indians who practiced traditional ways diminished, and in some tribes these traditions no longer survive. It is no surprise that mental health among American Indians has been poor (Brucker & Perry 1996; Peacock & Wisuri 2002). But although mental health issues exist at high rates in American Indian communities (Mason 2001), mainstream models have proven ineffective from assessment to treatment (Bullock 2001; Struthers & Lowe 2003). Some studies have suggested that American Indians may have a conception of mental health that differs from that of mainstream clinicians (U.S. Department of Health and Human Services 1999).

According to the U.S. Surgeon General's report on mental health care for American Indians and Alaska Natives, there have been no published "large-scale studies" done on the incidence of mental health problems among American Indians and Alaska Native adults. Other national studies of mental health disparities tend to represent American Indians inaccurately because of the small sample size, cultural differences in definitions of mental health, and the wide diversity among native tribes (Redford 2002; U.S. Department of Health and Human Services 1999). Smaller-scale studies that have been done with American Indian adults have indicated mental health disorders at rates higher than those of other minority groups. Suicide rates have been found to be 1.5 times the national rate (U.S. Department of Health and Human Services 1999). Some American Indians have been found to have high incidences of pathological gambling addictions (Zitzow 1996), which has been associated with depression.

Although American Indians have been found to have high rates of mental health distress, they have limited access to mental health services (Mason 2001). American Indians who do seek mental health services from mainstream providers have been found to terminate these services after an average of three visits (Ball 2001; Duran 2001; Struthers & Lowe 2002). All these mental health conditions have been directly tied to historic grief and trauma, so it is essential that providers are aware of this connection (Leininger 1995; Weaver & Yellow Horse Brave Heart 1999).

INDIAN HEALTH SERVICE

One of the rights guaranteed to American Indians by treaty and clarified through the years in court rulings and Acts of Congress is the right to health care. The Indian Health Service, according to their website, was established to provide health care to federally recognized tribal members. "The mission of the Indian Health Service, in partnership with American Indians and Alaska Natives, is to raise their physical, mental, social, and spiritual health to the highest possible level" (Indian Health Service 2001a). This is done through the provision of public health services to "promote healthy American Indians and Alaska Natives, communities, and cultures and to honor and protect the inherent sovereign rights of tribes" (ibid.).

Currently the majority of American Indians (55 percent) rely solely on the Indian Health Service for their health care. It has been estimated that the Indian Health Service only meets 60 percent of the health care needs of the American Indian population because of inadequate funding levels (Indian Health Service 2001b). Only 1 percent of Indian Health Service funding is targeted to urban areas even though 50 percent of the American Indian population lives there (Forquera 2002).

Long-term care was not included in the original Indian Health Service funding formula and has never been added, even though in 1992 the National Indian Conference on Aging identified long-term care as the number one health concern for American Indian elders across the nation (Redford 2002). Most American Indian elders who live on tribal lands still receive their health care from the Indian Health Service. If they are located close to an Indian Health Service facility once they enter a nursing home, the Indian Health Service may continue to provide the health care they are entitled to, such as dental care and pharmacy services. Tribal elders may also be eligible for Medical Assistance or Medicaid or both. However, a report by the Henry J. Kaiser Family Foundation found that many American Indians did not apply for these programs even though they were eligible. The same report indicated that American Indians in general were one of the least insured groups (Forquera 2002).

Mrs. Jones, like most American Indians, had no health insurance. While living on the reservation, her health care was provided by the local Indian Health Service clinic and Medicare benefits. Her income consisted of a small

Social Security check. Until she moved in with her daughter, she lived in her home, which she owned on property that her mother had received during the Indian Allotment Act era. When she moved to her granddaughter's home, she continued to receive some services, such as prescription benefits from the local Indian Service urban clinic. When she moved into the nursing home, however, she ended up having to sell some of her property to pay for her nursing home care.

PREFERENCES FOR ELDER CARE

As American Indians live longer and extended family members are not available to care for them, many elders find that chronic illnesses and old age require them to seek long-term care (Smith 1993). American Indian elders tend to develop disability and functional impairment from chronic health conditions that can cause a significant burden to family caregivers who lack the appropriate resources to assist them (Indian Health Service 2001b). According to census projections, the American Indian population aged sixty-five and older will grow by 250 percent in the next fifty years (ibid.). As this population grows, obviously the need for nursing homes will increase as well.

Elders who live on reservations have unique barriers in receiving care. Nursing homes in rural areas tend to be long distances from families and tribal communities (Jervis, Jackson, & Manson 2002; Manson & Callaway 1988; Begay 2002), which results in many elders not receiving needed care as families are reluctant to place elders far from home. Elders that are placed in nursing homes far from their families often feel isolated and abandoned, since their families cannot visit regularly. The lack of nursing homes run by American Indians also means that the cultural needs of American Indian residents are met inadequately or not at all by nursing home staff. Most American Indian elders who need to live in a nursing home are placed in a non-Indian nursing home. American Indian elders primarily want to remain close to family members, but, if that is not possible, they want at least to retain some normalcy in their lives by eating the foods they are accustomed to eating, for example, and practicing traditions that bring them comfort (Jervis, Jackson, & Manson 2002; Begay 2002).

Although tribes recognize the need for long-term care, only a few have the resources to develop tribal nursing homes (Administration on Aging 2002), which is why most American Indian elders are either cared for at home or reside in non-Indian nursing homes. Some reservations are so remote that it would be very difficult for tribes to financially maintain a nursing home facility. Further, many physicians and other skilled nursing home staff are reluctant to reside in the isolated, rural areas where reservations are located. Because of these factors, there are fewer than fifteen American Indian nursing homes across the country (Benson 2002; Finke 2002; Smith 1993). Those that exist often have limited services and lack certified doctors and staff. They tend to be relatively small with an average bed capacity of only fifty (Fink 2002). There are no known urban tribal nursing homes (Forquera 2002).

In the Southwest the Navajo tribe has tried to meet the needs of their older adult population for long-term care through group homes and their own nursing home. Even with these efforts, it is estimated that more than six hundred Navajo elders seek nursing home care outside the reservation (Begay 2002). Tribes acknowledge the need to build new nursing homes on reservations, support or enhance existing tribal nursing homes, and work with non-Indian homes to bring traditional foods, language, and activities to the elders who reside there. These identified needs, however, cannot be filled with current limited resources (Benson 2002).

There are many benefits for American Indian elders who are in tribal nursing homes: they are happier living among other American Indians; most tribal nursing homes are closer to family members; traditional practices are understood and accessible; and they can continue to eat traditional foods. Although one might think that this last item is minor, one American Indian elder in a non-Indian nursing home was reported to have said, "their fish doesn't taste like our fish" (Carnahan 2003); as a result, her appetite lessened and she became more fragile. Because the role of elders is understood and valued in a tribal nursing home, elders tend to feel more respected there (Smith 1993).

One such tribal nursing home in the upper Midwest, like others, was developed in an effort to "keep elders close to home." Elders from many other regional reservations also make the nursing home their home. Prior to the establishment of this nursing home, elders needing nursing home care were sent to other communities, some hours away from family members. Because the nursing home is small and most of the staff are community members, they have a lot of informal contact with family members. "The feeling [here] is good! The care is good, it is "in your heart" to care for these elders as if they were your own [family]." When having to make a decision, the social worker often asks the staff, "if this were your gramma, what would you do?" (Goodwin 2003).

A unique feature of a tribal nursing home, as noted, is the acceptance of traditional religious practices. Non-native staff has described this as "religious freedom" that they do not see in mainstream nursing homes. It is common for staff and residents to burn sage, and then use it to "smudge," and thus purify, the room of a resident who has died. Families are allowed to enlist people who practice traditional medicine or an Indian doctor to care for their family member in the nursing home. If a family wants their elder to use traditional medicine, such as tea, the staff can dispense it. American Indians tend to use humor in dealing with many situations, and so the tribal nursing home is often filled with laughter among both its staff and residents.

Elders who come to the tribal facility from other nursing homes often talk about the differences. One American Indian elder, for example, had become severely depressed while residing in a mainstream nursing home. She would not feed herself and did not want to eat. She sat in her room and would not participate in any activities. When she came to the tribal facility, she told the staff, she realized that she had "felt discriminated against" in the mainstream facility. When she saw that most of the staff at the tribal nursing home was American Indian and that the environment was so much more familiar, she regained her appetite and began to eat again. She now participates in many activities, including bingo at the casino twice a month!

The activities available at the tribal nursing home are varied and culturally appropriate. The community and local Department of Natural Resources donate food so the elders maintain seasonal foods in their diet, including wild rice, maple syrup, fish, and deer meat. Fry bread is cooked at the nursing home, and families are permitted to use the kitchen facilities to make meals for their family member. There are weekly powwows and other community social events such as day trips to other reservations. Elders sometimes attend elders' conferences overnight. The local tribal community informs the tribal nursing home of events and actively seeks the involvement and attendance of American Indian elders. Through this ongoing community involvement, elders feel that they are still contributing to society; they also feel wanted and respected by the community.

ISSUES WITHIN NURSING HOMES

The reality is that, given the growing American Indian elderly population, larger numbers of American Indian elders will be placed in mainstream long-term care facilities. It is important, therefore, to be aware of potential conflicts that can occur when elders are in non-Indian nursing homes.

The worldview of most American Indian elders is that they are to be highly respected and valued (Garrett & Garrett 1994). They expect family members to take care of them. When this is not possible, a family conflict may arise. Once in a nursing home, the elderly still expect that they will be treated with the utmost respect at all times. Although nursing homes seek to care for their residents with "respect," American Indian elders define this term in a unique way. What is considered appropriate respectful behavior in mainstream culture may be seen as disrespectful in American Indian culture. Most nursing home staff is not trained to respond to elders in the manner they expect. For example, making prolonged direct eye contact with an elder is considered respectful in mainstream culture, but American Indian elders may view this as intimidating or disrespectful. Direct confrontations are also avoided in American Indian families (Garrett & Garrett 1994). Family members, out of respect, usually never disagree with an elder, even if they see things differently. Elders in nursing homes are often made to follow directions or keep to a routine not of their choosing. If they refuse, they may still be required to do as asked. It is inherently disrespectful, in the American Indian worldview, to tell an elder what to do. It is counter to the belief of noninterference (Garrett & Garrett 1994, Joe & Malach 1992). Understanding this may encourage staff to take a nondirective approach whenever possible.

At home and at tribal community gatherings, most American Indian elders are given special treatment. For example, they are usually the first to be served food. Most nursing homes are understaffed and so cannot respond to an elder's request to be treated in a manner to which he or she is accustomed. It is often necessary for staff to work with families to help American Indian elders understand that their requests will be met but not, perhaps, immediately, as they might expect. In this way they can continue to feel respected and valued. Family members can also help to insure that their elder is receiving the care they are entitled to.

Although nursing homes may try to be respectful of traditional ways, sometimes conflicts may arise when staff is informed of traditional practices. These practices may go against organizational policies. For example, some elders in the nursing home may want to keep their sacred medicines with them (Brucker & Perry 1998; Dubray & Sanders 1999), but this may conflict with the facility's policy. Other American Indian elders may want to be treated with traditional folk medicine, which might involve a ceremony or ritual or the burning or ingesting of traditional medicines. This may also be seen as unacceptable in an institutional setting. Still other elders may want to be treated with Western medicine as well as traditional native doctoring (Indian Health Service 2001b). Policies should be in place to support and encourage these practices, so that American Indian elders can continue traditional practices at this time in their lives.

Some American Indian elders have learned to practice Christianity rather than traditional religion, something which many learned at boarding schools. It is important not to assume which practice an American Indian elder follows. Some elders practice, or at least respect, both Christianity and traditional customs (Dubray & Sanders 1999). Others, because of the trauma of boarding school or other oppressive experiences, may exhibit severe adverse reactions to anything associated with Christianity. Practitioners should be aware of this history and respect it.

To some American Indian elders, the gender of the caregiver is very important, especially when the care concerns personal matters (Mercer 1996). It may be taboo for a staff member to bathe an elder of the opposite sex. Some male American Indian elders may expect that a woman is supposed to care for them. Other elders may feel more comfortable with a man, as he is seen as stronger and more able to provide physical assistance. The gender of the caregiver should be taken into consideration as much as possible.

Living with a roommate or in an institutional setting may bring back memories, conscious or subconscious, of an elder's time in a boarding school. Some may feel what other residents or staff might label an "irrational" fear of other residents or staff. Staff members who are not aware of the elder's past history may dismiss the resident's fears. One American Indian nursing home resident felt that she always had to "keep an eye" on her roommate (Carnahan 2003).

Time is seen as more fluid by American Indians than by non-Indians (Brucker & Perry 1998; Dubray & Sanders 1999), especially by elders. One elder explained, "The spirits don't recognize time" and therefore many elders see something as happening "in its own time," when it is supposed to happen and not by the "clock." This clearly has implications for elders regarding schedules and appointments with family members.

American Indians also tend to be more group-oriented than individualistic (Joe & Malach 1992; Brucker & Perry 1998) and may be seen as more concerned with other residents than with themselves. They value, and have a tendency toward, generosity and may wish to share what they have with others. For example, sometimes an American Indian elder will consistently express concern about other residents. An elder might also give away food, perceiving that another resident needs it more. American Indians demonstrate honor and respect through the act of sharing (Brucker & Perry 1998; Garrett & Garrett 1994), but this cultural value may run counter to policies regulating what and how much a resident eats.

END-OF-LIFE ISSUES

American Indian elders do not like to talk about end-of-life issues, and this obviously makes it difficult to discuss long-term care (Redford 2002). It is even harder to talk about living wills and advance directives (Mercer 1996). American Indians generally do not like to talk directly about death. Many American Indian groups participate in cleansing and other ceremonies after the death of a loved one (Mercer 1996). The avoidance of discussions about end-of-life issues may present a conflict with what is needed by nursing homes and their licensing agencies who want to see evidence of these discussions reflected in patients' charts (Goodwin 2003). This conflict can be addressed, however, when the social worker is aware of this cultural taboo. The social worker can respectfully provide the opportunity to talk about end-of-life issues but honor the elder and the family's wishes if they choose not to do so. This can be noted in the patient record indicating the cultural norm of not discussing these issues in depth. In this way the social worker can educate the licensing agencies and other professionals about these norms.

COPING WITH CARE RECEIVING

American Indians, in general, believe in several key concepts that influence an elder's experience in a nursing home. One is their view of the world as a circle, with all things beginning and ending in the same place. One elder described the circle in the following way, relating it to the elderly: "If you live long enough and are lucky to become very old, you become a baby again. This means you have lived a very good life" (Stillday 2003).

Many American Indian elders accept their "fate" without question. One American Indian elder who resides in a mainstream nursing home kept assuring family members that she was okay living there: "Time passes quickly, I don't hurt anywhere, I am okay here." This acceptance comes from the belief that one must deal with what life offers (Joe & Malach 1992). Humor is often culturally based. It is important to American Indians, in general, to maintain a sense of humor throughout their lives. Indians laugh easily and enjoy stories about themselves that show them in humbling situations (Garrett & Garrett 1994). Creating an environment in which elders can share stories about themselves aids in their adjustment.

When American Indian elders need nursing home care, the issues they face are similar to those faced by other elders. These include a lack of privacy, loss of independence, and changes in one's identity and family role. Some issues, however, have culturally specific elements, and it is important for practitioners to be aware of these. Most American Indian elders play a strong role in their families and communities, and so when they move into a nursing home, a loss is felt not only to the elder and the elder's family but often to the tribal community as well (Henderson 2002). This loss may have been acknowledged prior to the elder's nursing home care, or it may come as a surprise to those who rely on this person. Family members may have been used to their elder relative taking care of everyone else and providing guidance for the family. This sudden role reversal can be upsetting and bring grief upon the family. Thus the family's responses to nursing home care can range from acceptance and support to guilt and avoidance (Goodwin 2003).

A deeply held cultural value in American Indian families is that elders are cared for at home, and so some families may worry about what others think of their decision to place an elderly family member in a nursing home. It is vital, therefore, to help the elder and family understand why nursing home care is essential and to work with them to accept this decision. Of course, families that must seek outside assistance for their elders will experience considerable conflict because of their inherent value system. When practitioners understand this reaction as a natural cultural response, they can help family members cope with the change. Because it is the tradition in American Indian communities that elders take care of you, when it becomes necessary you are now to take care of them. This increasingly includes making the difficult decision to place an elderly family member in long-term care when that is the most appropriate choice.

COMMUNICATION AND INTERACTION

Understanding the nonverbal communication patterns of American Indians is crucial. Whereas non-native providers may interpret indirect eye contact and silence as signs that the patient is not listening or is expressing disrespect, that response is actually quite common among American Indians as a sign of listening respectfully (Brucker & Perry 1998; Garwick, 2000). American Indian elders often use nonverbal communication which can lead to miscommunication if it is not recognized (Crowe 1997; Dubray & Sanders 1999). Another nonverbal cue is nodding as if in agreement, when, in fact, the elder is only indicating that he is listening. When nonverbal cues are misunderstood, elders can also be seen as being resistant (Sue & Sue 1990).

"We are always taught to be respectful of the doctor like you would be of the medicine man and you don't question them. . . . I think that piece is still there and more so with the elders" (Garwick 2000, p. 7). This attitude has implications for American Indian elders who may be reluctant to question or advocate for their own needs. Studies have shown that American Indians, before responding in a conversation, tend to pause an average of five seconds after another person stops talking to make sure that the person has finished speaking, whereas non-Indians tend to pause only one second (Brucker & Perry 1998). This cultural difference can result in a conversation being interrupted or a speaker moving on to another topic before the elder has had a chance to respond. Family and staff may need to be advocates for elders with medical personnel to ensure that the elder has a chance to ask questions and understands what is happening.

Their history of oppression has made many American Indian elders hesitant to trust providers (Dubray 1992; Locke 1992; Dubray & Sanders 1999; Joe & Malach 1992), especially in an institutional setting. Providers need to understand that American Indian elders and their families have not only been oppressed historically but have had to deal with racism and cultural insensitivity to this day. This makes it even more important to deal with American Indians in a culturally competent manner. Sometimes an organization's lack of cultural competence can result in a family feeling uncomfortable at the facility, and it is not uncommon for American Indian families either to stop visiting their elder relative altogether or simply decide to put up with their feelings of discomfort with the staff. As one member of an American Indian family stated, "I see my gramma in spite of the staff [at the nursing home]. I ignore them and they ignore me" (Medina 2003). The elder may or may not be aware of the tension between relatives and the nursing home staff, but surely it cannot be a positive experience for the resident. Nursing home staff should ask themselves: "Do all families feel equally welcome at our facility?" If American Indian family members appear to be less comfortable than other groups, then the institution is obliged to address this concern (Weaver 1999).

FOOD PREFERENCES

Long ago indigenous peoples utilized the food that surrounded them, and this varied depending on where they lived. For example, in Minnesota, Anishinabe people ate wildlife like deer, bear, moose, rabbit, and other game. They enjoyed many species of fresh water fish, birds, and food that could be gathered from under the ground, in the waters, and on the land, such as mushrooms, berries, and wild rice. Food was often gathered depending on the season, for instance, netting, spearing fish, and tapping maple trees for sugar and syrup in the spring; berry picking, gardening, and gathering other food stuffs during the summer; wild rice harvesting in the fall; and hunting and trapping during the winter. Today these traditional foods and ways of gathering still exist in tribal communities.

The food preferences of American Indian elders vary across tribal groups depending on the land where they lived. Many tribal elders who live in nursing homes grew up eating traditional foods such as fish, bison, berries, wild rice, corn, beans, nuts, and squash (Ambler 1999). These foods are often associated with family gatherings, and community and ceremonial functions (Norrel 2004). It can be very meaningful for these elders to be able to continue to eat these foods.

Providers should ask the resident and family members about individual food preferences and make efforts to accommodate them. For instance, in our case example, Mrs. Jones enjoyed eating wild rice, fish, venison, maple syrup, and blueberries. Although it was difficult to accommodate all these preferences, the nursing home did, on occasion, serve wild rice (mixed with white rice) and fish. Family members could bring in freshly picked blueberries and candy made from maple sugar. This may seem like a minor issue, but Mrs. Jones got a lot of pleasure and comfort from eating foods she had grown up eating. Some nursing facilities are able to allow residents' families to prepare entire meals on site to eat with their elder. Others may allow families to bring an occasional meal to the resident. Allowing people to eat foods that bring them good memories should be encouraged whenever possible.

CROSS-CULTURAL PRACTICE WITH AMERICAN INDIANS

There are several critical components for providers in the ongoing process of developing effective cross-cultural skills. The three main components are knowledge about American Indians, skill development specific to working with American Indians, and values that foster effective cross-cultural practice with American Indians.

KNOWLEDGE

Dr. Hilary Weaver (1999) has conducted research specifically on working with American Indian clients in a culturally competent manner. Her findings identified four important knowledge areas:

1. Practitioners must be aware of the differences between and among native groups. As previously stated, there are more than five hundred different tribes in the United States, each with distinct cultural and linguistic traditions. What is true for Mrs. Jones who grew up on a reservation in the northern Midwest may not be true for an elder of the same age who grew up in an urban area in California.

2. Practitioners must learn about historical federal policies and practices that have impacted tribal groups, especially pertaining to the impact of boarding schools. The historic trauma experienced by many American Indian elders impacts each elder in different ways.

3. How native people interact, communicate, see the world, and identify themselves is important. Universal American Indian key values include the "importance of family and extended family, respect for elders, matriarchal structures, spirituality, importance of tradition, and issues of death and mourning" (p. 221). The collective worldview versus the individualistic worldview was also identified.

4. It is essential to understand the contemporary realities of American Indians such as the sovereign status of tribes and the structure of local tribal governments and federal agencies such as the Indian Health Service that serve American Indians. By doing so, practitioners will learn what is locally available to assist native people (p. 221). They will also gain an awareness and understanding of the grief and loss issues that impact American Indians and affect their health adversely. Equally important is knowing about and being able to draw on the cultural strengths and resources in native communities.

SKILLS

Weaver (1999) also identified two major thematic areas when working with American Indian clients: general skills and containment skills. General skills involve being able to view, communicate, and solve problems from an American Indian worldview. Using a strengths-based approach was seen as most appropriate. The Administration on Aging also supports the "emic" approach of using a strengths perspective and strategies "which elders and their families identify for themselves as being most effective" (p. 5). This approach takes a holistic view of communities of color and encompasses the positive aspects of those communities in order to have a more accurate interpretation, and therefore intervention, when working with an elder of another culture. This in-depth understanding will ultimately lead to more effective cross-cultural practice (Administration on Aging 2002). To achieve this, it is important to ask elders and their families about their preferences and to accommodate these requests whenever possible.

Containment skills involve "patience, the ability to tolerate silence, and listening," as well as the use of humor (ibid., p. 222). Because American Indians tend to rely greatly on relationships with others, taking the time to listen and develop relationships with American Indian elders is very important.

VALUES

Four central themes emerged in the area of values: helper wellness and self-awareness; humility and a willingness to learn; respect, open-mindedness, and a nonjudgmental attitude; and an appropriate perspective on social justice (Weaver 1999).

The first theme, helper wellness and self-awareness, means that staff who work with American Indians should be "grounded in their own culture and spirituality" and conscious of their own beliefs, values, and biases about other cultures (ibid., p. 222). The second, humility and a willingness to learn, means to continually seek out knowledge about other cultures. This includes attending American Indian community events such as powwows. The third theme, respect, open-mindedness, and a nonjudgmental attitude, are self-explanatory. The final theme, social justice, may seem unrealistic for some staff, but it is important, especially when working with American Indian elders. Understanding the impact of historic and contemporary oppression on clients and their families is critical (ibid., p. 222), as it heightens an awareness to seek opportunities to impact policies and practices within one's own organization. Without this awareness and willingness to act, the power and control of staff and institutions may resemble causes of the loss of control and helplessness felt by American Indian elders throughout their lives.

CONCLUSION

The following interventions would help American Indian elders make a positive transition to living in a nursing home (Administration on Aging 2002; Joe & Malach 1992; Garrett & Garrett 1994; Garwick 2000; Seideman et al. 1996; and Weaver 1999). Although many of these suggestions are obviously valid for any resident in a nursing home, they are especially relevant to American Indian elders.

- Before the actual nursing home placement, ask the elder who she or he wants included in the meeting for her initial assessment and at future health appointments and meetings. For Mrs. Jones, this will likely include her granddaughter and may include her daughter if the latter's health allows. Other extended family members may also be included.
- Explain the reasons for questions that may be interpreted as "intrusive" so that the resident and family understand why the information is needed and how it will be used.

- At the initial assessment, ask if there are any traditional American Indian health practices that are important to the elder. Try to get a sense of the person's commitment to traditional cultural practice, as well as her or his values and beliefs. Rely on your overall impression rather than asking specific questions. Be aware and appreciative of the diversity within and between tribes, and make no assumptions about the elder's degree of cultural practice; instead, encourage her to tell you about her beliefs over time.

- Be aware of how the history of having been sent to a boarding school as a young child might affect the elder's adjustment in the institutional setting of a nursing home.

- Although an American Indian elder may identify herself as Catholic, as did Mrs. Jones, she may also take comfort from traditional American Indian practices. Inform the elder and the family as to whether the nursing home is open to bringing in traditional American Indian practitioners.

- Pay attention to how the resident and family communicate, especially nonverbally, and take time to listen. Understand that American Indians often express respect by listening quietly, which does not necessarily indicate agreement. If they do not ask questions, do not assume that they are aware of information or resources. To best serve American Indian clients, practitioners need to learn about and be able to provide American Indian resources and referrals for support.

- Ask about barriers to family participation at the nursing home and to the elder's potential adjustment. Be responsive to issues raised, and be honest about the extent to which these can be addressed.

- For some American Indian elders, having an interpreter may be a consideration.

- Ask about the kinds of traditional foods that the elder enjoys and find out if these can be prepared at the facility, either by the kitchen staff or the family.

- Encourage the family to attend events at the nursing home. Make a special effort to welcome extended family members.

- Inform the elder and family if there are other American Indian residents to interact with or American Indian staff who might visit the elder or his or her family.

- When cultural misunderstandings arise, be open to suggestions and to improving your own practice and institutional policies and practices.

The decision to place an American Indian elder in a nursing home is a difficult one, given the strong cultural practice of caring for elders within the context of family and community. The information presented in this chapter can assist with this transition if staff is attuned to the unique history, cultural characteristics, and needs of American Indian elders.

REFERENCES

Administration on Aging (2001). A guidebook for providers of services to the older Americans and their families. www.aoa.gov/monorityaccess/guidebook2001/intro.html.

Ambler, M. J. (1999). Dine College students research diabetes for their people. *Tribal College Journal* 11 (1), 18–21.

Anderson, C. M., & Stewart, S. (1983). *Mastering resistance: A practical guide to family therapy.* New York: Guilford.

Associated Press (1999). *Falling apart: Nursing homes scarce for America's Indians.* Pine Ridge, S.D. http//:www.rai.to/native%20/tc.htm.

Ball, T. (2001). Termination: The holocaust of the Klamath. Paper presented at the meeting of the Takini Network, Santa Ana, N.M.

Begay, S. (2002). Elders seek nursing home on the rez. *Navajo Times,* July 25. Window Rock, Ariz.; from www.thenavajotimes.com/eldrhome.html.

Benson, W.F. (2002). Long-term care in Indian country today: A snapshot. *American Indian and Alaska Native Roundtable on Long-Term Care: Final Report.* Albuquerque, N.M.: National Indian Council on Aging.

Bernard, M.A., Lampley-Dallas, V., Smith, L. (1997). Common health problems among minority elders. *Journal of American Dietetic Association* 97, 771–776.

Brucker, P. S., & Perry, B. J. (1998). American Indians: Presenting concerns and considerations for family therapists. *The American Journal of Family Therapy* 26, 307–319.

Bullock, A. (2001). *Connection of stress/trauma to diabetes and the insulin resistance syndrome.* Unpublished manuscript.

Burkhardt, M. A., & Nagai-Jacobson, M. E. (2000). Spirituality and health. In B. A. Dossey, L. Keegan, & C. E. Guzetta (Eds.), *Holistic Nursing: A Handbook for Practice,* pp. 91–121. Gaithersburg, Md.: Aspen.

Carnahan, E. (2003). Interview, June.

Clarke, T., Zales, T., & Stacco, F. C. (1982). *Outreach family therapy.* New York: Jason Aronson.

Cleary, M., Miller, L., & Peacock, T. (1998). *Collected wisdom: American Indian education.* Needham Heights, Mass.: Allyn & Bacon.

Cook, N. D. (2001). *Born to die: Disease and new world conquest, 1492–1650.* Cambridge: Cambridge University Press.

Crowe, T. A. (Ed.) (1997). *Application of counseling in speech-language pathology and audiology.* Baltimore, Md.: Williams & Wilkins.

De Graf, T. (2001). Mechanisms in the transgenerational transmission of (grand) parental trauma to their descendants. Paper presented at the meeting of the Takini Network, Santa Ana, NM.

Dubray, W. (1992). *Human services and American Indians.* St. Paul, Minn.: West.

Dubray, W. (1993). *Mental health interventions with people of color.* St. Paul, Minn.: West.

Dubray, W., & Sanders, A. (1999). Interactions between American Indian ethnicity and health care. In P.A. Day & H. N. Weaver (Eds.), *Health and the American Indian.* Co-published simultaneously as *Journal of Health and Social Policy* 10 (4), 67–84.

Duran, E. (2001). Native veterans and post-traumatic stress: Wounding seeking wounding. Paper presented at Takini Network Meeting, Santa Ana, N.M.

Duran, E., & Duran, B. (1996). Native American–post colonial psychology. Albany: State University of New York.

Fink, B. (2002). Nursing home survey report. *American Indian and Alaska Native Roundtable on Long-Term Care: Final Report.* Albuquerque, N.M.: National Indian Council on Aging.

Forquera, R. (2002). How do we address the long-term care needs of urban Indian elders? *American Indian and Alaska Native Roundtable on Long-Term Care: Final Report.* Albuquerque, N.M.: National Indian Council on Aging.

Garrett, J. T., & Garrett, M.W. (1994). The path of good medicine: Understanding and counseling Native American Indians. *Journal of Multicultural Counseling and Development* 22 (3), 134–145.

Garrett, M.D. (2002). Census information on American Indian and Alaska Natives: Implications for long-term care. *American Indian and Alaska Native Roundtable on Long-Term Care: Final Report.* Albuquerque, N.M.: National Indian Council on Aging.

Garwick, A. (2000). What do providers need to know about American Indian culture? Recommendations from urban Indian family caregivers. *Systems and Health: The Journal of Collaborative Family Healthcare* 18 (2), 177–190.

Goodwin, C. (2003). Telephone interview, May.

Henderson, J. N. (2002). How do we understand and incorporate elder's teaching and tribal values in planning a long-term care system? *American Indian and Alaska Native Roundtable on Long-Term Care: Final Report.* Albuquerque, N.M.: National Indian Council on Aging.

Indian Health Service (2001a). *Health and Heritage.* http:/info.ins.gov.

Indian Health Service (2001b). *Indian Health Service Profile.* http:/info.ins.gov.

Indian Health Service (2002). *American Indian and Alaska Native Roundtable on Long-Term Care: Final Report.* Albuquerque, N.M.: National Indian Council on Aging.

Jervis, L. L., Jackson, Y., & Manson, S. M. (2002). Need for, availability of, and barriers to the provision of long-term care for older American Indians. *Journal of Cross-Cultural Gerontology* 17, 295–311.

Joe, J. R., & Malach, R. S. (1992). Families with Native American roots. In E. W. Lynch & M. J. Hanson (Eds.), *Developing cross-cultural competence: A guide for working with young children and their families,* pp. 89–119. Baltimore, Md.: Paul H. Brookes.

Kinew, P. (2003). Presentation. Fond du Lac Tribal and Community College, American Indian Project, University of Minnesota Department of Social Work Conference, Cloquet, Minnesota.

Leininger, M. (1995). *Transcultural nursing: Concepts, theories, research, and practices.* 2nd ed. New York: McGraw-Hill.

Locke, D. C. (1992). *Increasing multicultural understanding: A comprehensive model.* Newbury Park, Calif.: Sage.

Lowe, J. (1996). The self-reliance of the Cherokee adult male. Doctoral dissertation, University of Miami, Miami, Fl.

Lowe, J., & Struthers, R. (2001). A conceptual framework of nursing in Native American culture. *Journal of Nursing Scholarship* 33 (3), 279–290.

Lum, D. (1996). *Social work practice and people of color: A process-stage approach.* Pacific Grove, Ca.: Brooks/Cole.

Mankiller, W. (Ed.) (2004). *Every day is a good day: Reflections of contemporary indigenous women.* Goldon, Colo.: Fulcrum.

Manson, S. M., & Callaway, D. G. (1988). Health and aging among American Indians: Issues and challenges for the biobehavioral sciences. In S. M. Manson & N. G. Dinges (Eds.), *Behavioral health issues among American Indians and Alaska Natives,* pp. 160–210. Denver: University of Colorado Health Science Center.

Mason, M. (2001). *Minorities shorted on mental health.* St. Paul, Minn.: Pioneer.

Medina, P. (2003). Interview, June.

Mehl-Madrona, L. E. (1999). Native American medicine in the treatment of chronic Illness: Developing an integrated program and evaluating its effectiveness. *Alternative Therapies* 5 (1), 36–44.

Meisenhelder, J. B., & Chandler, E. N. (2000). Faith, prayer, and health outcomes in elderly Native Americans. *Clinical Nursing Research* 9 (2), 191–203.

Mercer, S. O. (1996). Navajo elderly people in a reservation nursing home: Admission predictors and culture care practices. *Social Work* 41 (2), 181–189.

Norrel, B. (2004). Native super foods and healing ways. *Indian Country Today* 24 (18), D1.

Peacock, T., & Wisuri, M. (2002). *Ojibwe waasa inaabidaa: We look in all directions.* Afton, Minn.: Historical Society.

Poupart, J., et al. (2000). *To build a bridge: An introduction to working with American Indian communities.* 2nd ed. St. Paul, Minn.: American Indian Policy Center.

Red Horse, J. (1997). Traditional American Indian family systems. *Families, Systems, & Health* 15 (3), 243–250.

Red Horse, J. G., et al. (2000). *Family Preservation: Concepts in American Indian Communities.* Seattle, Wash.: Casey Family Programs and the National Indian Child Welfare Association.

Redford, L. (2002). Long-term care in Indian country: Important considerations in developing long term care services. *American Indian and Alaska Native Roundtable on Long-Term Care: Final Report.* Albuquerque, N.M.: National Indian Council on Aging.

Seideman, R. Y., et al. (1996). Assessing American Indian families. *MCN* 21, 274–279.

Smith, T. D. (1993). The elderly Native American—Forgotten again. *Aging* 365, 50–52. Department of Health and Human Services.

Stiffarm, L. A., & Lane, P., Jr. (1992). The demography of Native North America: A question of American Indian survival. In M.A. James (Ed.), *The state of Native America: Genocide, colonization, and resistance,* pp. 23–53. Boston, Mass.: South End.

Stillday, T. (2003). Interview, April.

Struthers, R., & Littlejohn, S. (1999). The essence of Native American nursing. *Journal of Transcultural Nursing* 10 (2), 131–135.

Struthers, R., & Lowe, J. (2003). Nursing in the Native American culture and historical trauma. *Issues in Mental Health Nursing* 24 (3), 257–272.

Sue, D. W., & Sue, D. (1990). *Counseling the culturally different: Theory and practice.* 2nd ed. New York: Wiley.

Trujillo, M. H. (2000). *Indian Health Service Fact Sheet.* Rockville, Md.: Author.

U.S. Census Bureau (2001). *Demographic trends in the 20th century.* http://factfinder.census .gov.

U.S. Department of Health and Human Services (1999). Surgeon General's Report: *Mental Health for American Indians and Alaska Natives.* http://www.mentalhealth.org/cre/ch4.

Utter, J. (2001). American Indians: Answers to today's questions. Norman: University of Oklahoma Press.

Weatherford, J. (1988). *Indian givers.* New York: Ballantine Books.

Weaver, H. N. (1999). Indigenous people and the social work profession: Defining culturally competent services. *Social Work* 44 (3), 217–224.

Weaver, H. N. (2005). *Explorations in cultural competence: Journeys to the four directions.* Belmont, Calif.: Brooks/Cole.

Weaver, H. N., & Yellow Horse Brave Heart, M. (1999). Examining two facets of American Indian identity: Exposure to other cultures and the influence of historic trauma. *Journal of Human Behavior in the Social Environment* 2 (1/2), 19–33.

White Shield, R. (2001). Historical trauma response. *The Circle* 21 (1), 8–9.

Wilkinson, C. (2005). *Blood struggle. The rise of modern Indian nations.* New York: Norton.

Yellow Horse Brave Heart, M. (1999). Gender differences in the historical trauma response among the Lakota. In P. A. Day & H. N. Weaver (Eds.), *Health and the American Indian.* Co-published simultaneously as *Journal of Health and Social Policy* 10 (4), 1–21.

Yellow Horse Brave Heart, M. (2001). Historical trauma theory and historical trauma and intervention research. Paper presented at the meeting of the Oregon Social Learning Center, Lincoln City, Oreg.

Zinn, H. (2003). *A people's history of the United States.* New York: Harper Collins.

Zitzow, D. (1996). Comparative study of problematic gambling behaviors between American Indians and non-Indians in a northern plains reservation. *American Indian and Alaska Native Mental Health Research* 7 (2), 27–41.

RESOURCES

Organizations and Websites

Bureau of Indian Affairs, www.doi.gov/bureau-indian-affairs.html.

Indian Health Service. www.ihs.gov.

National Indian Council on Aging, www.nicoa.org.

National Resource Center for American Indian, Alaska Native, and Native Hawaiian Elders. http://elders.uaa.alaska.edu.

National Society for American Indian Elderly. www.nsaie.org.

3

Chinese American Elders

Rhoda Wong

MY GRANDMOTHER

My grandmother lived with my family of eight in Hong Kong until she passed away at ninety years of age. She was hospitalized only once in her life, and she never returned home. She was sent to the hospital at midnight, and when the ambulance team transferred her to the stretcher from her bed, she stared at them and held the bedside stand very tightly. She believed that once she was in a hospital, she would never go home again. She wanted to die at home surrounded by her son and grandchildren. She thought that would be the greatest blessing in her life.

My family had never discussed a nursing home or adult home placement for my grandmother. My parents assumed the traditional Chinese practice of caring for my father's old mother, and they served her needs at home. If they did not take care of her at home, they would be criticized and shamed by our relatives. In fact, there were very few nursing homes, adult homes, or senior hostels in Hong Kong in the 1980s. The British-ruled government encouraged the Chinese tradition of caring for one's own elders, and only people with no families or children would have to reside in an institution and that would be considered a misfortune.

I entered a nursing home for the first time in April 1994 in New York City. I was going for an interview and asked myself whether I wanted to work in a nursing home, a place where I had never imagined placing my grandmother or my parents. During the interview, the Director of Social Work told me that the facility had 240 beds and that about a quarter to one-third of the residents were monolingual Chinese-speaking. Sixty to eighty Chinese residents! This was a surprise. The home employed a Chinese chef, a Chinese dietitian, a Chinese recreation assistant, and some Chinese-speaking nursing staff but did not have a Chinese social worker. The Social Work Director was Caucasian American and spoke no Chinese dialect. She did not understand Chinese culture or customs, but she was eager to communicate with the Chinese residents and their families and understand their needs. She had a strong desire to recruit a bilingual, Chinese-speaking social worker to her department in order to help the Chinese residents and their families.

I did not have any nursing home experience before beginning employment there, but I held onto the principle of a client-oriented approach and learned by trial and error. I worked there for more than three years, and it was important to nursing home residents and their relatives that I, as the social worker, understood their culture and languages. In the farewell party organized by the Chinese Family Support Group, for example, Mrs. C. said that the Chinese residents had become more alive since a bilingual Chinese social worker was hired because the social worker spoke with the residents in their own languages. She stated that her ninety-six-year-old great grandmother looked for the social worker to talk to and for assistance. Mr. T. said that he had never complained in the past, as he did not speak English and staff did not understand him. Also, he was afraid that staff would retaliate against his mother if he complained. But after I arrived, he could come to me to discuss his concerns.

Ms. J. said that her mother strongly requested to go home as soon as she arrived in the facility, as she believed that her children were going to abandon her there. Ms. J. felt very guilty about leaving her mother there, but she felt better later on when she learned that her mother was visited frequently by a Chinese-speaking social worker who comforted her in her own language, led her to the Chinese women's support group, and helped her adjust to life in the nursing home. The social worker comforted and supported the family as well. Ms. J. was encouraged to participate in the Chinese Family Support Group, and she did so in mutual support with other residents' families. Because many Chinese American residents and relatives believe that "harmony is valuable," they don't wish to make trouble and so choose to remain silent about problems that may arise between the nursing home staff and residents, but Ms. J. hoped that the Family Support Group would assert and protect the rights of their family members who resided in the home. Through group activities, the residents and their families achieved mutual support, using their own language, and they established support networks for residents and relatives.

These family comments reflect my experiences working in the nursing home. I had advantages because I know the origin, history, culture and customs, languages, thinking processes, family and interpersonal relationships, social roles and expectations, emotions, food preferences, behaviors, and so forth. This knowledge was useful in assisting residents and their families in adjusting to the nursing home, and it is a key component of culturally competent practice with Chinese American elders and their relatives. My experience should be helpful to social workers from diverse backgrounds who are working with older adults and their relatives.

DEMOGRAPHIC INFORMATION

The Chinese American population in 2000 was estimated at 2.7 million, and Chinese Americans at that time comprised 23.8 percent of the Asian population in the U.S, the largest Asian group in the country (Reeves & Bennett 2004). Because of immigration, this population doubled from 1980 to 1990, and doubled again from 1990 to 2000 (Lee & Mock 2005). Almost 10 percent are sixty-five years of age and older (Reeves & Bennett 2004) and most live in California, followed by substantial numbers living in New York and Hawaii. According to Census 2000, among Chinese Americans who do not speak English at home, almost 50 percent speak English less than "very well" (Reeves & Bennett 2004). Regarding education, 23 percent have attained less than a high school degree, 13.2 percent are high school graduates, 15.8 percent have achieved some college or an associate's degree, and 48.1 percent have completed a bachelor's degree or higher (Reeves & Bennett 2004).

China, known to the Chinese as the Middle Kingdom (Zhong Guo), is the third largest country in the world, following Russia and Canada, and covers an area of 3.7 million square miles in eastern Asia. There are four central administrative municipalities, twenty-three provinces, five autonomous regions, and two special administrative regions, Hong Kong and Macau. China had a population of 1.287 billion in July 2003, and, in 2000, 36 percent of the population lived in urban areas and 64 percent in rural areas.

The Hans comprise 91.9 percent of the population, and 8.1 percent includes sixty-five minority groups such as Zuang, Uygur, Hii, Yi, Tibetan, Miao, Manchu, Mongol, Buyi, and Korean. There are seven major language groups, and every group has a wide range of dialects. The group that speaks Mandarin (Standard Chinese, or Putonghua) is the largest. Early immigrants to the United States were mostly from the Guangdong area, where Cantonese is spoken. Other major languages include Shanghaiese, Fuzhounese, and Minnan (Hokkien-Taiwanese). The written form of all Chinese dialects is the same, with approximately fifty-six thousand characters. A simplified writing system is used in mainland China, whereas the traditional script dominates Hong Kong, Taiwan, and overseas Chinese communities. Although a northerner may not be able to communicate verbally in dialect with a southerner, each can read the other's writing.

IMMIGRATION HISTORY

The experiences of Chinese residents in the two nursing homes in New York City where I worked reflect part of the immigration history of Chinese people in the United States. The residents in these two nursing homes were between the ages of sixty and one hundred, with most between eighty-one and ninety years of age, having been born between 1900 and 1940. Around 91 percent of the residents for whom I provided social work services were from the Canton/Toisan area, 7 percent were from Shanghai and other parts of China, and 2 percent were from Taiwan. About 70 percent were women. In researching this chapter I contacted additional nursing homes in New York City to learn about their Chinese residents. Six provided data, and four had Chinese resident populations similar to the nursing homes where I worked.

To understand the ways in which pre-migration and immigration experiences influenced the lives of Chinese American nursing home residents, the immigration framework provided by Dr. Evelyn Lee is useful. The historical stages of Dr. Lee's framework include the First Wave (1850–1919): The Pioneer Family; the Second Wave (1920–1942): The Small Business Family; the Third Wave (1943–1964): The Reunited Family; the Fourth Wave (1965–1977): The Chinatown and Dual-Worker Family; and the Fifth Wave (1977 to the present): The New Immigrant, Refugee, and "Astronaut" Family (Lee 1996b; Lee & Mock 2005).

THE FIRST WAVE (1850–1919): THE PIONEER FAMILY

There were Chinese immigrants in the United States in the 1700s, but it was not until gold was discovered in California, in 1848, that many more Chinese immigrants arrived. Young male farmers from the provinces of southern China settled in the "Golden Mountain," the United States of America, to dig for gold, build railways, or work on the farms (Lee 1996b; Lee & Mock 2005). In the early nineteenth century major famines, civil unrest, military defeat, and foreign occupation occurred throughout China, forcing many Chinese to leave their country in search of a better life. These early immigrants worked hard and sent money home, and many returned to China after they had saved enough money.

Immigration from China was banned when the U.S. Congress passed the Chinese Exclusion Act in 1882 (Lee 1996b; Lee & Mock 2005). This Act, and its subsequent fourteen extensions, decreased the number of Chinese immigrants for sixty years, and Chinese immigrants were also forbidden from becoming naturalized U.S. citizens (Hraba 1994). Many Chinese laborers were forced to separate from their families. The Chinese community became a "womenless" (Lee 2000) and "familyless" world.

In 1898 the U.S. began to recognize American-born people of Chinese ancestry as U.S. citizens. In 1906 the San Francisco earthquake caused the destruction of all immigration papers in that city, and many people of Chinese ancestry claimed that they were U.S. citizens (Hraba 1994). As citizens, they could visit China and marry there, and when they returned to the U.S., many left their wives and children at home; some later sponsored their family to come to the United States. At least four or five generations of Toishanese entered the U.S. through a network of so-called paper sons and paper daughters from 1906 to 1950 (Wong 1999). These Chinese immigrated to the U.S. on the basis of a sheet of paper purchased in China identifying them as sons or daughters of Chinese Americans (Chin & Chin 2000).

THE SECOND WAVE (1920–1942): THE SMALL BUSINESS FAMILY

The Ch'ing dynasty of China ended in 1911, but the establishment of the Republic of China did not change the life of the Chinese people, as political conditions in China were still chaotic. The Chinese people continued to suffer from the Warlord Partition and the Japanese invasion.

U.S. immigration law was changed in 1930 to allow wives of Chinese merchants or of U.S. citizens married before 1924 to immigrate, but sometimes reunification was difficult after so many years of separation (Lee & Mock 2005). Some first-generation immigrants left their families in China, and others brought only their sons, some of them "paper sons." In some cases husbands lost contact with their children, remained single, or married other women after years of separation from their wives. Nevertheless, after 1930, many men were reunited with their wives and children, with the result that second-generation Chinese immigrants could be reared in the U.S. Simultaneously many laborers who had worked in the mines and railroads began businesses, including laundries and small fishing businesses, and immigrants and their children began to function as a productive unit (Chang 2003).

THE THIRD WAVE (1943–1964): THE REUNITED FAMILY

Changes in U.S. immigration laws created opportunities during this phase for many Chinese to come to this country, and they are now older adults. In 1943 the Chinese Exclusion Act, and its extensions, were repealed; in 1945 a War Brides Act was passed, allowing spouses and adopted children of U.S. personnel to enter the United States after World War II; and in 1952 the Walter-McCarran Act gave preference to immigration for family reunification (Hraba 1994, 445).

Sixteen thousand Chinese Americans had served in the U.S. Armed Forces during World War II, and in 1947 the War Brides Act was amended to allow Chinese American veterans to bring brides into the U.S. In 1948 the Displaced Persons Act allowed thirty-five hundred people who had come to the U.S. from China, including students, visitors, and seamen, and were unable to return to China because of the Chinese Civil War, to remain in the U.S. as permanent residents. In 1949 the People's Republic of China (PRC) was established, the U.S. terminated diplomatic relations with the newly formed PRC communist government, and five thousand highly educated Chinese in the U.S. were granted refugee status.

Land Reform in China in 1950 caused many people to flee to Hong Kong, and in 1952 a quota was established for people considered skilled "aliens" whose services were urgently needed. In 1953 Hong Kong allowed the entry of 2,777 refugees of the Chinese Revolution and further granted a total of 2,000 visas to the Nationalist Government in Taiwan. In 1962 the Presidential Directive of May 25 permitted Hong Kong refugees to enter the U.S. immediately as "parolees."

Most of the Chinese immigrants to the U.S. during this period were women. Some immigrated to reunite with their husbands after a long separation. Powerful bonds had been established between mothers and their children prior to their arrival in the U.S. (Lee & Mock 2005). Many of the early immigrants returned to China or Hong Kong to marry and then returned to the U.S. with their wives. These women were usually ten to twenty years younger than their husbands, and their average age when they entered the U.S. was between twenty and thirty years of age. Most of the current nursing home residents immigrated during this period.

THE FOURTH WAVE (1965–1977): THE CHINATOWN AND DUAL WORKER FAMILY

The 1965 Immigration and Naturalization Act amendments repealed the national origin quotas in the U.S., and the seven-category preference system based on family unification and skills was established, with a limit of two thousand immigrants per country established for the Eastern Hemisphere. Many of the Chinese immigrants who were able to come because of this Act came as families (Lee & Mock 2005). From 1966 to 1976 the "Cultural Revolution" took place in China, and during this time most Chinese immigrants entered the U.S. based on family reunification. Many immigrants during this wave lived in Chinatowns or nearby, working primarily in restaurants and garment factories. They generally spent most of their time in Chinatown or going to and from Chinatown and did not have opportunities to learn about mainstream society. Many found it very difficult to acculturate or assimilate to their new surroundings. Year after year they remained unable to speak or read English. The people in this cohort, primarily women, are now approximately between the ages of sixty and eighty, and comprise the young elderly in nursing homes.

THE FIFTH WAVE (1977 TO THE PRESENT): THE NEW IMMIGRANT, REFUGEE, AND "ASTRONAUT" FAMILY

The reestablishment of diplomatic relations between the PRC and the U.S. in 1978 allowed many long-separated Chinese American families to reunite with relatives who lived in China. In 1980 the U.S. established the first permanent and systematic procedure for admitting refugees, and asylum status was codified. Many foreign students and professionals pursued studies in the U.S., and most stayed after they graduated.

The passage of the Immigration Reform and Control Act in 1986 raised the ceiling on immigration from Hong Kong from six hundred to five thousand annually, and, after the June Fourth Tiananmen Square Movement in 1989, the U.S. government allowed Chinese residents already in the U.S. to remain and become permanent residents. In 1997 Hong Kong was returned to China, and many Hong Kong residents, worried about political instability, migrated to the U.S. Instability of the political environment in Taiwan also resulted in immigration to the U.S., and many Taiwanese foreign students stayed in this country after graduation. Other Chinese, attracted by the "Internet revolution," immigrated during the 1990s (Chang 2003). Almost all the immigrants sponsored their families still in China to come to the U.S. for reunification. Some families, referred to as "astronaut families," set up a household for their children in the U.S. and another in their home country for adult relatives who had received their green cards (Lee 1996b; Lee & Mock 2005).

The Chinese population in the U.S. has become increasingly diverse, as many refugees from Vietnam, Laos, and Cambodia during the fifth phase have been ethnically Chinese, and many are survivors of hunger, rape, incarceration, forced migration, and torture. Ethnic Chinese have also immigrated from Japan, Korea, the Philippines, Singapore, Malaysia, Thailand, Mexico, Canada, and other countries in South American and Europe (Lee 1996b; Lee & Mock 2005).

IMMIGRATION HISTORY AND NURSING HOME PLACEMENT

Previous life experiences of nursing home residents influence their attitudes about nursing home placement, their levels of acceptance and adjustment, and their responses to service delivery. Residents' pre-migration experiences have been affected by their city or village of origin, family composition, major political changes, socioeconomic status, educational level, employment status, and support systems (Lee 2000), and have shaped their thinking and behaviors throughout their lives. Adjustment to the new surroundings is also influenced by the immigration experience, including the reasons for emigration, the means of leaving one's homeland, hardships endured during the trip, and types of losses and traumas (Lee 2000).

Many female residents of nursing homes came to the U.S. to reunite with their husband and children after long years of separation. Thus, in addition to the challenges of adjusting in this country, many had problems in their relationships with husbands, children, or in-laws after immigration and reunification. Women whose husbands had died before the wives arrived in the U.S. had to depend on their children. Whatever other circumstances they encountered, they were also faced with the overwhelming task of redefining their roles as wife or mother or both. Some found it difficult to adapt to new lifestyles and patterns to which other family members had already adapted, especially older women and those who had been separated from their husband for many years. Without adequate support systems, many Chinese immigrant women struggled to become self-sufficient and self-reliant (Kao & Lam 2000). Residents with this history who want to maintain a high level of independence may experience conflict with nursing assistants attempting to provide care, as the assistants may think that these women are stubborn and uncooperative with services. Social workers can provide assistance by serving as "culture mediators" (Fandetti & Goldmeier 1988). In that role they can help staff understand residents' need to achieve self-determination as much as possible, and can work with residents and their relatives directly regarding these issues.

Some Chinese immigrants now in nursing homes have experienced war trauma and political turmoil. The Sino-Japanese War occurred in the 1930s to

1945, and the civil war between Communists and Nationalists in 1945–49 was followed by numerous political movements and persecutions, and the "Cultural Revolution" from 1966 to 1976 (Lee 1996a).

In addition to clients' pre-migration and immigration history, caregivers should understand their post-migration experiences, including those related to culture shock and acculturation. Many older Chinese nursing home residents are from agricultural backgrounds, and their exposure to Western culture has been very limited. They are "un-acculturated" immigrants who were older at the time of immigration. As noted previously, they lived in Chinatown and maintained their social life in that community, rarely leaving the community after their arrival. Their contacts and lifestyle remained similar to their experiences before migration; they do not speak English and have had very few opportunities to connect with mainstream society. Many worked for Chinese employers, received community resources and services in Chinatown, and their children went to school in that community. They received social support from relatives and people from the same town or village in China. For interdisciplinary services to be provided adequately to this cohort of nursing home residents, cultural sensitivity training for staff is critical. Monolingual English services are not a viable option for residents who never learned English skills or have lost these skills because of dementia.

Other Chinese older adults immigrated to the U.S. during the last twenty years, but there may be relatively few nursing home residents in this group currently. They came to the U.S. to reunite with their children, and some sponsored their children who were still in China or Hong Kong in their efforts to immigrate to the U.S. Many members of this older adult cohort have experienced problems in adjusting to their new life in the U.S., and some have returned to their place of origin.

CHINESE CULTURAL CHARACTERISTICS

During the five-thousand-year history of China, culture has been developed, accumulated, adapted, changed, and internalized. Primarily an agricultural society, Chinese culture developed with the family as a basic unit of living and production, and many generations of the family lived together and formed the extended family structure. Family members have traditionally depended on the family unit for their livelihood and to maintain the integrity and equilibrium of the family.

In the nursing homes where I have provided social services, over 50 percent of the Chinese American residents came to the U.S. directly from their hometown villages. They led self-reliant and self-sufficient lives as farmers in their villages, and life was simple and maintained on a basic level. They lived and sat on the ground and might never have entered a building prior to immigrating. Consistent with their agricultural backgrounds, many Chinese immigrants have grown vegetables in the backyards of their homes in the U.S.

VIEWS OF FAMILY RELATIONSHIPS, FILIAL PIETY, AND AGING AND THE ELDERLY

Roles are very clearly delineated in traditional Chinese families. The family emphasizes harmonious interpersonal relationships, interdependence, and mutual obligation in order to maintain inner harmony and family security (Lee 2000). To maintain the integrity and reputation of the family, individual feelings and interests are modified. Familial interactions, moreover, are governed by prescribed roles defined by family hierarchy, obligation, and duties (Lee & Mock 2005). In the patriarchal traditional family, men have dominant roles; husbands deal with the outside world, and, as fathers, are stern disciplinarians (Lee & Mock 2005). Lee and Mock also point out that parents use measures of "respect, shame, and face saving" to control their children (p. 305).

Women in traditional Chinese families are instructed to obey their mother-in-law and husband. They take care of in-house affairs and home chores, and are expected to meet the family members' need for affection and care. The eldest son is expected to carry on the family name and enjoy special privileges, and the eldest daughter is taught to assist her mother with household chores and attend to younger siblings. Chinese mothers have historically been described as "self-sacrificing, suffering, guilt inducing, and over involved with their children" (Lee & Mock 2005, p. 305). Women are to be "Thrice Obeying," which means that, when young, they are expected to comply with their fathers' or elder brothers' wishes, and with their husband's when they marry. After their husband's death, they are expected to obey their sons (Lee & Mock 2005).

Old age has traditionally been a symbol of honor and status representing life experience, wisdom, authority, and high status in the Chinese social hierarchy (Tsai & Lopez 1997). It is believed that "having a senior at home is a treasure to the family." Growing old and living surrounded by younger generations is considered a blessing, and parents expect to be taken care of in their old age (Lee & Mock 2005).

The Chinese have traditionally shown filial piety to parents and to older members of the family, as they gave life to the younger members and are expected to join the family's ancestors after death. Each family member is considered a link with past and future generations, and Confucian teaching supports the idea that filial piety is the foundation of all virtues and that this begins with service to one's parents. Filial piety supports parents' expectations that care will be provided by their children when the parents grow old (Lee & Mock 2005).

Many Asian elders have immigrated to the U.S. so that they can be close to their children and maintain family ties, and so their children can continue to fulfill responsibilities to serve their parents until they mourn their parents' death. However, the past generation of Chinese families in the U.S. has undergone tremendous changes as a result of high immigration rates from China, Hong Kong, and Taiwan; "the massive economic and political changes in these countries have had a dramatic impact on Chinese families in the U.S." (Lee & Mock 2005, p. 305). These changes have greatly affected intergenerational roles and relationships within families and have influenced the need for nursing home placement of older relatives in some families. Lee and Mock suggest that changes in contemporary Chinese American families include the following factors:

(1)   The traditional Chinese extended family has gradually yielded to a more nuclear family; (2) the traditional patriarchal family has transformed, in many cases, into a system in which a mother shares decision-making with the father; (3) the parent-child dyad has diminished in importance, and importance of the husband-wife relationship has increased; (4) the favoring of sons has slowly decreased; daughters now attain comparable education and careers and can be counted on to take care of aged parents; (5) there has been a change in the family life cycle from arranged marriages to marriages preceded by romantic love; (6) adult children now leave the home, when, previously, there was no empty nest phase; (7) successful child rearing is now measured mostly by the children's academic and career achievements; and (8) earning power is no longer solely the father's responsibility, but is shared with other adult family members. (2005, p. 306)

VIEWS OF LIFE AND DEATH, HEALTH AND ILLNESS

Because the primary precipitating factors in nursing home placement relate to illness, it is important for social workers who are working with Chinese nursing home residents and their relatives to understand their cultural views of life and death, health and illness. Similarly, in social work with relatives, service providers are frequently engaged in addressing family members' concerns about their own physical and emotional well-being.

Traditional Chinese society sees birth, aging, sickness, and death as aspects of the natural process of life. Many Chinese believe that they do not have control over nature and so maintain a fatalistic outlook on life. They often pursue harmony and peace with nature and accept the world as it is. They desire a long life and good death, and these are believed to be blessings.

In Chinese culture, people have traditionally accepted the theory of yin and yang and the balance of bodily functions. In this view, yin and yang represent the powers that regulate the universe and also exist within the body. Yin is represented by femininity, darkness, coldness, and water. Yang symbolizes masculinity, the sun, heat, and fire. An imbalance in yin and yang within the body is believed to cause illnesses and discomfort. Yin symptoms can be a cough with lung congestion, rheumatic pains, or dizziness. Yang symptoms can be a fever, rash, or sore throat. Restoring the balance of yin and yang is fundamental in Chinese medicine, and traditional Chinese believe that herbal medicine and diet regulate the body system and bring the body to its original equilibrium. Popular indigenous healing practices among Chinese in the U.S. include nutrition, herbal medicine, acupuncture, and therapeutic massage; geomancy and fortune-telling to prevent or remove a bad spirit; and religious faith healing (Lee 1996b: 257). Chinese immigrants have tended to deny their emotional concerns or to express them in physiological terms (Lee 1996b).

Lee and Mock (2005, p. 307) suggest that traditional religious and spiritual beliefs and concepts of health and disease still strongly influence many Chinese people in the U.S., and include the following common explanations regarding the development of mental illness and emotional problems:

1. *Imbalance of yin and yang and disharmony in the flow of chi*....[discussed above]
2. *Supernatural intervention.* Mental illness is seen as a form of spiritual unrest meted out to the individual through the agency of a "ghost" or vengeful spirit. . . .
3. *Religious beliefs.* Mental illness is viewed as negative karma, caused by deeds from past lives or punishment from God. . . .
4. *Genetic vulnerability or hereditary defects* caused by bad genes passed down or a tainted hereditary lineage. . . .
5. *Physical and emotional strain and exhaustion* caused by extreme stresses such as failing in a business, ending a love affair, death of a family member, and so on. . . .
6. *Organic disorders.* Mental illness is conceptualized as a manifestation of physical disease, especially brain disorders, diseases of the liver, hormonal imbalance, and so on. . . .
7. *Character weakness.* Mental health is achieved through self-discipline, exercise of will-power, and the avoidance of morbid thoughts. Persons who are born with weak character will not be able to practice these disciplines and are more vulnerable to emotional problems.

PERSONALITY AND SELF-EXPRESSION, SOCIAL VIEW AND SOCIAL MANNER

Pursuit of love *(Yen)*, righteousness *(I)*, decorum *(Li)*, wisdom *(Zhi)*, and honesty *(Xing)* are the fundamental Confucian teachings that have tradition-ally guided many Chinese people to establish and maintain harmonious rela-tionships with others. Rites of decorum *(li)* entail both rights and responsi-bilities toward one another. Conformity and accommodation are praised and admired more than confrontation, and public debating of conflicting ideas and opinions is considered unacceptable. A person is expected to be sensitive to what people think and be gracious toward others so as not to make them "lose face." Self-expression and individualism are discouraged; modesty, self-control, self-reliance, self-restraint, and face-saving are frequently taught, and shame and guilt are crucial psychological influences guiding interper-sonal relationships among many Chinese people.

In Western culture, Chinese people are described as pleasant, polite, hard-working, shy, and unassertive. Silence and lack of eye contact are common forms of indirect communication; silence is a sign of respect and direct eye contact is considered a sign of lack of respect and attention, particularly when directed toward people in authority and older people. In order to avoid con-frontation, the word "no" is rarely used. Hesitation, ambiguity, subtlety, and implication are often apparent in Chinese speech. Understanding nonverbal cues and contextual meanings is necessary in social work practice with Chi-nese elders and their relatives. When Chinese elders and their relatives do not ask for assistance, this does not mean that they do not need help. Recip-rocation or treating others as one would wish to be treated is often used in interpersonal relationships, and some people apologize frequently because they think they are inconveniencing others.

I have seen female residents in nursing homes push away staff members who have tried to bathe them, and these residents were reported as combat-ive and physically abusive. Chinese people do not ordinarily touch one anoth-er during conversations. Touching someone is considered shameful and dis-respectful, especially toward women and the elderly. People greet others by bowing instead of shaking hands, and nodding the head may indicate "yes," whereas shaking the head may indicate "no."

RELIGION AND CELEBRATIONS

The nursing home admission form may include a space for indicating the religion of the person being admitted. Buddhism is frequently indicated as the religion for Chinese residents, but this response is poorly informed. Many

Chinese themselves have had a false belief that they are Buddhist when they worship their ancestors and ghosts, gods and goddesses, in the temple. Nowadays Chinese people practice different religions, among them Buddhism, Catholicism and other Christian religions, and Islam. There is no major religion that originated from the fundamental Chinese culture. If there is one, it is the worship of heaven and ancestors. The *Book of Rites* (*Li Chi*) indicates that, "to worship the Heaven and ancestor is to requite one's origins, their kindness and virtue." Farmers are superstitious because they survive on all available resources in nature and depend on changes in natural forces.

Chinese are widely believed to practice Buddhism, as Buddhist rituals and philosophy are compatible with traditional Chinese philosophy and agricultural and civil customs. Following the establishment of the People's Republic of China in 1949, the Chinese Communist Party prohibited the civilian practice of religion. Consequently many Chinese immigrants may not practice any religion at all.

The traditional Chinese belief is that supernatural forces exist on three levels: gods, ancestors, and ghosts. When confronted with a specific problem, people petition the god, as they would petition an Imperial official with relevant jurisdiction to grant a favor. Ancestors are considered a person's relatives, and they are owed continuing loyalty and support; in turn, ancestors reciprocate by granting their relatives good fortune and by tacitly agreeing not to cause them mischief in daily life. Death is not seen, traditionally, as the annihilation of the individual, and ghosts are deceased individuals who did not belong to one's family. In practice, the most feared ghosts tend to be those who died without anyone to care for them.

It is important to know about major festival celebrations because they are part of the life of nursing home residents:

LUNAR NEW YEAR

The most important festival for Chinese occurs on the first day of the first lunar month (between late January and late February). This date marks the beginning of spring, so it is also known as the Spring Festival. A reunion dinner with certain foods is required, and people dress in new clothes to visit relatives where they receive little red packets with money inside. Nothing unpleasant is allowed to happen on this day in order to ensure good fortune for the rest of the year. Chinese may celebrate the New Year for the entire month.

LANTERN FESTIVAL

This festival occurs on the fifteenth day of the month and is also known as Chinese Valentine's Day. People hang lanterns in their homes to celebrate the birth of newborns that year. A special food called sticky rice balls is also served.

DUANWU JIE (DRAGON BOAT FESTIVAL)

Held on the fifth day of the fifth lunar month, this festival commemorates a patriotic poet who drowned himself because his state was taken over by a neighboring state. To remember this, dragon boat races are held and rice dumplings are eaten.

ZHONGQIU JIE (MOON FESTIVAL)

The fifteenth day of the eighth lunar month marks the occasion of the fullest and brightest moon. Moon cakes made of a thin pastry filled with sweet mashed lotus seeds are eaten and given as gifts. The night is also filled with lights from paper lanterns. Legend has it that a lady, Chang Er, became immortal after drinking a potion stolen from her husband, a tyrannical king. She then flew to the moon where she remains today.

TRADITIONAL FOODS AND LEISURE ACTIVITIES

Food has played a major role in the Chinese lifestyle and culture from earliest Chinese history. Chinese people have valued their way of dining as an art. A popular phrase I learned in childhood was, "Food is as important as heaven to civilians." Rice is the basic grain staple for the Chinese, and *Fan* denotes both cooked rice and a meal. *Fan* is eaten with *Cai,* which denotes both vegetable dishes and others that accompany rice. Chinese traditionally use chopsticks to eat, with the exception of soup. Chopsticks were invented three thousand years ago and are used to push rice from the bowl into the mouth and to pick up bite-sized pieces of food.

Less rice is eaten in the north, as wheat grows better in that region. Food made from flour includes plain steamed buns (*mantou*), filled steamed buns (*baozi*), wheat pancakes, wheat dumplings and wonton, and Cantonese thin egg noodles. Other common foods include congee, soybeans, and soymilk. Rice congee, soymilk, wheat pancakes, *mantou,* and *baozi* are served for breakfast. For lunch and supper there is boiled rice with side dishes, either a stir-fried dish or a steamed dish and a thin soup. In the north, noodles, thick pancakes, or steamed buns are the traditional starch staples. At any formal celebration, eight to ten dishes of special foods are served as a banquet.

Another habit is drinking tea, the most important traditional beverage in China. This gradually developed into a custom with people visiting Tea Houses, where a large variety of dim sum is served with different types of tea. Traditional Tea Houses are centers for kin to get together for social events. There are three types of teas—green, red, and oolong—and 350 to 500 varieties of processed teas. Traditionally any time is teatime in a Chinese home, and the drink is offered as soon as a guest enters. Serving tea is a matter of politeness, a symbol of togetherness, and the sharing of something enjoyable (Kramer 1994).

On several occasions in a nursing home I observed Chinese residents drawing hot water from the water tap to make tea, although Chinese rarely drink water that is not boiled. Chinese residents would clearly enjoy hot Chinese tea served in nursing homes as a daily drink.

During China's long history, its culture has been influenced by historical legends and tales, which are frequently the subject of operas. There are opera schools and different styles of regional opera. The best known are Peking, Kun, Shaoxing, and Huangmei. Chinese immigrant nursing home residents tend to be from the Guangdong area, including Toisan and other counties, and prefer Cantonese opera. In the past, people did not go to theaters to watch operas, as many were peasants living in the villages, but circuit opera teams moved from village to village and performed operas. In the agricultural areas, opera performances were traditionally major events. Chinese operas are available on videotapes, CDs, and DVDs for sale or rental and may be enjoyed by nursing home residents.

CHINESE CULTURE AND ADAPTATION TO NURSING HOME PLACEMENT

Older immigrant residents, as already pointed out, may not easily alter their values in a new culture, depending on whether they immigrated as older adults, in middle age, or as youths. The level of urban experience is also a factor affecting acculturation of older adults (Ross-Sheriff 1992), and so some older immigrants remain at low levels of acculturation.

Kim (1991; cited in Wong & Ujimoto 1999) suggests there are three types of disadvantageous experiences for some Chinese American older adults: the substantial loss of pre-immigration socioeconomic resources or ties, the continuous attachment to significant parts of their pre-immigration lifestyle and belief system, and their limited experience of Americanization. After immigrating to the U.S., older adults may feel neglected when family members go to work or school. Some maintain their belief in family integrity and filial piety, and expect adult children to take care of them without assistance. Many older immigrants are confronted with differences in how older adults are viewed in Chinese and U.S. cultures, and some do not understand that modern education and socioeconomic complexity have changed the practice of traditional values and life patterns across generations. Some may become frustrated and confused.

Many Chinese immigrant older adults seek support from their ethnic community as protection from the stress of acculturation. Many senior centers and kinship associations are located in Chinatowns, and the socialization function and services provided by these organizations satisfy needs of older immigrants who want to associate with people of the same ethnic background. Many older people live in their own residences in Chinatowns in order to avoid language barriers, potential conflicts, and difficulties that may arise from living with their children. They can maintain their original lifestyle, practice their usual customs and celebrations, enjoy their own leisure pattern, and meet friends easily. Younger relatives with more formal education may have moved out of Chinatown to new towns and suburbs, and Chinese American adults may maintain relationships with their parents by visiting them frequently, taking them to a Tea House, or contributing some financial support.

Families face major challenges when their parents get older. In addition to debilitated health, older persons may also experience the loss of a spouse, relatives, and close friends. Some relatives arrange for their family elders to move into their homes, where they supply care with the assistance of a home attendant or home health aide. For these relatives, institutionalization is not acceptable, as they fear that their parents might interpret placement as rejection and abandonment. And, as noted earlier, members of the younger generations may feel ashamed and guilty if they do not fulfill the duties required by filial piety. When these older family members become more frail and debilitated, however, their relatives can no longer provide care at home, and nursing home admission becomes inevitable.

Yee, Huang, and Lew (1999) have written that Asian American families have generally become more accepting of institutionalizing their elderly relatives. They may be reluctant to place relatives in nursing homes, but there is a point at which they can no longer cope with infirmities such as incontinence, wandering behaviors associated with dementia, or secondary illnesses that overwhelm the capacity of family members to manage everyday functions.

CULTURAL CONFLICTS AND NURSING HOME PLACEMENT

The following case illustrates the problem that many Chinese American elders have because they do not want to die in a hospital or nursing home instead of surrounded by their family at home, as is expected within Chinese culture.

The first week of Mrs. Q.'s placement was chaotic. She cried all day and was in conflict with the staff at all times. She left the unit on several occasions and attempted to travel to Queens where her family lived. She was angry with her children and grandchildren, and reprimanded them during their visits. Her sixty-year-old son and daughter-in-law expressed their feelings of guilt to the social worker and requested that the social worker arrange for Mrs. Q. to be discharged to her home, despite her debilitated physical and mental condition. After several meetings, the family arranged for at least one family member to stay with Mrs. Q. for at least half a day, every day, after her return home. The family assured her that she could go home after she recovered, and a month later Mrs. Q. was discharged.

The following case shows how I responded to the difficulties that Chinese residents and their relatives have regarding misunderstandings with staff.

Mrs. W. washed her clothes in the sink in her room, and then she hung the wet clothes by the window. A staff member found the clothes and took them away, concerned that Mrs. W. was not following nursing home regulations and that a complaint about the staff member would be made to the administration. Mrs. W. was supposed to place her clothes in the hamper so that they could be sent to the laundry. She became very upset and agitated and did not understand why the staff was angry and had taken her clothes away. She felt that she should wash her own clothes in order to avoid troubling other people. Mrs. W. saw no problem if she hung her clothing by the window, for she had washed her clothes by hand all her life. Mrs. W. and the nursing staff both complained to the social worker.

After I learned about the situation, I oriented the staff about Mrs. W.'s psychosocial development and early life experiences in rural China prior to immigration. I also explained that Mrs. W. did not want to ask other people for help with tasks she could manage for herself, and that her attitude was very common among Chinese females of her generation. I also comforted Mrs. W. and provided emotional support, because she was upset. She felt that she had been accused of doing something wrong, and she did not understand why. I explained the facility rules and regulations, and that it was the responsibility of staff to take care of her and send her clothes to the laundry. If she always did things on her own, staff members could be criticized for not doing their job. When Mrs. W.'s daughter visited, I also spoke with her about the conflict; she understood the situation and also explained it to her mother. Mrs. W. gradually understood and became more compliant with facility rules and regulations. It is important to keep in mind, however, that in a nursing home in which cultural change is taking place, opportunities for Mrs. W. to participate in washing some of her clothes might be explored.

In this situation, Mrs. W.'s behavior was influenced by her social values, attitudes, lifestyle, and experiences. As service providers, it is necessary to understand the influence of cultural expectations on behavior of Chinese American residents that may result in conflict with staff, and social workers can function as culture mediators to help interdisciplinary staff understand residents (Fandetti & Goldmeier 1988).

The experiences of Mr. R., a family caregiver for his grandmother, reflect the maintenance of values related to filial piety at the same time that his family moved toward acceptance of his grandmother's permanent placement in a nursing home:

I have a big family, and I am the oldest grandson. My grandmother is the head of my family, and she sponsored my whole family to come to the U.S. I want to fulfill her desire to feel cared for by others. I visit her every Saturday. I want to light up her hope to live longer. Every time I visit, she asks when I will come again. "I will come next Saturday," I tell her. After I leave, she asks the nursing staff every day, "What day is today?" If she had not fallen so frequently at home, hitting her head and burning her thigh, my family would not have placed her in the nursing home.

At first, she was very unhappy about the placement. She asked when she would go home. I tried to encourage her about the advantages of staying in the nursing home. I promised to visit her every day in the beginning and then weekly after the first month. Gradually she has accepted the placement, and now she even forgets where she lived in Chinatown. She has been in the nursing home for seven years. I can accept now that my parents or I will be placed in a nursing home when it becomes necessary. I think that, after my grandmother's placement, my mother will also agree to that. I hope there will be more culturally sensitive programs and activities in the home for my grandmother. My dream is to have a "cultural corner" on the unit for the Chinese residents. Non-Chinese residents would also be able to experience and explore Chinese culture.

SOCIAL WORK PRACTICE WITH CHINESE RESIDENTS AND THEIR RELATIVES

When families consider alternatives for care they may be afraid to discuss nursing home placement with their elders. They may tell older adults that they will be in the nursing home for rehabilitation only. Newly admitted residents may have strong emotional reactions. This author has met Chinese American residents who said that they were depressed following placement, were unable to accept placement, felt abandoned and angry, and lacked adequate knowledge of English to communicate with staff. Many complained that they did not have Chinese food or meals in their nursing home and said that they disliked the American version of Chinese food.

In this initial stage of placement, what can a social worker do to help residents and their relatives adjust to nursing home placement? To Chinese immigrant elders, nursing home placement implies a "second immigration" process (Kolb 1999). In addition to debilitated health conditions, residents may experience stressors similar to those experienced during their immigration from their homeland to the U.S. These include cultural conflict, minority status, environmental change, isolation, loss of power, lack of language proficiency, lack of respect, lack of care provided by relatives, fear of racial discrimination, and adjustment to an unfamiliar culture. The social worker is often the front-line person most able to address these issues. It is very important for a social worker to be available to residents and their relatives in the new surroundings as a helper, supporter, and problem solver.

Older generations of Chinese American immigrants may not understand the profession or role of the social worker. Several times I was addressed as "Doctor" by residents and their older relatives. Social workers need to explain their professional roles from the start. Residents and relatives should be addressed in a polite and formal manner with warm expressions of acceptance, especially if very few staff members speak Chinese dialects. In order to establish a "culture connection" (Lee 2000), social workers who are Chinese American or have extensive experience working with Chinese Americans can disclose their familiarity with the culture. Social workers who are not Chinese or are unfamiliar with Chinese culture should still show interest and appreciation of the resident's cultural background (Lee 2000). Occasionally residents and relatives may ask the social worker personal questions, and if the social worker is comfortable with disclosing appropriate information, this may facilitate a cultural alliance and positive level of trust (Lee 2000). For a long time after placement, residents may continue to perceive the social worker only as staff and helper and not as the resident's social worker. Still, engagement is being established.

To these "second migrated" residents, experiencing language barriers or communicating in a second language can be very stressful. If the social worker communicates with residents in their Chinese dialects, speaking even a few words or sentences, the connection can more easily be established and residents' stress relieved. Non-Chinese social workers can learn simple

Chinese words from residents in order to establish rapport, as residents may be pleased to teach social workers their languages. It is also important to recognize nonverbal cues and their cultural meanings.

The adjustment of newly admitted residents can be made easier if they are taught about their rights as residents of a nursing home. A copy of residents' rights in the Chinese language should be given to residents and relatives, and the social worker should educate the resident and family about Western concepts of community care and medical treatment approaches. Social workers should be encouraged to actively participate in planning the resident's care and be assertive in protecting the resident's rights. They should be assured that the resident will receive good care. Because residents may not be able to maintain attention easily or may have only limited cognitive functioning, the social worker may want to avoid giving detailed explanations during orientation. Simple wording and concepts should be used if a resident's knowledge of English is limited.

Chinese American older adults may have difficulty accepting the structure of group life—residing with people who they do not know—especially when those people do not speak their language and the environment is unfamiliar, and they may talk about missing their home. By listening to residents' descriptions of physical or psychological concerns, and by addressing their needs, social workers provide emotional support and help to maintain residents' optimal level of social functioning. The social worker can engage residents in "small talk" (Lee 2000) and encourage them to express their feelings of isolation, loneliness, anxiety, or depression. The social worker can also provide a safe environment that allows residents to work through losses in areas such as independence, status and power, and they can provide opportunities for residents to discuss their feelings. Use of the multiple helping roles of social workers can assist in the resident's adjustment. Residents will adjust more readily by meeting residents and staff who already know their culture, social background, and lifestyle, and social workers can make these introductions.

CLINICAL ISSUES AND INTERVENTIONS

Crucial aspects of the assessment of Chinese American residents are the psychosocial-cultural background and immigration history. Social workers should thoroughly explore the residents' backgrounds, and assessment should include the components that shaped the individual's upbringing, current functioning, and hopes for the future (Fong, Spickard, & Ewalt 1996). Consideration of residents' ethnicity and cultural attributes in the clinical assessment can contribute to the accuracy of the diagnosis and appropriate planning of individualized treatment strategies. As noted above, the assessment of Chinese American elders should emphasize pre-migration sociopolitical influences, immigration experiences, and the traditional roles of women.

Because Christianity, Buddhism, Taoism, and ancestor worship are the most prevalent teachings underlying the worldviews of Chinese Americans, Lee and Mock (2005, p. 312) provide examples of concepts related to these teachings that are useful in working with families. They suggest that "the concepts of *karma*, reincarnation, and compassion are effective in working with Buddhist clients. The Confucian teaching of 'the middle way,' the Buddhist teaching of *karma*, and the Taoist teaching of 'the way' are examples of how religious and philosophical teachings can be helpful in coping with life stresses." Lee and Mock recommend that clinicians "encourage family members to share their cultural beliefs on the causes of their problems, their past coping style, their help-seeking behavior, and their treatment expectations" (ibid.).

MENTAL HEALTH OF CHINESE NURSING HOME RESIDENTS

Depression in Chinese American elderly has been studied by several researchers (Mui 1998; Casado & Leung 2001; Stokes et al. 2001). In the clinical assessment, residents' symptoms of depression may be misunderstood and dismissed as signs of aging. Chinese Americans rarely report experiencing depression, but their mental health or psychological concerns are usually revealed through physical complaints such as tiredness, lack of energy, loss of interest in ordinary activities, sleep problems, sharp changes in appetite and weight, continuous bodily aches and pain, and poor concentration and memory. They also may express anger, sadness, anxiety, fear, loneliness, and feelings of emptiness and hopelessness. Upon admission to the nursing home, some residents might also feel helpless, worthless, irritable, and agitated, and experience suicidal ideation. The suicide rate among Chinese American older adults is high (Casado & Leung 2001).

Social workers should always be alert to residents' emotional changes and make referrals for psychological and psychiatric evaluations, as needed. Misdiagnosis may occur if information is not fully or accurately translated. If a resident's psychological difficulties arise from the inability to accept placement, the social worker should involve the resident's family and encourage the resident to discuss his or her viewpoints and feelings with relatives.

Mental illness related to war traumas and political persecution is found in some Chinese American older adults, and schizophrenia is found among

Chinese immigrants from the mainland who have been isolated or separated from family and relatives for prolonged periods (Murase 1992). In working with Chinese residents with schizophrenia or Alzheimer's disease, the social worker can provide support and social stimulation in order to maximize functioning, as well as support family members who feel guilty about their loved one disturbing other residents.

INDIVIDUAL SUPPORT AND COUNSELING

Showing respect and demonstrating empathy and a nonjudgmental attitude, social workers should encourage Chinese residents to verbalize their concerns and emotional reactions during counseling sessions. When I began to work in a nursing home, Ms. I., a monolingual Toisan-Cantonese resident, stayed alone all day and had no interactions with her peers. She either lay in her bed or sat next to the pay phone, waiting for her son to call. According to staff, she was the same every day, year after year. The social worker took the initiative and spoke with her in her dialect. After rapport was established, Ms. I. responded voluntarily to the social worker's weekly visits and supportive counseling. A few months later, she began to participate in the support group and interact with her peers.

GROUP WORK

Peer or mutual support is very important in helping residents to adjust to nursing home life. A mutual support group provides a sense of belonging and offers structured opportunities for residents to talk and share the norms and values of their culture. Although many activities may be organized by the recreation department of the nursing home, it is often the social worker who organizes and facilitates therapeutic groups for residents. I organized a Chinese women's reminiscence group, where the participants were ten women who were functioning cognitively at medium to high levels and spoke the same dialects. Most shared the same geographical and cultural background, as they were from the same county, Toisan, in Guandong province. The goals in forming the group were to promote mutual support, identity development, and a sense of belonging, and maximize daily functioning through reminiscences about similar experiences in their hometown and as immigrants in the U.S. Residents were given a private, quiet room for their weekly group meetings, with no formal structure; all residents had equal opportunities to share their opinions and feelings. The social worker encouraged each resident to speak and interact, with the understanding that traditional Chinese women usually do not express their thoughts and feelings in front of other people.

Activities included sharing experiences, as well as games and exercises, watching old Chinese movies and operas, drinking Chinese tea, and making simple Chinese snacks. In each session, residents were served various Chinese teas and traditional dim sum. They talked about folk customs and celebrations in the villages when they were young, and they shared their experiences about the loneliness they suffered when they were still living on the farms in China and their husbands were working in the U.S. They shared their viewpoints on the stories in the old Chinese movies, and they made simple Chinese handicrafts and shared with peers the handicrafts they had made in the past. The social worker supplied materials including sticky rice balls that participants could use to make traditional dim sum. They also talked about their experiences as farmers and planting vegetables in their backyards after coming to the U.S.

Another useful group activity is the resident council. Where I worked, however, Chinese residents had been a voiceless minority in resident council meetings because of language barriers. Social workers should actively assist residents to participate in these meetings. A Chinese-speaking social worker can translate and encourage residents to speak their concerns and opinions regarding their placement and care in the nursing home, and social workers who do not speak Chinese should also work with staff and residents to facilitate participation by Chinese-speaking residents.

CARE PLANNING

Federal law requires all nursing homes that receive Medicare funds to develop an individual care plan for each resident. Both residents and relatives (or responsible parties) have the right to participate in the development of the care plan and can examine all medical records pertaining to the residents' treatment and care. Residents and their relatives have the right to make important decisions on residents' behalf and advocate for appropriate high-quality care. The major focus of the care-planning meeting is to discuss the resident's individualized plan of care and review the results of the previous care plan. Both the residents and their designated responsible party should be invited to attend the meetings, which, routinely, are held four times a year. However, many Chinese American residents and relatives do not know their rights.

It is important for social workers, as participants in the interdisciplinary team responsible for residents' care, to be advocates for Chinese-speaking residents and their relatives in the care planning process. Because of the language barrier and their busy work schedules, many Chinese American families may not be able to attend the care-planning meetings. Nevertheless, the social worker should advocate and encourage family members to attend the meetings and speak up for their loved one's care and treatment. Social workers can also assist residents and family members to interpret and understand the presented medical interventions and plan of care, providing problem-solving alternatives that are culturally sensitive, identifying problems and solutions that the treatment team can address, and providing additional information about community or facility resources for the resident, family, or team. In addition, a social worker may provide required mediation for issues that arise between the resident/family and staff around problems with care. Medical terminology, especially in English, is not always familiar or understandable to residents or their family members, and care plans should be presented in a manner that is understood by all.

There are principles that social workers must uphold when participating in the care planning process for all residents. Social workers must respect the residents and support their self-esteem, privacy, dignity, and self-determination. When the care plan is formulated, residents' wishes must be respected. Chinese American residents and relatives may be unaware of their rights in care planning because of language barriers and lack of familiarity with the medical and caring system in the U.S. The social worker may need to alert others to respect the resident's wishes regarding the practice of religious beliefs, life patterns, daily activities, food preferences, and choice of clothing.

DAY-TO-DAY PRACTICE

COMMUNICATION

The biggest concern in working with monolingual Chinese-speaking residents is language barriers. While there are hundreds of dialects, Cantonese and Mandarin are the two major spoken dialects among Chinese immigrants in the U.S. However, residents speaking Cantonese may not be able to communicate with staff members who speak Mandarin. Failure to understand or misinterpretation of a resident's language and some of their expressions may cause inaccurate assessments of residents' actual concerns and care needs.

In nursing homes, many Chinese residents do not or cannot seek help voluntarily because of language barriers or medical conditions. By the time a Chinese resident's problem is brought to the attention of nursing or medical staff, it may have become a critical situation. Miscommunication or lack of communication can cause neglect and mistreatment. This was true of Ms. S, who had never raised her concerns to the nursing staff. She always smiled sweetly to the staff who attended to her needs. It seemed that she did not want to disturb anyone by voicing her needs or problems. The truth was that she did not speak any English. Thus, unintentionally, she misled staff to believe that she never had any problems. Another resident, Ms. U., stayed in her room the entire day because of leg pain until I visited and discovered the problem.

Social workers, therefore, should be sensitive to residents' unspoken needs (Mui 1998) and aggressively explore their concerns. Many Chinese American older adults present their problems implicitly. They may deny that their problem or stress is serious, and they may also be superstitious. Residents should be educated to address their problems as soon as possible. Moreover, to communicate with some nursing home residents, one must be patient with residents' limited ability to concentrate and impaired cognitive functioning. Communication boards or flash cards can be useful. Instead of writing characters on the boards and cards, pictures are recommended to translate the messages; older Chinese Americans may be unable to read in either Chinese or English. Bilingual Chinese-speaking family members are resources to help staff communicate with residents, but confidentiality needs and traditional expectations of intergenerational relationships and responsibilities must be kept in mind.

Another role that social workers may need to play is to facilitate communication and help reduce miscommunication between residents, relatives, and staff during daily interactions, routine care planning, and regular family meetings between staff and family members. It is also important to remember that residents who were bilingual in Chinese and English prior to admission may lose their ability to speak English as a result of deteriorated cognitive functioning. Ms. Z. was observed listening to staff talking in English, but she responded in Mandarin. She was not aware that she was speaking in Mandarin to staff who did not speak Chinese. At other times I needed to communicate with residents, who suffered from aphasia or had lost their hearing, by writing in Chinese.

RESIDENTS' INTERACTION WITH OTHER RESIDENTS AND STAFF

Some Chinese American residents of nursing homes have never before lived with non-Chinese people or in a group setting. Furthermore, many of these residents are not familiar with concepts pertaining to group life and institutional rules and regulations. Misunderstandings and conflicts probably will occur between roommates from different cultural backgrounds, and even between those with the same background. In daily care, staff may misunderstand residents' messages because of language barriers or misinterpretation of gestures. At times, different interpretations of a situation result in conflict. In Mrs. W.'s situation, described above, she felt that washing clothes in her room was a trivial matter, but staff saw her behavior as a failure to adhere to instructions and nursing home regulations. In another situation, staff complained that Ms. S. tried to help residents wash themselves using a basin, but the nursing home policy is to shower residents with staff assistance or supervision. The social worker explained to staff that showering is a Westernized way of washing, and Chinese older women from villages are accustomed to washing themselves in a traditional manner by using a basin.

DISCHARGE PLANNING

Discharge planning can mean helping residents arrange to enter an acute care setting, another nursing home, or return to their home in the community. Important components include resident and family involvement, continuation and coordination of care and treatment, and timely notifications and follow-up. When working with Chinese American residents, social workers need to make referrals to agencies that provide culturally sensitive care and treatment. Social workers should be familiar with appropriate service providers in the community and establish ongoing connections with these providers.

FAMILY INVOLVEMENT

Many relatives of Chinese American residents are involved throughout the resident's entire stay in the nursing home. Mr. R. and his mother visited his ninety-seven-year-old grandmother daily until she had adjusted well. She gradually came to accept the placement, understanding that her family had not abandoned her but were just not able to provide the care she needed at home.

A Chinese-speaking social worker, or, if unavailable, another social worker, can try to help Chinese American families deal with feelings of shame and guilt about their relative's placement in the home. Approaches may include supportive counseling, education, and empowerment, the process of increasing personal, interpersonal, or political power.

In supportive counseling, the social worker can provide empathy and opportunities for relatives to verbalize feelings of guilt and shame, and also encourage and support efforts to return to normal life. Also, by educating relatives about normal aging processes and the bio-psycho-social needs of dependent older adults, social workers can increase the family's awareness of factors that contribute to relocation stress and institutional adaptation. Moreover, when a resident is diagnosed with a chronic disease, it is important that the family become as knowledgeable as possible about the progression of the disease. Finally, social workers can encourage empowerment so that individuals, families, and communities can take action to improve their situations (Gutierrez 1996). In the nursing home, Chinese families can play an active role through participation in the care planning process. This can help protect residents' rights and assure quality of care, as family members can complain when the care is inadequate.

Chinese American families in which spoken English is very limited may want to consider forming their own family support group, and social workers can help with this process. In a support group that I facilitated, Chinese American relatives met once a month, on weekends, to listen to invited speakers talk about skilled nursing care, health and mental health issues, and community resources. Relatives raised concerns about the quality of care, and younger family members who spoke English assumed responsibility for communicating all family members' opinions to the nursing home administration.

The person who makes the placement decision may be the resident's son, but frequent visitors tend to be the resident's daughters or daughters-in-law. In Ying's (1994) study of intergenerational contacts in Chinese American families, daughters maintained greater contact and provided more support to their aging parents than sons did.

ETHICS AND END-OF-LIFE PLANNING ISSUES

In working with Chinese American residents and their relatives, social workers may experience difficulties in their efforts to address ethical decision making and end-of-life planning concerning advance directives, care in the end stage of life, and funeral arrangements. A traditional Chinese belief is that a sick person should be protected from additional emotional suffering that might result from knowing that they are dying. Traditionally children usually did not discuss funeral arrangements with their parents before a parent's death. To talk about dying, resuscitation, and hospice care and funeral arrangements when a relative's health was still stable would be considered disrespectful or a curse. When residents reach a medical crisis, relatives may still feel guilty if they make a critical decision that implies giving up hope and preparing for their relative's death.

A health care proxy is considered acceptable by some Chinese American families, and an adult child is often assigned this role. In most situations Chinese families assign decision-making duties to the eldest son (McLaughlin and Braun 1998). Opting for a "Do Not Resuscitate Order" (DNR) is a difficult decision, as children may feel that they are helping to cut short the life of their parents, which would result in feelings of guilt. When a resident suffers from a great deal of pain or reaches the end of life, relatives of Chinese American residents consider palliative or hospice care to be appropriate.

RESIDENTS WITHOUT FAMILY

In almost every large city, Chinese American older adults live and die alone, in poverty (Wong 1999). Early immigrants may not have family or may have experienced circumstances in which it was impossible to reunite with relatives who remained in China. No one visits or brings them food that they are accustomed to eating. I provided social services to several residents who had no families. One was unable to verbalize his feelings as a result of a stroke and aphasia and frequently expressed his anger in destructive behaviors. Social workers empathized with him and explored ways to address his needs. He became calmer and was able to open up to other people, including relatives of other Chinese American residents. Members of the family support group began to visit him and bring him Chinese food.

CONCLUSION

It is hoped that this discussion of Chinese American immigration history, origin and culture, lifestyle, and social work practice issues will help social work professionals who serve Chinese American nursing home residents and their relatives develop a greater understanding of this service population and improve the quality of services.

When working with Chinese American nursing home residents and their relatives, establishing a "social and cultural connection" is essential. To accomplish all social work–related tasks during a resident's placement, social workers should be ready to assume multiple helping roles (Lee 2000), including that of advocate, interpreter, counselor/therapist, facilitator, mediator, educator, and trainer. Extra patience, flexibility, and creativity are requisites in working with members of an unfamiliar group. Social workers also need to develop an understanding of the gestures and expressions of Chinese American elders, culturally appropriate communication skills, and responsiveness to observable nonverbal needs.

Social workers need to be aware of how their own ethnic and cultural socialization and experiences affect their values and emotions when serving residents and their families of a different culture. Social workers should be opened-minded and willing to learn about and develop respect for other cultures. They should avoid subjective feelings, be nonjudgmental, and be empathetic toward residents.

When available, a bilingual Chinese-speaking social worker should take a proactive role with the nursing home administration to develop culturally sensitive programs and services for residents and their families. Social workers should also advocate that more bicultural staff be hired for positions such as admissions officer, dietitian and cook, and nursing and recreation staff. A bilingual Chinese-speaking social worker can serve as trainer and educator to help nursing home staff more clearly understand and develop sensitivity to the needs, values, and behaviors of Chinese American residents and their relatives, but often bilingual and bicultural social workers are not available, and all social workers must work to meet the needs of Chinese American residents and their relatives through culturally sensitive practices.

It is important to value and acknowledge the individuality of Chinese American residents and their relatives, and not rely on stereotypes. Adult children and younger generations of Chinese immigrants are more receptive to institutional care as a result of acculturation and assimilation, are more knowledgeable about nursing homes, and have more exposure to information about facilities providing long-term care. Many Chinese older adults, moreover, who are experiencing debilitating health conditions, have begun to face the reality that younger members of their families may not be able to care for them at home.

Underutilization occurs when services are either insensitive or are believed to be insensitive to cultural differences. Many institutions practicing "culturally sensitive" programs hire bilingual staff knowledgeable about the cultural and historical background and values of the target population to help residents maintain a good quality of life. Some Chinese families believe that it is preferable that nursing homes assign a specific unit for Chinese residents, whereas others disagree. Of utmost importance is that the needs and wishes of residents are addressed with respect to their culture and ethnicity in order to achieve social and psychological well-being.

REFERENCES

Anderson, E. N. (1994). Food. In D. Wu & P. Murphy (Eds.), *Handbook of Chinese popular culture*, pp. 35–53. Westport, Conn.: Greenwood.

Asian American Federation of New York (2003). *Asian American elders in New York City: A study of health, social needs, quality of life and quality of care.* New York: Asian American Federation.

Asian American Health Forum (1990). Asian and Pacific Islander population statistics. Monograph series 1. San Francisco: Author.

Barnes, J., & Bennett, C. (2002). *The Asian population: 2000.* Washington, D.C.: U.S. Census Bureau.

Barnhart, R. M. (1993). *Li Kung-lin's classic of filial piety.* New York: Metropolitan Museum of Art.

Bond, M. (1992). *Beyond the Chinese face: Insights from psychology.* Hong Kong: Oxford University Press.

Bond, M., & Hwang, K. (1986). The social psychology of Chinese people. In M. Bond (Ed.), *The psychology of the Chinese people,* pp. 213–263. New York: Oxford University Press.

Browne, C., & Broderick, A. (1996). Asian and Pacific Islander elders: Issues for social work practice and education. In P. Ewalt, E. Feeman, & D. Poole (Eds.), *Multicultural issues in social work,* pp. 322–335. Washington, D.C.: NASW Press.

Burr, J., & Mutchler, J. (1993). Nativity, acculturation, and economic status: Explanations of Asian American living arrangements in later life. *Journal of Gerontology: Social Sciences* 48 (2), S55–S68.

Casado, B., & Leung, P. (2001). Migratory grief and depression among elderly Chinese American immigrants. In. N. Choi (Ed.), *Social work practice with the Asian American elderly,* pp. 5–26. New York: Haworth Social Work Practice Press.

Chai, C., & Chai, W. (1967). *Li Chi: Book of rites. An encyclopedia of ancient creed, usages, religion, and social institutions.* Translated by James Legge. New Hyde Park, N.Y.: University Books.

Chang, I. (2003). *The Chinese in America: A narrative history.* New York: Penguin.

Cheung, F. (1989). Psychopathology among Chinese people. In M. Bond (Ed.), *The psychology of the Chinese people,* pp. 171–212. New York: Oxford University Press.

Cheung, M. (1989). Elderly Chinese living in the United States: Assimilation or adjustment? *Social Work* (September), 457–461.

Chin, J. (1983). Diagnostic considerations in working with Asian-Americans. *American Journal of Orthopsychiatry* 53 (1), 100–109.

Chin, T., & Chin, W. (2000). *Paper son: One man's story.* Philadelphia: Temple University Press.

Chung, D. (1992). Asian cultural commonalities: A comparison with mainstream American culture. In S. Furuto et al. (Eds.), *Social work practice with Asian Americans,* pp. 27–44. Thousand Oaks, Calif.: Sage.

Clinical Indicators in Nursing Homes Work Group (1993). *NASW clinical indicators for social work and psychosocial services in nursing homes.* Washington, D.C.: NASW Press.

Dai, Y., et al. (1999). Cognitive behavioral therapy of minor depressive symptoms in elderly Chinese Americans: A pilot study. *Community Mental Health Journal* 35 (6), 537–542.

DeBary, W. (Ed.) (1964). *Sources of Chinese tradition.* 2 vols. New York: Columbia University Press.

Fandetti, D., & Goldmeier, J. (1988). Social workers as culture mediators in health care settings. *Health and Social Work* 13 (summer), 171–179.

Fong, R. (1992). A history of Asian Americans. In S. Furuto et al. (Eds.), *Social work practice with Asian Americans,* pp. 3–26. Thousand Oaks, Calif.: Sage.

Fong, R., & Mokuau, N. (1996). Not simply "Asian Americans": Periodical literature on Asians and Pacific Islanders. In P. Ewalt et al. (Eds.), *Multicultural issues in social work,* pp. 269–281. Washington, D.C.: NASW Press.

Fong, R., Spickard, P., & Ewalt, P. (1966). A multiracial reality: Issues for social work. In P. Ewalt et al. (Eds.), *Multicultural issues in social work,* pp. 21–28. Washington, D.C.: NASW Press.

Goodman, C. (1990). The caregiving roles of Asian American women. *Journal of Women and Aging* 2 (1), 109–120.

Gutierrez, L. (1996). Understanding the empowerment process: Does consciousness make a difference? In P. Ewalt et al. (Eds.), *Multicultural issues in social work,* pp. 43–59. Washington, D.C.: NASW Press.

Hikoyeda, N., & Wallace, S. (2001). Do ethnic-specific long-term care facilities improve resident quality of life? In N. Choi (Ed.), *Social work practice with the Asian American elderly,* pp. 83–106. New York: Haworth.

Hraba, J. (1994). *American ethnicity.* Itasca, Ill.: Peacock.

Jang, M., Lee, E., & Woo, K. (1998). Income, language, and citizenship status: Factors affecting the health care access and utilization of Chinese Americans. *Social Work* 23 (2), 136–145.

Jernigan, H., & Jernigan, M. (1992). *Aging in Chinese society: A holistic approach to the experience of aging in Taiwan and Singapore.* New York: Haworth.

Kamo, Y., & Zhou, M. (1994). Living arrangements of elderly Chinese and Japanese in the United States. *Journal of Marriage and the Family* 56, 544–558.

Kao, R., & Lam, M. (2000). Asian American elderly. In E. Lee (Ed.), *Working with Asian Americans: A guide for clinicians,* pp. 3–36, 46–787. New York: Guilford.

Kolb, P. (1999). A stage of migration approach to understanding nursing home placement in Latino families. *Journal of Multicultural Social Work* 7 (3/4), 5–11.

Kramer, I. (1994). Tea drinking and its culture. In D. Wu & P. Murphy (Eds.), *Handbook of Chinese popular culture,* pp. 55–76. Westport, Conn.: Greenwood.

Lee, E. (1996a). Asian American families: An overview. In M. McGoldrick, J. Giordano, & J. Pearce (Eds.), *Ethnicity and family therapy,* pp. 227–248. New York: Guilford.

Lee, E. (1996b). Chinese families. In M. McGoldrick, J. Giordano, & J. Pearce (Eds.), *Ethnicity and family therapy,* pp. 249–267. New York: Guilford.

Lee, E. (2000). Overview: The assessment and treatment of Asian American families and Chinese American families. In E. Lee (Ed.), *Working with Asian Americans: A guide for clinicians,* pp. 3–36, 46–78. New York: Guilford.

Lee, E., & Mock, M. (2005). Chinese families. In M. McGoldrick, J. Giordano, & N. Garcia-Preto (Eds.), *Ethnicity and family therapy,* pp. 302–318. NewYork: Guilford.

McLaughlin, L., & Braun, K. (1998). Asian and Pacific Islander cultural values: Considerations for health care decision making. *Health and Social Work* 23 (2), 116–126.

Mui, A. (1998). Living alone and depression among older Chinese immigrants. *Journal of Gerontological Social Work* 30 (3/4), 147–166.

Murase, K. (1992). Models of service delivery in Asian American communities. In S. Furuto et al. (Eds.), *Social work practice with Asian Americans,* pp. 101–120. Thousand Oaks, Calif.: Sage.

Ow, R., & Katz, D. (1999). Family secrets and the disclosure of distressful information in Chinese families. *Families in Society: The Journal of Contemporary Human Services,* 620–628.

Paper, J. (1994). Religion. In D. Wu & P. Murphy (Eds.), *Handbook of Chinese popular culture,* pp. 55–76. Westport, Conn.: Greenwood.

Proctor, E., & Davis, L. (1996). The challenges of racial difference: Skills for clinical practice. In P. Ewalt et al. (Eds.). *Multicultural issues in social work,* pp. 97–106. Washington, D.C.: NASW Press.

Reeves, T. J., & Bennett, C. E. (2004). *We the people: Asians in the U.S. Census 2000 Special Reports.* Washington, D.C.: U.S. Census Bureau.

Reid, D. (1986). *Chinese herbal medicine.* Boston: Shambhala.

Roberts, J. (1999). *A concise history of China.* Cambridge, Mass.: Harvard University Press.

Roberts, J. (2000). *Modern China: An illustrated history.* Phoenix Mill, Thrupp, Stroud, Gloucestershire: Sutton.

Root, M. (1999). Women. In N. Zane & L. Lee (Eds.), *Handbook of Asian American psychology,* pp. 211–231. Thousand Oaks, Calif.: Sage.

Ross-Sheriff, F. (1992). Adaptation and integration into American society: Major issues affecting Asian Americans. In S. Furuto et al. (Eds.), *Social work practice with Asian Americans,* pp. 45–64. Thousand Oaks, Calif.: Sage.

Segal, U. (2002). *A framework for immigration: Asians in the United States.* New York: Columbia University Press.

Serby, M., Chou, J., & Franssen, E. (1987). Dementia in an American-Chinese nursing home population. *American Journal of Psychiatry* 144 (6), 811–812.

SSu shu. (1971). *The four books: Confucian analects, The great learning, The doctrine of the mean, and The works of Mencius.* English translation and notes by James Legge. Taipei, Taiwan: Chengwen.

Stokes, S., et al. (2001). Screening for depression in immigrant Chinese-American elders: Results of a pilot study. In N. Choi (Ed.), *Social work practice with the Asian American elderly,* pp. 27–44. New York: Haworth.

Tsai, D., & Lopez, R. (1997). The use of social supports by elderly Chinese immigrants. *Journal of Gerontological Social Work* 29 (1), 77–93.

Uba, L. (2003). *Asian Americans: Personality patterns, identity and mental health.* New York: Guilford.

Weiner, R. (1994). Lifestyles: Commercialization and concepts of choice. In D. Wu & P. Murphy (Eds.), *Handbook of Chinese popular culture,* pp. 9–33. Westport, Conn.: Greenwood.

Wong, P., & Ujimoto, K. (1999). The elderly: Their stress, coping, and mental health. In N. Zane & L. Lee (Eds.), *Handbook of Asian American psychology,* pp. 165–209. Thousand Oaks, Calif.: Sage.

Yee, B., Huang, L., & Lew, A. (1999). Families: Life span socialization in a cultural context. In N. Zane & L. Lee (Eds.). *Handbook of Asian American psychology,* pp. 83–133. Thousand Oaks, Calif.: Sage.

Ying, Y. (1994). Chinese American adults' relationship with their parents. *International Journal of Social Psychiatry* 40 (1), 35–45.

Yutang, L. (1998). *My country and my people = Wu guo yu wu min.* Peking: Foreign Language Teaching and Research Press.

Zhang, A., et al. (1997). Family and cultural correlates of depression among Chinese elderly. *International Journal of Social Psychiatry* 43 (3), 199–212.

RESOURCES

Chinese Classic

The classic of filial piety (Hsiao Ching). Translated by Liu Ruixiang & Lin Zhibe (1992). 2nd ed. Shangdong: Friendship.

Websites

www.english.peopledaily.com.ch/50years/glance.
www.chinalanguage.com/Language/Chinese.html.
www.siu.edu/~ekachai/culture.html.
www.umanitoba.ca/faculties/arts/anthropology/courses/122/module/culture.html.
www.tandy.sbu.tcu.edu/~stephens/teaching/mana4223/culture.
www.askasia.org.
www.beyond.com/LearnEnglish/BeAD/Readings/A WomenA1Library.html.
www.ailf.org/heritage/chinese/essay01.htm.
www.asianamericanhistory.org/timeline.html.
www.education.yahoo.com/reference/factbook/ch/popula.html.

4

Italian American Elders

Patricia J. Kolb and Rosemarie Hofstein

ROSEMARIE'S GRANDMOTHER

I can recall the stories my grandmother would tell of her large family. She was somewhere in the middle of nine children, half of them born in Italy and the other half here in the U.S. She was born in New York, in the Bronx. Her parents spoke Italian but the children were only allowed to speak English. My grandmother was a rambunctious child usually on the other side of parental direction. She was the only one of nine to care for her parents in their infirmity.

My grandmother passed away three months short of her ninety-first birthday. She died at home surrounded by her family. We were able to do that because she had spent two and a half months in a nursing home receiving sub-acute rehabilitation after a stroke. She was financially secure which enabled us to provide round-the-clock care. Not everyone is that fortunate, and not everyone can have their needs met at home.

When my grandmother's mother suffered a stroke, my grandmother went to her house every day to bathe her and feed her. She put her into the wheel chair and took her to the bathroom. She walked her a few steps every day and cooked all her favorite meals. This was sometime in the early 1940s. She later died in 1948 of a massive stroke. Nursing home placement was never a consideration.

Several years later my grandmother's father was diagnosed with colon cancer and underwent a colostomy. No one else in the family could bring themselves to do the colostomy care, but my grandmother learned how to do it and mastered the technique. She cared for her father throughout his decline until his hospitalization at Calvary Hospital, which at that time was on Edgecombe Avenue in the Bronx. He died two weeks after his admission, in 1951. My grandmother had a calling to care for people, and she did so throughout her life. When it was her time for the end-of-life journey, we were able to have her at home. Not everyone is that blessed.

These experiences illustrate important realities in the lives of many Italian Americans when family members reach later adulthood. Rosemarie's grandmother and great-grandparents were able to remain at home despite illnesses because relatives were actively committed to helping them be there. Care of older relatives at home by family is a deeply held cultural value that continues over generations in many families of Italian ancestry. Rosemarie's great-grandparents encouraged their daughter's acculturation when they required that she speak English rather than Italian at home during her childhood, but she also learned and maintained traditional Italian cultural expectations, namely, that she was to assist her parents as they became older and ensure that they remain at home. She did everything that she could to help her parents avoid long-term nursing home placement, and she was successful.

As Rosemarie's grandmother became older and ill herself, consistent with traditional Italian cultural expectations, her family actively supported her desire to remain at home. When she had a stroke and her needs exceeded the assistance that relatives could provide, she temporarily received rehabilitation services in a sub-acute facility and then returned home with the support of family. Her relatives and she were flexible enough to use nontraditional resources, sub-acute care and assistance from a paid round-the-clock non-relative caregiver but maintained the traditional commitment to family involvement and caregiving at home.

Differences in life circumstances of contemporary Italian American families result in variations in the potential for an older adult in need of assistance to remain at home. While many Italian Americans have a strong preference for the traditional practice of family care provided for older adults at home, in some situations nursing home care is the only viable option. Because of this reality and the authors' belief that social workers can maximize the use of their practice knowledge and skills if they are culturally competent, we have written this chapter.

There are many reasons why nursing home care may become necessary. At least one family member must be available with the time, knowledge, energy, and commitment to coordinate care at home and secure needed resources, and financial resources are also a critical factor. The reality is that changes have occurred in the social structure of the United States and of many other countries, and they have created impediments for families of many ethnic groups that want to maintain traditional caregiving roles. One change is the increased life expectancy, so that more people live to ages where they are more likely to need a great deal of assistance. Another is that more and more women, the traditional family caregivers in many cultures, are gainfully employed either for their own fulfillment, out of financial necessity, or for other reasons, and are less available to be caregivers (Kolb 2003).

The need for nursing home placement comes as a shock to many Italian families. The traditional belief is that life often requires sacrifices, and one is that children will provide care for their parents at home when they become old. When family circumstances result in nursing home placement, the option considered the last resort, the decision can cause children to feel guilty. The social worker is a crucial resource for residents and relatives who are reacting to events that create such distress.

This chapter includes information that the authors, who have had extensive contact with Italian American families, believe is fundamental in beginning to develop cultural competence in social work with Italian American nursing home residents and their relatives. The information we can provide in a brief chapter is limited, of course, and in all ethnic groups there are great variations in the experiences of individuals and families. It is important, however, to know about the collective history of people with a shared ancestry, as this knowledge provides insight into current values, attitudes, and behavior. This chapter, therefore, summarizes Italian immigration history, including conditions influencing departure from Italy and experiences following arrival in the United States. Additional topics in the chapter are traditional customs and expectations regarding family relationships, food, religion, and issues and interventions in social work practice with Italian American nursing home residents and their relatives.

IMMIGRATION HISTORY

Northern Italians were the first Italians to immigrate to the United States, settling primarily in California, Louisiana, and New York, but relatively few Italian immigrants came to this country prior to 1881 (Hraba 1994). The 1878 edition of the U.S. Census Bureau's Statistical Abstract reported that 23,998 "alien passengers" arrived in the U.S. from Italy between October 1, 1819, and December 31, 1870 (U.S. Census Bureau 2006a). Large-scale Italian immigration to the U.S. began in the last quarter of the nineteenth century as a part of Italian emigration to many countries. Immigration to the U.S. became primarily a phenomenon of southern Italians, whereas Italians living in northern Italy immigrated mostly to European countries.

Seasonal and temporary immigration of northern Italians to France and Switzerland has a long history, and this pattern of European destinations continued during the mass emigration that started in the 1880s. These patterns were repeated in chain migrations as southern Italians who migrated overseas brought their relatives to non-European countries, and northern Italians brought relatives to European countries (Sassen 1999).

Emigration patterns from the north and south were influenced by the 1880 agricultural crisis, differences between the north and south in industrial development, and differential transportation costs. During the initial period of mass emigration, travel to New York from southern Italy was cheaper on average than travel to northern Germany. Early patterns were reinforced in the south for several reasons: industry was hurt by a free trade policy, people searched for wage labor when peasant economies generated little money, and an international labor market developed in which cheap labor was sought, particularly in the face of growing trade unionism (Sassen 1999).

Describing conditions in southern Italy at the beginning of mass Italian migration to the United States, Gambino (1974, pp. 42–43, 63–64) wrote:

> The successful unification of Italy, along with a number of other events, was to mangle the life of the people of Southern Italy, who at the time of national unification constituted at least two-fifths of the population of Italy. Because of a concurrence of political and economic, social and natural disasters that defy the laws of probability, their condition was to deteriorate to fatal depths. . . . [The southern Italians'] love of life in the face of its adversities was tested anew in the severe agricultural depression of the Mezzogiorno that reached calamitous proportions by the 1880's. The price of wheat produced by the contadini [peasants], already at a depressed low of 22 lire a quintal in 1888 (a quintal equals about 220 pounds) fell to 13.5 lire in 1894. During this same period, the national government, in a policy that could not have done more to kill the contadini if it had been purposely designed to do so, increased both the tax on grain and the price of salt, a government monopoly except in Sicily. (In a land without ice and before the age of refrigerators, salt was essential to preserve meats and fish.)

Disastrous conditions also resulted from disease and geological forces. Addressing the impacts of these conditions on southern Italians, Gambino (ibid., p. 65) wrote:

> In the volcanic triangle of Vesuvius, Etna, and Stromboli, one can deepen the understanding of the Italian-American spirit of quiet determination, love and awe, hope and guardedness in the face of life. Above all, one can feel his fierce energy and his irrepressible will to prevail in whatever life presents.

Disease and natural disasters resulted in death and destruction for massive numbers of southern Italians during the 1800s and early 1900s. Cholera came to southern Italy on top of widespread malaria, resulting in hundreds of thousands of victims from 1860 to 1925. Natural disasters resulted from devastating events in the early 1900s in the volcanic triangle. Vesuvius erupted in 1906 and Etna in 1910. Earthquakes struck the provinces of Basilicata and Calabria in 1905, and, in 1908, a major earthquake and tidal wave in the Strait of Messina, between Sicily and the Italian mainland, caused tremendous loss of lives and property. More than three hundred towns were leveled, and about twenty thousand people were killed in the city of Reggio di Calabria, which was largely destroyed. The national government was ineffective in its relief efforts, and animosity toward the government was fueled by government troops that prevented survivors from returning to Messina to dig out trapped relatives (Gambino 1974).

The *contadini* also experienced relentless pressure from the *latifondisti* [landed gentry]. Efforts to implement genuine land reform had been attempted since the second century B.C., and measures in the late 1800s actually resulted in the lands of the southern Italian Mezzogiorno falling into fewer hands. The *latifondisti* were richer and more powerful than ever. In the far southern province of Calabria, in 1882, the ratio of landlords to the population was 121 landowners per 1,000, and in 1901 it was 91 landowners per 1,000. In Basilicata, in 1882, the ratio was 168 landowners per a population of 1,000, and in 1901 the ratio was 159 per 1,000. In Sicily the ratio of landlords to the population was 114 to 1,000 in 1882, and in 1901 it was 94 per 1,000. Almost 90 percent of the southern land was owned by large landowners by 1901, and the average holding of independent *contadini* was too little for economic viability. The tax system was crippling, and owners of large estates monopolized water rights and owned most of the few decent roads, charging prohibitive rates for the use of both (Gambino 1974).

As the great landowners became more powerful, they moved to the cities, leaving *gabelotti* (overseers) to manage their estates, and the overseers extracted kickbacks and imposed other forms of extortion on the *contadini* working on the estates. Ninety percent of the *contadini* worked on the estates or in the sweatshops of businesses owned by landowners who had moved to the cities, and many became day laborers. From 1870 to 1890 the average income of *contadini* in Sicily declined, but the cost of living doubled (Gambino 1974). After Italy was unified as one nation in 1870, the implementation of laws beneficial to northern Italians further impoverished southern Italians. These laws, in addition to volcanic eruptions, earthquakes, and malarial outbreaks, spurred the emigration of large numbers of southern Italians in the late 1800s (Giordano, McGoldrick, & Klages 2005).

Italians were the largest nationality group to immigrate to the United States in the late 1800s and early 1900s. More than 4.1 million Italians arrived in the U.S. between 1881 and 1920 and settled primarily in a pattern described by Parrillo (2005, p. 106):

> Settling mostly in "Little Italys" in cities large and small, immigrants from the same region, even village, clustered in the same city sections. This chain migration pattern resulted in the creation of cohesuve neighborhoods with village, family, and communal orientations built around their parallel social institutions of church, newspapers, social organizations, and stores. Although assimilation would gradually occur—particularly among their children pursuing *la via nuova*—in those communities, Italian was the daily language and ethnicity an everyday reality, leading many native-born Americans to view negatively the presence of too many "unassimilable" newcomers.

Many Italians were sojourners, sometimes referred to as "birds of passage," that came to the U.S. "to make enough money to return home and buy land, redeem the family mortgage, or provide dowries for sisters or daughters" (Parrillo 2005, 106–107). A large proportion of Italian immigration to the U.S. between 1880 and 1920 is considered to have been a "shuttle migration." That is because, in the 1880s and 1890s, half of all Italians returned to Italy, and often 60 to 70 percent of Italian immigrants were returning between 1908 and 1920. Many sojourners decided to remain in the United States, however, or returned there with their wives and children (ibid.).

Italian immigration declined significantly beginning in 1921 with the passage of the National Origins Quota Act in that year and its amendment in 1924. The 1921 Act reduced immigration to 3 percent of a nationality's population in the U.S. in 1910, and the 1924 amendment lowered the limit to 2 percent of the group's population in 1890. The limit became 3 percent in 1929, but the ceiling was limited to 150,000 total immigrants. This legislation was intended to favor northern and western Europeans and was supported by nativist Americans who, in their terms, wanted to "keep America American" in the face of the very large southern, central, and eastern European immigration from 1880 to 1921 (Parrillo 2005, p. 108). Migration to the U.S. from Italy increased notably, however, after new immigration legislation was enacted by Congress in 1965.

Emigration from Italy to the U.S. declined significantly by the 1980s in a trend consistent with the general decline in European emigration as a proportion of overall immigration to the United States. Parrillo (2005) has noted that "push" factors contributing to the desire to leave home had become greater in other parts of the world by that time. For the period from 1992 to 1994 Congress set an overall limit of 700,000 immigrants annually, and beginning in 1995 a limit of 675,000 annually, although immediate family members were admitted in addition to these caps. Despite significant declines in European immigration as a proportion of all U.S. immigration, almost 1.5 million European immigrants arrived between 1993 and 2003, including 25,000 Italians (Parrillo 2005, pp. 113, 116, 133).

PREJUDICE AND DISCRIMINATION AGAINST ITALIAN AMERICANS

An enormous clash of cultures burst forth as Italians arrived in the U.S. in large numbers in the early 1900s. The immigrants' values emphasizing group affiliation contrasted with values in the U.S. emphasizing individualism, independence, and personal achievement. As the number of Italians grew, prejudice against Italians increased, and they were considered inferior, dangerous, uneducated, violent, and criminal (Giordano, McGoldrick, & Klages 2005). Immigrants were blamed for "all existing social discontents," including an increase in crime, despite the fact that the crime rate for the rest of the country was higher than among immigrants (Parrillo 2005, p. 106). Although few Italian Americans belonged to the Mafia, the Mafia stereotype that developed continues to exist (Giordano, McGoldrick, & Klages 2005).

As sojourners decided to remain in the U.S. and others returned with their families, the generally high birth rates among southern, central, and eastern European immigrants alarmed nativists. Describing this alarm, Parrillo (2005) explains:

> Some cited population statistics to project the "old" Americans becoming a minority to the "inferior" newcomers. Eugenicists like Madison Grant, president of the New York Zoological Society, argued in *The Passing of the Great Race* (1916) for those of Anglo-Saxon, Nordic, and Teutonic origins to marry only among themselves to prevent racial hybridism and reversion to the "lower type" through contamination of their "racial purity." . . . Organizations such as the American Protective Association (APA) and the Ku Klux Klan drew widespread popular support in their campaigns for a "pure" America.

The Ku Klux Klan, reconstituted in 1915 after its sympathetic portrayal in D. W. Griffiths' silent film classic, *Birth of a Nation*, reached a membership of almost five million by 1926. Membership was strongest in Indiana and Ohio, with loyal support from thousands of Pennsylvania Dutch Klansmen, who held intense feelings against Roman Catholics. Dedicating itself to white supremacy, Protestant Christianity, and Americanism, the new Klan used intimidation, violence, and politics to influence voters, employers, schools, and textbook content, seeking moral regulation and a stabilization of the old order (Parrillo 2005, pp. 107–108).

The "Great Migration" from Southern, Central, and Eastern Europe was deliberately ended by nativists during the 1920s with the passage of the National Origins Quota Act and its amendments in the 1920s.

DEMOGRAPHIC CHARACTERISTICS

In 2003, 16,728,000 people of Italian ancestry lived in the U.S., with 47 percent living in the Northeast, 16 percent in the Midwest, 21 percent in the South, and 16 percent in the West (U.S. Census Bureau 2006b). The states with the largest percentage of Italian American residents as a proportion of the state population are Rhode Island (19.0 percent), Connecticut (18.6 percent), New Jersey (17.9 percent), New York (14.4 percent), and Massachusetts (13.5 percent) (The National Italian American Foundation 2006c). The states with the largest number of Italian Americans are New York, New Jersey, California, Pennsylvania, and Florida (ibid.). Counties with the largest number of Italian Americans (more than two hundred thousand) are Suffolk County and Nassau County (Long Island), New York; Cook County (Chicago), Illinois; Los Angeles County, California; Middlesex County, Massachusetts; and New Haven County (Connecticut) (National Italian American Foundation 2006a).

Italian Americans tend to remain in the city where they were reared and to be evenly divided among Democrats, Independents, and Republicans (National Italian American Foundation 2006b). The average family income is around $33,000 annually; a majority are pro-choice, and a majority believe that more funds should be spent on health, education, and assistance for poor people (ibid.).

A relatively small proportion of Italian Americans were born in Italy, but one million people in the U.S. speak Italian at home (Schaefer 2005). Of people who speak Italian at home, 69.5 percent speak English very well, 19.4 percent speak it well, 9.8 percent do not speak it well, and 1.2 percent do not speak English at all (U.S. Census Bureau 2006a).

FAMILY RELATIONSHIPS

Large-scale southern Italian immigration in the late 1800s and early 1900s, as previously indicated, resulted from poverty and the hope of a better life. Because the vast majority of Italians who immigrated to the United States have come from southern Italy, the attributes considered "Italian" by most people in this country are representative primarily of southern Italy. The customs, lifestyles, nuances in language, and food preferences of southern Italians are different from those of northern Italians as a result of geography and economy. Compared to northerners, southern Italians have benefited less from industrialization and tended to rely more on farming and to be poorer, less educated, and have a somewhat more fatalistic orientation (Giordano & McGoldrick 1996).

Family has provided continuity for Italians in all situations and training to cope with a difficult world. *La via vecchia*, "the old way," symbolizes "a value system organized primarily around protecting the family . . . for Italians, family is an all-consuming ideal" (Giordano & McGoldrick 1996, p. 567). The family system in southern Italy was the fundamental unit of social structure, and *onore della famiglia*, "honor of the family," was highly valued (Johnson 1985). *Onore della famiglia* includes family solidarity and maintenance of traditions through service, respect, and devotion (Covello 1967; Johnson 1985). According to Johnson (1985, p. 43), in southern Italian families "there is widespread agreement on the supreme importance of the family, the submersion of the individual within the family, limited opportunities for nonfamilial interests, and strong means to enforce conformity to family goals." Although many second- and third-generation Italian Americans see the family as a strong source of security and identity, some individuals feel that it stifles individual needs and desires for success (Giordano & McGoldrick 1996; Messina 1994; Rolle 1980).

According to Giordano, McGoldrick, and Klages (2005, p. 621), upwardly mobile third- and fourth-generation Italian Americans may experience feelings of shame, self-hatred, and identity confusion because of conflict between Italian values of family solidarity and the emphasis placed on autonomy and individuation by the dominant culture in the U.S. However, third- and fourth-generation Italian Americans experience family in diverse ways, with some continuing to obtain a strong sense of security and identity from family, but others experiencing family as stifling their individual needs and desires for success (Giordano, McGoldrick, & Klages 2005, p. 616).

The experience of repeated invasions from foreign armies throughout the Middle Ages and into the Renaissance may have contributed to a cultural resilience among southern Italians, encouraging the belief that they could only rely on people from their own town and ultimately only on family (Giordano & McGoldrick 1996). According to Giordano and McGoldrick:

> Value was placed on the personality traits that would provide a cushion against external instability. Adaptability and stoicism became ethnic trademarks. Rather

than attempting to alter the course of events, Italians took pride in their ability to cope with difficult situations. Resilience became more than an attitude; it became a way of life. To counter the harshness and fatalism in their daily lives, Italians mastered the ability to fully savor the present, particularly with family gatherings and community festivals. (1996, p. 568)

Italian immigrants settled primarily in cities in the mid-Atlantic states and New England, a pattern strongly influenced by the importance placed on neighborhood connections and family relationships in which children felt obliged to be close to aging parents and often did not move or travel. As time went on, however, intergenerational conflicts frequently erupted because parental identity was weaker, peer pressure often stronger, socializing networks existed outside the neighborhood, and popular culture promoted values antithetical to traditional Italian family values (Giordano & McGoldrick 1996). Hraba, citing Ware (Ware 1935; in Hraba 1994, p. 329), wrote:

A rift between generations occurred in Italian families. The American experience had individualized family members, wives as well as children, and this showed up in different values concerning arranged marriages, size of families, dating, husband's authority at home, divorce, and the children's role in the family.

Public school education also contributed to the rift because children learned American ways in the schools. A further rift appeared, as families were no longer working as a unit as they had in southern Italy (ibid.).

Italian immigrants viewed upward social mobility negatively and saw the "American Dream" only as opportunities for food and shelter for the family and steady work. Often family businesses were started only because Italians did not want to work for outsiders, and this contributed to family solidarity. Educational training was viewed as secondary to the security, affection, and sense of relatedness of family and was considered a threat to family values. The third and fourth generations now embrace education, although in some working-class and poorer families there are still negative attitudes toward education (Giordano & McGoldrick 1996).

The nuclear family has been the subject of much research about Italian families (Cronin 1970; Douglas 1984). The dominance of the nuclear family has been attributed to immigration rates, age of marriage, patterns of land tenure, and family size, with the extended family functioning primarily as a social rather than economic unit (Covello 1967; Douglas 1984; Gans 1962; Johnson 1985; Silverman 1968). In reporting the results of an exploratory study based on interviews of spouses and adult children assisting family members with Alzheimer's disease in Italy, Vellone, Sansoni, and Cohen (2002) described a profound sense of family duty.

Johnson (1985) suggests that studies of Italian American immigrants reflect the functional importance of the extended family and that this was adaptive to the situation of immigrants. In her study, she found that adults of Italian descent were inclined to live relatively close to their parents, and therefore there was frequent interaction. Grandchildren also remained involved with their grandparents, and Italians reported numerous rewards from their grandchildren. It appeared that elderly Italians did not need to seek out social organizations or senior clubs because they had "the family."

Although Johnson (1985) suggests that elderly Italians generally do not need to seek out social organizations or senior clubs because they have "the family," Kolb has known male Italian immigrants who spent substantial periods of time in Italian social clubs with friends. Hayes, Kalish, and Guttmann (1986), moreover, emphasize that, during major Euro-American waves of immigration, federal health and income assistance programs did not exist, and neighborhood beneficial associations often developed to help residents in the event of accidents, illness, or death. These expanded into fraternal organizations, and many eventually became social and cultural clubs. Among Italians, assistance provided by mutual benefit societies included insurance and loans, welfare services such as immigrant aid, and assistance for elderly community members.

According to Hraba (1994, p. 324), community development by early Italian immigrants was extensive:

> One could attend musicals and operas and watch marionette shows in Italian neighborhoods. There were also Italian communal organizations that spread across specific locales to include virtually all Italians in America. For example, there were over 110 Italian newspapers in the country in 1918, and many had circulation far beyond a local area. . . . The Missionary Sisters of the Sacred Heart established hospitals, schools, and orphanages for Italians throughout the country. Fraternal societies became national organizations; for example, the Order of the Sons of Italy once had 3,000 lodges across the country. The purposes of this organization . . . are a combination of assimilationist and ethnic preservation themes.

Relatives continue to gather for ritualized religious and lifecycle events. For the Italian Americans in Johnson's (1985) study, these occasions were frequent. Clarke's (2001) study of Italian Canadians in nursing homes supports the idea of continuing interaction between residents and their relatives, as he found high levels of family interaction among participants in his study, and nursing home residents able to travel often spent weekends with relatives. Of the ninety-two Italian Catholic nursing home residents in Clarke's (2001) study, 92 percent reported that their ties with relatives were very close.

ROLES WITHIN ITALIAN AMERICAN FAMILIES

Italian American families have been described as adult-centered (Covello 1967), with children expected to conform to adult demands enforced by an explicit system of rewards and punishments. Traditionally, male children had freedom to form relationships outside the family, whereas females' activities were more restricted because of the value placed on maintaining family honor by preserving the virginity of unmarried females and the fidelity of married females. A hierarchical structure resulted from segregated sex roles within an adult-centered home, with males, at least nominally, of higher status than females, and parents of higher status than children (Johnson 1985). As in many cultures, families expect that daughters will provide care for sick or aging parents (Giordano & McGoldrick 1996).

In traditional families the father is the undisputed head of the household and authoritarian and rigid in setting rules and guidelines for behavior, whereas the mother offers emotional sustenance and is revered (Giordano and McGoldrick 1996). Families in Italy have been described as father-dominated and mother-centered, with mothers exercising power at home (Johnson 1985). This pattern can be observed in Italian American families, but studies present a mixed view, and roles and relationships vary among families. Role changes among some Italian American women have included a shift toward more active mastery and concerns for achievement (Johnson 1985).

Social interactions of immigrant and first-generation Italian families are guided by a complex code of obligations for familial and extra-familial relationships, *l'ordine della famiglia,* which requires that the family is the top priority, which means remaining physically and psychologically close, coming together in times of crisis, and caring for vulnerable family members (Giordano & McGoldrick 1996). Family members are taught that they must not disgrace the family, take advantage of relatives, talk about the family to outsiders, or openly express emotion outside the family. However, secrets and alliances do develop at times within families, and sometimes intergenerational conflicts occur if third- and fourth-generation Italian Americans rebel against these dynamics (Giordano & McGoldrick 1996; Papajohn & Spiegel 1975).

Parents in traditional families expect their children to assume responsibility for themselves outside their home, and children are expected to please adults by talking and behaving in an adult manner. Ties between father and daughter, mother and son, are often the strongest, especially the latter. The family code dictates that family members "should owe nothing to those outside the family, be unconcerned with the activities and behavior of 'outsiders,' and show respect—but not trust—for outside authority" (Giordano & McGoldrick 1996, p. 574). As is true in many cultures, daughters are expected to provide care for sick or aging parents. The value placed on intergenerational relationships throughout the lifecycle is apparent in the following statement (Giordano & McGoldrick 1996, p. 574):

> Throughout the life cycle, they [Italians] think of relationships from an extremely inclusive perspective, and their primary life cycle difficulties have to do with stages involving separation, in particular "launching" and death. Indeed, it has been said that there is no such thing as launching in an Italian family, that the parents just send their children out far enough to find partners who are then brought into the family circle, which then is expanded. The network of significant others is usually large, including aunts, uncles, cousins, *gumbares* (old friends and neighbors), as well as godparents, who assume a role of great importance in child rearing.

Although it is widely believed that the male figure is the head of the Italian or Italian American family, many who have grown up in an Italian household believe that, actually, the mother is in charge. Children are highly valued, and the culture applauds filial accomplishment. As adults, children are expected to provide grandchildren, expanding the circle of family. It is expected that parents have laid the basis for respect and loyalty to themselves as elders, and this means that there is someone to care for them when they can no longer care for themselves (Johnson 1985, p. 58).

FOOD

My grandmother is in the kitchen cutting the Italian bread she has made. The bread my grandmother has made is a big bread, a substantial bread, one you can use for dunking, or for scraping the last bit of sauce from a bowl of pasta, or for breaking into soups or stews, or for eating with a little olive oil and a shake of salt, or with the juices of a very ripe tomato and some very green olive oil (pane e pomarole).

Louise De Salvo, "Cutting the Bread"

Food has a special place in Italian culture. As southern Italian culture developed, pleasure from food and eating became central to daily life and a source of emotional and physical solace (Femminella & Quadagno 1976; Mangione

& Morreale 1992; Giordano & McGoldrick 1996). With the lives of southern Italian families connected to uncontrollable events, Italians could at least have control over the food supply in their homes (Cronin 1970; Johnson 1985). The head of the household in southern Italian families achieved status if family members were plump, as this indicated success in his primary role, even if he did not succeed in other roles (Johnson 1985).

In Johnson's (1985) study, Italian American respondents indicated that meals provided an opportunity for sociability at a designated time within the nuclear family, and they identified eating patterns as an indicator of ethnicity. Respondents made comments such as, "if someone doesn't eat pasta twice a week and on Sunday, he's not Italian," "families become American when they stop serving lasagna with the Thanksgiving turkey," "a household that does not have at least two pots simmering on the stove does not have an Italian wife," and "whenever you find two Italians, you find food" (p. 91). Johnson's Italian American respondents frequently described Italian men who marry non-Italians as thin and hungry-looking. Responses also reflected a close association between food and mothering.

Food and its preparation are central in the experiences and identities of many Italian American women. The diversity and complexity of their personal experiences and the relationship of these experiences to food is explored from many perspectives in DeSalvo and Giunta's anthology, *The Milk of Almonds: Italian American Women Writers on Food and Culture* (2002, p. 11). As they write in the introduction,

If the cultural memory and collective unconscious of Italian Americans is of a land that did not provide sufficient sustenance for those who emigrated, then, in the New World, the central importance of food in Italian American life and culture and in the works of Italian American writers becomes more readily understandable. For this is a people who have undergone the trauma of emigration, with its devastating—but also its creative and culturally productive—results. And though this preoccupation with food is often interpreted reductively by outsiders to Italian American culture (and by some insiders also), still, it has a politicized significance, for it counteracts those negative images of Italian American life—Italian Americans as mobsters, as uneducated dimwits—that persist in popular culture.

RELIGION

After having experienced frequent disregard by Roman Catholic clergy in Italy, Italian immigrants to the U.S. from the late 1800s into the 1900s experienced hostility from the Irish who dominated the Catholic Church and ran the parochial schools. Many Italians placed great value on the pageantry and spectacle of Church rituals that foster family celebrations and rites of passage, and that contrasted sharply with the asceticism of the Irish Catholic Church. Clarke (2001, p. 29) notes that the literature indicates that Catholics of English or Irish cultural backgrounds tend to value self-direction more highly, and Catholics of Italian origin tend to value conformity more.

Many Italian Americans maintain a pattern of inactivity with the Roman Catholic Church (Schaefer 2005). Some Italians, however, continue to support the Catholic Church, as it represents tradition, family, and community, and view God more as a friend of the family (Giordano & McGoldrick 1996; Giordano, McGoldrick, & Klages 2005). Religious beliefs and practices remain important for many older Italian Americans.

Clarke (2001, p. 65) believes that the Catholic Church remains the focal point of the Italian community in Canada, although the influence of the Church is diminishing for the younger generations. He identifies the importance to Italian older adults of participation in activities associated with Catholicism that bring the community together. Activities binding the members of the community include masses, celebrations of festivals and holidays, feasts of patron saints, and the rituals of baptism, confirmations, weddings, and funerals. Intergenerational participation in these activities also takes place within many Italian American families in the U.S., including participation by family members who are highly acculturated to life outside Italian American communities.

ITALIAN AMERICAN FAMILIES AND NURSING HOME PLACEMENT

In many families, the sacrifice parents have made for their families is used as a device to secure proper care and respect for parents in their old age, with the implicit expectation that adult children will take care of elderly parents as a result of lifelong socialization patterns. If children fail to meet their parents' expectations, Italian American mothers may use techniques such as sighing, crying, or talking about friends who have been abandoned by their families. The following are examples of such strong feelings of abandonment on admission day and a social worker's responses.

Several years ago we admitted a lovely Italian woman who had been living at home with her daughter and son-in-law. She would not get out of the car on the day of admission but remained inside the parked car, at the front door of the facility. Her son tried hopelessly to get his mother out of the car. I proceeded to the car window where I pleasantly greeted the woman and said that I was there to escort her to her new home. She stared straight ahead and said, "No thanka you, I hava a home witha my daughta and—the husband." I again tried to coax her out by explaining that we were a Catholic facility with many nuns and many other people from the neighborhood. I even ventured to name a friend of hers who had been admitted a few months earlier. She rolled down the window and said, "Listen to me, you are a very nicea girl, but I hava seven children. Ifa this one doesn't want me anymore I go to the next, and ifa thata one doesn't want me I go to the next. Why can a mother raise seven children, but seven children can't take care of one mother?"

I eventually got the woman out of the car. Honestly, I think it was because she had to go to the bathroom, but once we got her in the front door we had a chance. She liked her room because it had a water view and reminded her of her hometown in Italy. We also quickly found one of our Italian-speaking Sisters to greet her and she collapsed into the nun's arms crying her woes, but she did stay. Years later we had a similar scenario, but that time it did not result in an admission. The applicant wound up going home with her son after four hours of coaxing. I informed the family that we really could not admit someone against their wishes if cognitively able to make that decision. Ironically the same person was admitted three months later after having suffered a stroke. She could no longer make independent decisions. She was very sad.

Contacts with middle-aged Italian Americans indicate that often their bond with older relatives is unwritten, motivated by duty or repayment, and sometimes by love. The possibility of a parent becoming totally dependent can create considerable anxiety for Italian American adult children. Community sanctions as well as filial values make nursing home placement a most undesirable option in many families. Relatives frequently worry about what others will say if they decide to place a parent in a nursing home, as nursing homes are often seen as existing for those without family. The following is an example of family interaction in a nursing home in New York City:

A resident who had lived in the facility for more than five years attended mass regularly, ate her meals in the main dining room, and attended many of the recreational programs offered. She interacted well with the staff and peers. As soon as her son arrived to visit she would start saying, "I want to go home. Please take me home. I want to go home. When am I going home?" She would badger her son until the end of his visit, and he would be distraught. This went on for more than a year. Finally, the social worker sat down with him and asked, "Why do you come to visit so often when you leave so dejected?" His response was, "She's my mother." The social worker met with him several times and discussed what his visits were accomplishing for either one of them. His response was that his mother had the opportunity to make him feel guilty and that made her feel good. His only consolation was that intellectually he knew he could not manage his mother's care at home. The day his mother died the social worker met the son in the hallway and offered her condolences. He asked her right then if he had done the right thing, or should he have taken her home?

Consistent with experiences of social workers in the U.S., Clarke (2001) found in his study that emerging themes in the expectations of Canadian Italian residents for their children were respect, appreciation, and keeping in contact. Children of the Italian residents generally provided some kind of assistance, and Clarke suggests that "the basis of this support may be embedded in the primary group nature [of Italian familial relationships] in which face-to-face interactions give members a sense of self-awareness, identity, and socialize them with the norms and values of the group" (p. 59). Many Italian residents described sacrifices in rearing their children, but the residents saw the other side of this effort when they experienced their children become helping sons or daughters. Clarke suggests that the adult children's acts of delayed reciprocity in helping their parents provide a model of the helping relationship for their own children, fostering an understanding of the behavior that will be expected from them as adults.

It is important to remember that Italian American elders constitute a diverse and resilient group of people possessing many strengths and abilities. They have survived challenges associated with their own immigration experiences, or have been challenged as children or grandchildren of immigrants, often dealing with intergenerational conflicts regarding values within their families. Many have reared children in unfamiliar surroundings and encountered hostile outsiders. Frequently the possibility of nursing home placement is not the first challenge to their traditional value system, and they may be aware of social changes, including the development of nursing homes, that have taken place in Italy as well as in the U.S. Many have experienced changes in their communities related to neighborhood deterioration, gentrification, a neighboring ethnic community expanding into their neighborhood as the population increases in the other community, movement of younger people out of the community, or urban renewal that has affected the physical, psychological, and social aspects of their community (Hayes, Kalish, & Guttmann 1986).

To facilitate adjustment and enjoyment of life in the nursing home, social workers and other staff need to offer Italian residents opportunities to participate in family activities, including those related to religious celebrations, when residents and their families express interest in these experiences. Visits of intergenerational family members to the nursing home should also be encouraged, as well as opportunities for residents to visit their relatives. Roberto (1990; cited in Clarke 2001, p. 66) suggested that interaction with descendants helps older adults to have a feeling of continuity of family and provides assistance with reflection and recalling earlier experiences.

It is important for all service providers to understand that many Italian American nursing home residents have experienced language barriers and age-old patterns of avoiding social contacts outside the family, and once inside the nursing home these feelings do not diminish. Two-thirds of the Italian residents in Clarke's (2001) study indicated that they expected their relatives to talk with the nurse about their care, and the dominant reason for this expectation appeared to be the need for relatives to serve as interpreters. He found that many caregiving relatives, aware of the older person's prior experiences and related expectations, did not relinquish the care of a loved one after they needed to choose a nursing home but instead appeared to want to direct the care. Many relatives visited several hours each day, and some relatives brought food from home and attempted to provide personal care even though the facility was already providing assistance.

NURSING HOME RESIDENTS, FOOD, AND RECREATION

For some older adults, eating may be the one area over which they still have some control. While they are experiencing losses and learning new routines in a nursing home, eating is an area in which Italian residents can continue to feel that they are competent, something they know more about than the social worker, doctor, or nurse. Most Italians in nursing homes can describe how to prepare a meal and the ingredients needed. They wonder why staff would dare to tell them what and how they should eat.

Nursing home food and its preparation is frequently a point of contention for Italian nursing home residents and their families. A home may advertise Italian cuisine, and although the fine print indicates that residents must adhere to therapeutic diets, prospective residents and their relatives may pay little attention to these words. Since food is highly revered in Italian culture, some older adults believe that if you can eat or are eating, then you are well or getting better, and if you do not eat or cannot eat, it is a sign to start mourning.

Growing up "healthy" in an Italian family means you have to eat. I recall frequent visits to my grandmother's house always resulting in a meal or snack of some sort. Even in her later years, when her vision was almost completely gone, she would have a cup of tea and a sandwich waiting for me. She was always looking to feed her great grandchildren. Despite her visual impairment and frailty she managed to have the french fries hot and ready with lots of ketchup!

Years earlier, when her own brother lay dying in the hospital, she would return from her visit saying, "He ate his soup and drank his coffee, he'll be okay." My grandmother was a bright and intelligent woman. She had nursed many people back to good health and held many a hand while they died. But as long as the person was eating, then he or she was okay.

When a resident no longer desires food or comprehends the act of eating, staff recommendations for meeting residents' nutritional needs may conflict with the preferences of family members. The relatives' priority may not be for the resident to eat, but rather the amount and kinds of foods they can give to their relative. The object of dispute may become the food itself, the flavor, consistency, and presentation, and not the ability to chew, swallow, or stimulate the appetite.

Assistance by relatives and friends at mealtimes can provide important opportunities for interaction between Italian residents and their informal caregivers. Clarke (2001, p. 67) observed the following in Canadian nursing homes:

> At meal times some adult daughters and friends volunteered to take residents to the dining room. They offered assistance in feeding, and they helped others to whom they were not related by blood. Special background music was played in the dining rooms at mealtime. On each table sat a vase with a beautiful flower. Fresh white tablecloths and decorated walls added brightness to the surroundings. Yet, without the presence of a loved one, some residents appeared sad and dreary. Mealtime was no longer a family get-together for some residents; rather, it was an unpleasant individual experience.
>
> Caregiving routine involved being wheeled to the dining room at a fixed time, and being taken back to the bedroom within a specified time. Some residents refused to leave their rooms for various reasons: the food was not appetizing, the food was considered too much, or because a relative was not able to visit.

Although it is difficult for many relatives and friends to be present at mealtimes, it is important for staff to understand the importance in many Italian families of being together at mealtimes and encourage this participation in the life of residents.

Many Italians and Italian Americans are accustomed to highly seasoned dishes and aromatic recipes. They may enjoy deep-fried foods covered in sauces, cheeses, lots of garlic, and olive oil. For many, the salt shaker is considered a necessary utensil. When an older adult enters an institution where meals are prepared for a very large number of residents and therapeutic diets must be maintained, the food often does not meet the expectations of Italian residents. Many residents come from homes where they either prepared scrumptious meals or lived in a house filled with the aromas of good meals prepared by relatives. When food is not served the way Italian residents want or prepared in the manner to which they are accustomed, many do not eat. Many older Italian Americans still can their own tomatoes, make their own sausage, prepare pickled peppers, and make their own wine. They do this in the yard, the garage, the cellar or the kitchen. It is difficult for nursing homes to compete with the home-grown ingredients of Italians' gardens and canned by their own hands.

Refusing to eat presents a host of problems for staff at a nursing home. In the case of restorative therapy, proper nutrition is essential for strength and muscle building, as well as for good skin integrity, wound healing, and cognitive functioning and reasoning. How then do we create gastronomical delicacies that are low salt, low fat, low cholesterol, dairy free, and sugar free? It is difficult to find a truly Italian recipe that is any of the above and still has the same flavor or consistency.

When food is brought from home, however, the staff can work with the resident's relatives and friends to make alterations consistent with dietary restrictions. Perhaps the diet might then include one flourish of the salt shaker rather than two, perhaps two tablespoons of olive oil instead of four. Skim may be substituted for whole milk ricotta cheese. These are only some examples of how family members can bring food from home and still conform to the doctor's recommendations.

One way to overcome disdain for therapeutic diets is to allow diet-free days or small breaks now and then. Residents may enjoy attending an "Evening-Out Dinner" program in the nursing home, when food is delivered from the local pizza shop or Italian restaurant, or they can occasionally dine out and order whatever they want.

It is important for service providers to explore Italian American residents' interests and knowledge related to their social, recreational, educational, and employment experiences in Italy and the United States. Educational levels achieved by Italian American older adults vary substantially, as do literacy levels in English and Italian, and it is essential to assess literacy levels to evaluate basic communication needs and recreational options. Some Italian-speaking nursing home residents have been assumed to have dementia, when, in fact, they did not respond to English because they did not understand the language.

Residents may experience a great deal of pleasure from listening either to Italian or other music, or singing, or discussing historical or current events in Italy and the U.S., or playing cards. If literacy is limited, many recreational activities that do not rely on reading and writing skills can be used, including listening to opera and other music. Although listening and discussing opera is frequently thought of in the U.S. as an activity of interest only to highly educated people, an interest in opera cuts across all Italian socioeconomic strata. People from rural and urban areas and diverse educational and socio-economic backgrounds have listened to opera in Italy and the U.S. Although not all Italian Americans are interested in opera, opportunities to listen to opera recordings or attend concerts can provide joy to some residents and be an activity shared with family members or groups of residents. Many beautiful Italian operas composed during the nineteenth and twentieth centuries remain extremely popular internationally, and there is a long and continuing history of renowned Italian opera singers, including Enrico Caruso, Mirella Freni, Luciano Pavarotti, Renata Scotto, and others, which is a source of ethnic pride and supports positive self-esteem.

SOCIAL WORK PRACTICE ADDRESSING RELATIVES' CONCERNS

Responses of Italian American residents and their relatives to nursing home policies and practices vary greatly. However, the example of Ms. S. provides a description of issues that arise in social work with some Italian American residents and their relatives. Ms. S. was admitted to a nursing home from her own home with a primary diagnosis of dementia. Her mental deterioration had become apparent after the death of her husband a few years before her admission. She had been cared for at home by home health aides paid for by the Medicaid program, and her daughter assumed responsibility for her care at night. Ms. S. has two adult children, a son and a daughter. She was born in Italy and immigrated to the U.S. in 1967; Italian is her primary language. Shortly before admission she started wandering and had become incontinent of bladder and bowel. Events leading up to her admission and stay in the nursing home reflect common problems of Italian American residents and their relatives and illustrate social work interventions.

The daughter works full-time and was displeased with home care and frustrated by sleepless nights, so she decided to pursue long-term placement for her mother. The admission process took two months. When the daughter was called about bed availability, she declined because her family was visiting from Italy and she did not want them to be present when her mother was placed. She declined the second available bed because of the impending holidays and the need for her mother to be present at all the family gatherings. The third decline was because the admission day would be a Friday, and "Fridays are unlucky days."

From the day the resident was admitted, her daughter had constant complaints. It started with food issues. Individual menu items were being selected by the daughter based on her mother's previous preferences. The clinical observation was that the resident could no longer discriminate between foods. She ate well and ate anything provided. The daughter insisted that staff conform to her selections. Staff attempted to educate the daughter about nutritional issues, especially those identified with advanced dementia. They have not been successful yet but remain patient. The daughter was also concerned with food consistency and how the food looked. "If it doesn't look like Italian food, my mother won't eat it." Despite staff efforts to educate her and share observations, she would not accept her mother's inability to discriminate between foods. The social worker needed to help staff understand the daughter's behavior from the perspective of her Italian American background.

The daughter's second focus had to do with the resident's incontinence. She denied stating at admission that her mother was incontinent of both bowel and bladder. Upon arriving for her visits, the daughter would ask that the resident be taken to the bathroom. She knew that her mother was on a toileting schedule and wore an incontinence brief. Even if the resident had been attended to, the daughter would insist that it be done in her presence. If it was not done quickly enough, she did it herself, and then complained that the staff was not taking care of her mother.

There was a request from the family that nursing home staff restrain the resident so she would not wander away. Staff informed the family that this is a restraint free facility. They did not understand that simply requesting it was not sufficient reason for its use. Staff again tried to educate the family about why restraints could not be used. Alternative methods to prevent elopement without denying the resident the right to move about the facility were also explained. Restraints were always a last resort and this resident had not needed them. The family was concerned with physical safety, not the psychosocial well-being of the resident, and that was why they felt they needed to take charge of the parent who could no longer manage alone.

Ms. S. adjusted well after the first few days of admission, became comfortable with the staff, and her physical aggression decreased. Her resistance to care was attributable to dementia. She attended sensory stimulating programs as well as daily spiritual activities. Although she could not participate, she benefited from the stimulation just by being present. Yet her daughter saw no benefit in her mother's attendance at these programs

The resident no longer wandered, perhaps because her ability to ambulate independently had deteriorated over the past seven months. She no longer communicated verbally and had difficulty maintaining eye contact. She was spoon-fed by the staff or her family when they were present. Her dementia continued to advance, and it became more difficult for her daughter to deal with it. Intellectually the daughter verbalized that she knew that nothing could be done for her mother. But when the social worker and other staff sat with her at interdisciplinary care conferences to discuss her mother's current status, she blamed the facility for the deterioration.

The assigned social worker met with the daughter numerous times, but the daughter was reluctant to acknowledge the disease process, and, referring to her family in Italy, she asked: "What am I supposed to tell them when they come to visit again? How am I going to explain what has happened?" Again the social workers attempted to educate her and offer to speak with other family members about dementia and the progression of the disease.

Social work staff believed that the underlying problems were the daughter's guilt regarding placement, her fear of developing dementia herself, and her inability to accept that she could no longer provide the twenty-four-hour care her mother required. She had to explain to various family members why she was "putting her mother away" and then felt the need to "prove that she had done the right thing." Italian American daughters are usually expected to take care of their mothers, and many are expected to be there to meet all their parents' needs, and then some. Because of traditional cultural expectations regarding the roles of family members, this mother and daughter could make no allowance for the working woman nor did they understand why the woman is out of the house. There are also Italian American families, however, that are able to adjust, with greater flexibility, to the realities of caregiving and life's circumstances.

Our roles as social workers require us to not only be caregivers to our clients but also educators to their families. When working with Italian Americans, the social worker will often have to engage relatives. In order for the resident who needs services to adjust and accept placement, it is important for relatives to accept the resident's need for services. Social workers and other staff often hear families say "she used to before" or "he did before he went into the hospital," but what relatives fail to acknowledge is that their relatives would not be in the nursing home if they could still do what they did "before." There is a period of mourning the old self and accepting the new. Sometimes residents and their relatives never achieve acceptance of their situation. They may remain in denial, requiring an inordinate amount of staff support and time, and they are often emotional, but the social worker must continue to work with residents and families with patience, compassion, cultural sensitivity, and, at times, a certain amount of firmness.

FAMILY ACCEPTANCE OF SOCIAL SERVICES AND MENTAL HEALTH SERVICES

Here we not only admit the resident but also the family. We consider the expectations of the family equally to those of the resident. We work together to find a way to meet their needs without losing sight of what the nursing home industry provides. Italians tend to be emotional. I speak from experience, being of Italian descent myself. Emotions may take over, and logical thinking may fall to the wayside. Today's nursing facilities try to provide a homelike setting. They try to provide for the daily needs of residents to the fullest. Yet it is impossible for one-on-one attention to be a standard as it is in their own homes. In one incident during my years working in a nursing home, I actually had a family say to me, "I don't care about the rest of them. I care about mama, my mama."

Rosemarie Hofstein

Italian Americans tend to delay seeking professional help and instead seek help within the family (Cleary & Demone 1988; Femminella 1982; Giordano & McGoldrick 1996). When seeking help outside the family, family members may feel ashamed about not being able to resolve the problem themselves or may approach the relationship with an attitude of distrust of everyone outside the family. In describing how to initiate work with Italian Americans in family therapy, Giordano and McGoldrick (1996, pp. 576–577) provide useful recommendations for professionals working with Italian Americans in many settings and regarding many issues, including ones that pertain to older family members:

- Honestly share common values
- Do not probe until trust is established
- Anticipate a lively first encounter because Italian Americans can be engaging and colorful speakers, and their expressiveness can become exaggerated when they experience stress
- Notice differences between style and content
- Be aware that the words may not be meant literally, that they "give expression to the moment"
- The emotional impact, social content of the problem, and related physical sensations may be described at length

- They may deny difficult problems because they may be unwilling to share private matters with a person outside the family
- Resolving a problem often means relieving stress without changing the family's equilibrium
- Family secrets must be dealt with carefully

Giordano and McGoldrick also urge professionals to keep in mind the strengths of many Italian Americans, including primacy of personal relationships, enjoyment of home life, and respect for parental authority in the home.

INTRAFAMILIAL AND STAFF DYNAMICS

Clarke (2001) found that, although parents expected their children to be devoted visitors and caregivers, parent-child relationships were mutual exchange relationships where children also had expectations of their parents. These included the expectation that parents will look after their own appearance, which Clarke interpreted as part of a broader expectation that parents should avoid embarrassing their children. He suggests, therefore, that "both generations play different roles that are rooted in the concept of shared responsibility" (p. 115).

In the two primarily Italian nursing homes in Clarke's study (2001, pp. 93–94), the presence of some nurses who spoke Italian and others who spoke Spanish made communication easier for the Italian residents. However, the demands of speaking these languages led to strain and overload for these nurses. As a result, conflicts developed among nurses and between nurses and residents. Although initially satisfied that residents preferred them as their nurses, Italian-speaking nurses later challenged residents as too demanding and also took issue with other nurses whom they believed were not doing as much work as they were. Clarke suggests that issues related to shortage of bilingual staff may be addressed by considering language facility when staff is recruited, but nursing homes can also address this issue through workshops and in-service education.

MEDICAL ISSUES AND END-OF-LIFE CARE

An important process for the welfare of nursing home residents and their relatives is the assignment of an individual or group of individuals as health care proxy, and specifying one's preferences in specific medical situations. A proxy is legally authorized to make medical decisions on behalf of a resident who is unable to make these decisions alone. Variations exist among states in policies regarding informal caregivers' right to make decisions on behalf of a person when there is no assigned proxy, but one type of situation in which no health care proxy had been assigned is described below. In this situation, no proxy form had been signed by the resident, and the wishes of the resident's son conflicted with those of the nursing home staff.

Ms. M. was born in Italy, was ninety-three years old, and was totally dependent on others for activities of daily living. She was unable to communicate and had been fed through a tube for the last two years. An insulin-dependent diabetic with peripheral vascular disease, she developed gangrene of the right great toe which was spreading. The surgeon recommended amputation below the knee.

Unfortunately this resident had no health care agent assigned to her. She had one son who visited daily. He was against the amputation and would not sign a consent form for the procedure, and, of course, the surgeon would not perform the procedure without consent. The clinical staff met with the family twice, and the physician has had numerous conversations with them.

In this situation, the family's concern was not about pain, discomfort, or death; they did not want the resident to die without a body part. Some Italian Americans believe, culturally, that in order to rest in peace the entire body needs to be intact. Losing a body part because of an accident is one thing, but agreeing to deliberately remove one is another. Social work staff at the nursing home desperately tried to educate the son about the pain and discomfort associated with his mother's condition, but he would not allow himself to accept it.

The thought of surgically removing a limb caused this family much anguish. They were reluctant to believe staff reports of pain and discomfort, as this would force them to select the alternative of amputation. Because they preferred not to make this choice, they refused to consider it. The cultural response was to leave the decision in God's hands.

As a formality the issue was referred to the Ethics Committee in the nursing home. The physician and administrator could move for an expedited guardian to be appointed to make the appropriate decision. The clinical team also needed to consider the benefit of the surgery and the quality of the resident's life once the amputation was performed.

If the resident had agreed to complete a form assigning a health care proxy when she was cognitively able, the decision would not have been an issue. In not signing the proxy form, the mother may have felt that she was maintaining control.

It is also important to understand the perspectives of many Italians regarding death and dying. As with many people, they often have difficulty accepting the end of life and seeing the goodness of the years spent. Because of the cultural stigma of nursing home placement, death in the nursing home comes with a double burden. Families find it difficult to explain to other relatives "how we let it happen" and face the community that knows about the relative dying while a nursing home resident.

CONCLUSION

Centuries of oppression, disasters, epidemics, and traumas experienced by people living in the geographic area that would become southern Italy shaped a widespread cultural belief long ago that no one outside the family could be trusted. Subsequently many Italian Americans have experienced prejudice and discrimination in the United States, reinforcing the belief in a need for family solidarity. Powerful cultural expectations requiring strong and lasting family bonds developed, and these bonds and expectations have accompanied Italians during emigration and resettlement in the United States and other countries. These expectations include beliefs that parents will make sacrifices for their children and that children will assist their parents as needed when they become old.

The need for nursing home placement is a shock to many Italian American elders and is often distressing for family members reared with the cultural mandate to provide all necessary care at home. Social workers need to understand the cultural expectations, as well as the potential for intergenerational conflict regarding these expectations, and provide opportunities for residents and their relatives to discuss and try to resolve their conflicts, concerns, and feelings. Nursing home placement may be seen as a stage of the migration process that includes experiences prior to placement (pre-migration and departure); the decision-making process and move into the home (transit); and the adjustment process (resettlement), all of which residents and relatives may find helpful to discuss (Kolb 2003), just as it is important to understand the earlier immigration experience as a process that includes pre-migration and departure, transit, and resettlement (Drachman & Ryan 2001). Furthermore, social workers may have to work with residents and staff as culture mediators to help resolve problems that may arise as a result of the emotionality and expressiveness of some Italian American residents and their relatives who view placement in a nursing home as a crisis;

the potential for insufficient cultural understanding by interdisciplinary service providers may also need to be addressed (Fandetti & Goldmeier 1988).

The authors believe that the information in this chapter will contribute to the development of cultural competence in social work with Italian American elders and their relatives. People of Italian ancestry live in many countries, and the discussion presented here may also be useful in providing services in other locales. Although this chapter generally addresses cultural beliefs and practices and social work interventions in broad terms, nursing home staff must remain aware that Italian American elders and their relatives are extremely diverse.

Seemingly endless variations are seen among individuals and experiences simply as a result of multiple influences on individuals and families. A resident may be a recent immigrant or may have immigrated in childhood, young adulthood, or middle age; or may belong to the second, third, fourth, or later generation of his or her family living in the U.S. Ties among nuclear and extended family members may be close or distant. The number of relatives who interact with the resident may be few or many. Residents may have lived only in a community with other people of Italian ancestry, may have participated in Italian American community activities, or may have had a partner of Italian ancestry. Friends may have included family members only or a broader circle of people. Individuals vary in their preference for traditional Italian foods and religious celebrations, as well as beliefs about advance directives. Older adults may or may not speak Italian, and if they do speak Italian and cannot speak English, they can be subject to misdiagnosis and erroneously thought to have dementia. Residents may have become acculturated to some U.S. cultural values that differ from traditional Italian values, yet maintain traditional expectations about intergenerational relationships between older and younger family members.

REFERENCES

Clarke, E. (2001). *Aging and caregiving in Canada*. Canadian Studies series. Vol. 30. Lewiston, N.Y.: Edwin Mellen.

Cleary, P., & Demone, H. (1988). Health and social service needs in a northeastern metropolitan area: Ethnic group differences. *Journal of Sociology and Social Welfare* 15 (4), 63–76.

Covello, L. (1967). *The social background of the Italo-American school child*. Leiden, Netherlands: Brill.

Cronin, C. (1970). *Sting of change: Sicilians in Sicily and Australia*. Chicago: University of Chicago Press.

De Salvo, L. (2002). Cutting the bread. In L. DeSalvo and E. Giunta (Eds.), *The milk of almonds: Italian American women writers on food and culture*, pp. 322–331. New York: Feminist Press at the City University of New York.

De Salvo, L., & Giunta, E. (Eds.) (2002). *The milk of almonds: Italian American women writers on food and culture.* New York: Feminist Press at the City University of New York.

Douglas, W. (1984). *Emigration in a southern Italian town.* New Brunswick, N.J.: Rutgers University Press.

Drachman, D., & Ryan, A. S. (2001). Immigrants and refugees. In A. Gitterman (Ed.), *Handbook of social work practice with vulnerable and resilient populations,* pp. 651–686. New York: Columbia University Press.

Fandetti, D., & Goldmeier, J. (1988). Social workers as culture mediators in health care settings. *Health and Social Work* 13 (summer), 171–179.

Femminella, F. (1982). Social psychiatry in the Italian American community. In R. Caporale (Ed.), *Italian Americans through generations.* New York: American Italian Historical Association.

Femminella, F., & Quadagno, J. (1976). The Italian American family. In C. Mindel and R. Halberstam (Eds.), *Ethnic families in America,* pp. 61–88. New York: Elsevier.

Gambino, R. (1974). *Blood of my blood: The dilemma of the Italian-Americans.* Garden City, N.Y.: Anchor Press/Doubleday.

Gans, H. (1962). *Urban villagers: Group and class in the life of Italian Americans.* New York: Free Press.

Giordano, J. & McGoldrick, M. (1996). Italian families. In M. McGoldrick, J. Giordano, and J. Pearce (Eds.), *Ethnicity and family therapy,* pp. 467–582. New York: Guilford.

Giordano, J., McGoldrick, M., & Klages, J. (2005). Italian families. In M. McGoldrick, J. Giordano, & N. Garcia-Preto (Eds.), *Ethnicity and family therapy,* pp. 616–628. New York: Guilford.

Hayes, C., Kalish, R., & Guttmann, D. (Eds.) (1986). *European-American elderly: A guide for practice.* New York: Springer.

Hraba, J. (1994). *American ethnicity.* Itasca, Ill.: Peacock.

Johnson, C. (1985). *Growing up and growing old in Italian-American families.* New Brunswick, N.J.: Rutgers University Press.

Kolb, P. (2003). *Caring for our elders: Multicultural experiences with nursing home placement.* New York: Columbia University Press.

Mangione, J., & Morreale, B. (1992). *La storia: Five centuries of the Italian American experience.* New York: HarperCollins.

Messina, E. (1994). Life-span development and Italian-American women. In J. Krase and J. DeSena (Eds.), *Italian-Americans in a multicultural society,* pp. 74–87. New York: American Historical Society.

National Italian American Foundation (2006a). Counties with highest amount of Italian Americans. Accessed October 12, 2006. http://www.niaf.org/research/2000_census_2.asp.

National Italian American Foundation (2006b). Italian American Contributions. Accessed October 12, 2006. http://www.niaf.org/research/contribution.asp.

National Italian American Foundation (2006c). States with the highest populations of Italian Americans (2006). Accessed October 12, 2006. http://www.niaf.org/research/2000_census_5.asp.

Papajohn, J., & Spiegel, J. (1975). *Transactions in families.* San Francisco: Jossey-Bass.

Parrillo, V. (2005). *Diversity in America.* Thousand Oaks, Calif.: Pine Forge.

Rabkin, J., & Struening, E. (1975). *Ethnicity, social class, and mental illness in New York City: A social area analysis of five ethnic groups.* Working Paper No. 17. New York: American Jewish Committee.

Rolle, A. (1980). *The Italian American: Troubled roots.* New York: Free Press.

Sassen, S. (1999). *Guests and aliens.* New York: New Press.

Schaefer, R. (2005). *Race and ethnicity in the United States.* Upper Saddle River, N.J.: Pearson Education.

Silverman, S. (1968). Agricultural organization, social structure and values in Italy: Amoral familism reconsidered. *American Anthropologist* 70, 1–20.

U.S. Census Bureau (2006a). *Statistical abstract of the United States: 2006.* Washington, D.C.: U.S. Government Printing Office.

U.S. Census Bureau (2006b). Table 1a. United States. Ability to speak English by language spoken at home for the population 5 years and over: 2000. Census 2000 PHC –T-37. Ability to speak English by language spoken at home 2000. Accessed October 12, 2006. http://www.census.gov/population/cen2000/phc-t37/tabola.pdf.

Vellone, E., Sansoni, J., & Cohen, M. Z. (2002). Experiences of Italians caring for family members with Alzheimer's disease. *Journal of Nursing Scholarship* 34 (4): 323–329.

RESOURCES

Organizations and Websites

Alzheimer's Association Resources. http://www.alz.org/resources.

American Association of Retired Persons International. http://www.aarp.org/international.

Italian American Writers. http://www._italianamericanwriters.com.

My Nursing Home. http://www.mynursinghome.com.

National Italian American Foundation. http://www.niaf.org.

Nursing Home Comparisons. http://www.Medicare.gov-nursinghomecompare.

Readings

Barzini, L. (1964). *The Italians.* New York: Atheneum.

Ciongoli, A. K., & Parini, J. (2002). *The story of Italian immigration: Passage to liberty and the rebirth of America.* New York: Regan Books.

Krase, J., & DeSena, J. (Eds.) (1994). *Italian-Americans in a multicultural society.* New York: American Historical Society.

Tommasini, A. (2004). *Opera: A critic's guide to the 100 most important works and the best recordings.* New York: New York Times Company.

5

Japanese American Elders

Tazuko Shibusawa

MRS. TANAKA

Mrs. Tanaka is an eighty-three-year-old, second-generation Japanese American woman recently admitted to an intermediate care facility after falling and fracturing her hip. She was referred to the social work department by her physical therapist, as she refused to participate in her rehabilitation program. The physical therapist was concerned that Mrs. Tanaka may be suffering from depression; the nursing staff reported that she had a poor appetite and had been socially withdrawn ever since admission to the facility. The recreational aides wheeled Mrs. Tanaka to attend daily recreational programs, but she only observed the activities and did not participate.

Mrs. Tanaka has a son who lives an hour away from the facility, and he and his wife visit every week. They are concerned with discharge plans, for they know that Mrs. Tanaka will not be able to return to her home where she had been living alone since her husband passed away five years ago. Although Mrs. Tanaka and her family have lived in the Midwest for the past fifty years, her son wondered if he should move his mother to an assisted living facility on the West Coast, where she would be among other Japanese American residents. Although Mrs. Tanaka was born in the United States and speaks English better than Japanese, her son thought that his mother would be happier in a setting that served Japanese food. The social worker wondered how Mrs. Tanaka would adjust to a new living situation, especially being so far away from her immediate family. She was uncertain about how she should counsel Mrs. Tanaka and her relatives.

MRS. KIMURA

Mrs. Kimura is a seventy-two-year-old Japanese woman who was admitted to a nursing facility following a stroke that left her body paralyzed on the left side. Her attending physician did not know whether Mrs. Kimura would be able to return to live with her daughter and son-in-law, especially as Mrs. Kimura also had signs of dementia in recent years. She had spent most of her life in Japan before moving, in her mid-sixties, to the United States to live with her only daughter. Mrs. Kimura's daughter is married to an American man who is not Japanese, and they have two children, one away at college and the other a senior in high school.

Mrs. Kimura does not speak English, and the facility staff depends on her daughter to translate for them. The daughter visits her mother every day after work, and spends longer periods with her mother on the weekends. The daughter is very concerned about having her mother in a facility where she does not understand the language, and she would like to care for her mother at home. She knows that this is not possible, however, given her mother's physical disabilities and possible onset of Alzheimer's disease. She has told one of the nurses that she feels badly about leaving her mother in the facility; the nurse would like the daughter to meet with the social worker, as the daughter is overwhelmed having to visit her mother and also care for an adolescent son.

Mrs. Tanaka and Mrs. Kimura obviously represent two different types of Japanese elders that social workers may encounter in long-term care facilities. The two women have led very different lives, growing up in two different countries (see Table 5.1), yet they may present similar adjustment difficulties when placed in nursing facilities where the residents are predominantly white. Because most nursing homes in the United States are not integrated (Berdes & Eckert 2001), they can pose difficulties for Japanese elders who do not live close to a Japanese community. Long-term care facilities serving Japanese American elders are located only on the West coast and Hawaii, close to the large ethnic concentrations of Japanese. Japanese American elders who live in other parts of the United States face the challenges of adjusting to facilities where they may be the only Japanese American resident.

EXPERIENCES OF JAPANESE AMERICANS IN THE U.S.: HISTORICAL BACKGROUND

Immigration from Japan to the United States began in the late 1800s (Kitano & Daniels 1987), with the first immigrants working on Hawaiian plantations and then moving to the West Coast when Hawaii was annexed by the United States in 1898. The first wave of Japanese immigrants was comprised of single men from poor rural areas in Japan who worked in agriculture and railroad maintenance (Kitano & Daniels 1987). Most came to the U.S. with the goal of making money and eventually returning to Japan, but making money

TABLE 5.1 Comparison of Mrs. Tanaka and Mrs. Kimura

	Mrs. Tanaka	Mrs. Kimura
Nativity	Born in the U.S.	Born in Japan
Primary language	English	Japanese
Cultural identification	Japanese American	Japanese
World War II	Internment camp in the U.S.	Japan
Food preference	Japanese food	Japanese food
Generational category	Second generation (*Nisei*)	New immigrant (*Shin Issei*)

was not easy and many of them ended up settling in the U.S. and marrying women in Japan through arranged marriages. Their wives are known as "picture brides," because their husbands knew them only through pictures when they arrived in the United States from Japan (Nishi 1995).

Japanese who immigrated in the early 1900s faced severe discrimination; they were not allowed to become U.S. citizens or own land, and hostility and housing segregation led the first-generation immigrants to form their own communities (Brooks 2000). Before World War II most urban Japanese Americans lived in ethnic enclaves, which offered physical and emotional protection from racial prejudice (Broom & Kitsuse 1973). At one time more than forty Japanese ethnic communities, known as "Japan Towns," existed on the West Coast, and besides offering a safe haven, these communities also provided services that Japanese Americans otherwise could not obtain. For example, a hospital was established in the Japanese American community in Los Angeles, as Japanese-born doctors were denied staff privileges at local hospitals and Japanese American patients were sometimes denied hospital care (Hospitals a pillar to Japanese Americans 1998).

All immigration from Japan came to a halt in 1924, when the U.S. government banned it. Immigration began again in the 1950s, when the Immigration Exclusion Act was revised, but anti-Japanese sentiment on the West Coast, during World War II, culminated in President Franklin D. Roosevelt signing an executive order that led to internment of all Japanese, including children of immigrants who were U.S. citizens during World War II. Close to 120,000 Japanese Americans on the West Coast were classified as "enemy aliens" and were incarcerated in internment camps in Arizona, Arkansas, California, Colorado, Idaho, Utah, and Wyoming. Most Japanese were forced to sell their belongings, and many lost their property. Internment lasted until World War II ended in 1945. A number of the second-generation immigrants who were U.S. citizens left camp during the war: young men were released when they enlisted in the U.S. army, and many of these men fought in Europe even as their parents remained incarcerated in camps; other second-generation Japanese Americans left camp to work in factories or on farms in Illinois and New Jersey. After the war some Japanese Americans moved to the Midwest and East Coast because of lingering anti-Japanese sentiment on the West Coast, as was the case with Mrs. Tanaka and her husband. The eastward move led to the development of small Japanese American communities in cities such as Chicago and New York. However, internment had devastating psychological effects on many Japanese Americans. Mental health professionals and researchers have noted that many Japanese Americans continue to feel that they are vulnerable to similar acts of racism and discrimination based upon racial-ethnic identity (Mass 1991; Nagata 1993; Yoo 2000).

Reactions to the experiences of internment during World War II may emerge in older Japanese Americans when they are forced to enter a nursing home, perhaps recalling their experiences of being separated from their communities and family members and interned. Mrs. Tanaka was interned with her mother and siblings in a camp in Colorado, and her father, who had been a pastor of a church, was interned along with other leaders of the Japanese American community in a prisoner-of-war camp in Crystal City, Texas. For elders such as Mrs. Tanaka, certain foods that were served in camp can evoke painful memories of internment—foods including, for example, corned beef and cabbage, apple butter, and spam (Nagata 1993). Other Japanese American elders may begin to prefer speaking Japanese and may desire familiar items from childhood, even though they are fully acculturated into mainstream U.S. society. This behavior can be related to the loss of short-term memory and retention of long-term memory, as typically occurs in the early onset of Alzheimer's disease.

DEMOGRAPHIC CHARACTERISTICS

According to the 2000 census close to 797,000 Japanese Americans live in the United States (U.S. Bureau of the Census 2000), mainly in Hawaii or on the West Coast. Japanese Americans have the highest life expectancy (82.1 years) among Asian Americans and Pacific Islanders in the United States (Department of Health and Human Services 1997), and, in contrast to other Asian ethnic groups, Japanese Americans tend to be highly acculturated. Because of low immigration rates after World War II, Japanese Americans have the highest proportion of U.S.-born elders among Asian Americans (Tanjasiri, Wallace, & Shibata 1995). The 1990 Census indicated, for example, that 63 percent of Japanese American elders were born in the U.S., in contrast to 16 percent of Chinese American elders (Elo 1997). Almost 90 percent of Japanese Americans have a high school education (U.S. Census Bureau 1993), and over 35 percent have a bachelor's degree or higher (Lee 1998). The poverty rate among Japanese Americans in 1989 was estimated to be somewhere between 3 percent and 7 percent, which is similar to the white population (ibid.). Japanese American families tend to be very small; the total fertility rate for Japanese American women is 1.1 (ibid.).

Japanese elders in the United States are categorized according to their immigration history (Table 5.2). First-generation Japanese immigrants are known as *Issei*, which means "first generation" in Japanese. Most *Issei* who immigrated prior to the 1924 Exclusion Act have passed away. The current elder group of Japanese Americans is comprised of *Nisei*, meaning "second generation," and new immigrants are known as *Shin Issei*, meaning "new" *Issei*. Some of the new immigrants may have lived in the United States for more than thirty years, and others may be newly arrived immigrants. The *Nisei* include those who grew up in the U.S., and those known as *Kibei Nisei*, who were sent back to be educated in Japan during childhood. The latter are less acculturated, prefer to speak Japanese, and share similarities with immigrants arriving from Japan later (*Shin Issei*). There is also a growing number of third-generation Japanese Americans known as *Sansei* who are entering late adulthood.

Nursing home staff needs to know that Japanese Americans exhibit different degrees of acculturation. Staff may be providing care to residents like Mrs. Kimura, who immigrated to the United States in their fifties (*Shin Issei*), someone such as Mrs. Tanaka, who was born and raised in the United States

TABLE 5.2 Categories of Japanese American Elders

Generation Category	Description
Issei	First-generation immigrants who came to the U.S. prior to the 1924 Asian Exclusion Act
Nisei	Second-generation children of *Issei*
Kibei Nisei	Second-generation children of *Issei* who were sent back to Japan to be educated (*Kibei* means "return to the U.S.")
Sansei	Third-generation immigrants (children of second-generation *Nisei*)
Shin Issei	New immigrants from Japan

and never even visited Japan (*Nisei or Sansei*), or a person who was born in the United States but spent their formatives years in Japan (*Kibei Nisei*). Even among the "new immigrant" (*Shin Issei*) group, some may have immigrated during adolescence, and others may have moved to the United States later in life.

It is also important to recognize individual differences based on personal histories and personalities. Although most elderly Japanese Americans prefer to be in long-term care facilities with other Japanese Americans, some may prefer non-ethnic facilities where they can remain anonymous and maintain privacy (Hikoyeda & Wallace 2001). In Japanese American communities on the West Coast, people tend to know one another because their communities are small. Especially among second-generation *Nisei,* such as Mrs. Tanaka, people know one another from internment camps. Other older Japanese Americans may have grown up in white neighborhoods and may feel more comfortable in a predominantly European American facility.

FAMILY RELATIONSHIPS

Despite acculturation, most Japanese Americans have retained values and norms of their original culture. Third- and fourth-generation Japanese differ from European Americans in family relationships and parenting styles (Ching et al. 1995; Kitano 1976, 1988), communication patterns (Johnson & Marsella 1978), and style of caring for elderly family members (Keifer 1974; Kitano 1976, 1993; Osako 1979).

In traditional Japanese culture the primary responsibility of caring for frail elders belongs to adult children. Filial obligation is based on Confucian norms, which dictate familiar roles and responsibilities according to gender, generation, and birth order (Johnson 1993). Respect for one's parents is also reinforced by Shintoism, the indigenous religion of Japan, which maintains that when elderly parents die they become spirits and protect the family (Kinoshita & Kiefer 1992).

The way in which Japanese Americans have retained the cultural values of filial obligation can be observed in community-based programs for elders. When the first generation Japanese immigrants began to age in the late 1960s and early 1970s, Japanese American communities throughout the U.S. developed ethnic specific services such as long-term care facilities and senior programs for their elders who were primarily Japanese-speaking. A number of these services were named *Keiro,* meaning "respect for the elders."

In traditional Japanese societies eldest sons never left the parents' home, and his wife, the daughter-in-law, was expected to care for his parents in old age. Although Japanese Americans did not retain this custom, living arrangements among Japanese American elders do differ from Euro-American cohorts. According to a study based on the 1990 Census data, 37 percent of older unmarried Japanese American women lived with their adult children (Kamo & Zhou 1994). This rate is higher compared to the co-residence rate of their non-Hispanic white counterparts, which was 9.4 percent. Japanese elders who lived with their adult children tended to be foreign-born, recent immigrants, and not as acculturated as those who lived separately (Kamo & Zhou 1994). Among married elderly Japanese American females, 6.9 percent lived with their children, and only 2.2 percent of their white counterparts did.

Nonetheless, *Nisei* do not expect to become dependent on their children despite the traditional cultural value of filial obligation (Tomita 1998). The *Nisei* have largely embraced the Western values of independence and autonomy. They also have fewer expectations of their children compared to their first-generation (*Issei*) parents who expected their children to grow up with a sense of Japanese identity. Many Japanese American elders also have sons- and daughters-in-law and grandchildren of diverse cultural backgrounds, as a result of the high rate of interracial marriages among later-generation Japanese Americans. The 1990 Census indicated 40 percent more Japanese/white births than mono-racial Japanese American births (U.S. Census Bureau 1990, as cited in Root 1996).

HEALTH ISSUES

Much information about the health of elderly Japanese Americans comes from longitudinal studies conducted in Hawaii (Curb et al. 1996); San Francisco, California; and Seattle, Washington (McCormick et al. 1996). Two cross-national studies conducted in Japan, Hawaii, San Francisco (Ni-Hon-San), and Seattle (Ni-Hon-Sea) also yielded data on the differences between Japanese elders in Japan and those in the United States. Japanese American men living in Hawaii have a life expectancy of seventy-nine years, which is one of the highest in the world (Reed et al. 1998). The Ni-Hon-San studies examined the relationships between genetic and environmental factors in the development of coronary heart disease, cerebral vascular disease, and different types of cancers (Reed et al. 1983); the results showed that Japanese Americans in Hawaii and San Francisco had a much higher risk for cardiovascular disease than their cohorts in Japan. Change from a traditional Japanese diet, which is high in fish and vegetables, to a Western diet, which is higher in animal fat, is thought to explain changes in disease rates among

Japanese Americans. In addition to cardiovascular disease, high rates of Type-II diabetes and prostate cancer among Japanese American men have also been attributed to increased fat intake (Fujimoto et al. 1987). On the other hand, the mortality rate from cerebrovascular diseases was found to be lower for Japanese Americans than their Japanese cohort. This may be attributed to less intake of salt in the Western diet. Both Japanese and Japanese Americans reportedly have relatively high death rates from stomach cancer, which may also be attributed to nitrite-rich, salty foods (Tanabe 2002).

The Seattle portion of the Ni-Hon-Sea study, which examined the prevalence and incidence of dementia among elderly Japanese in Seattle, Honolulu, and Japan, indicated a lower incidence of Alzheimer's disease among Japanese Americans who are less acculturated (Graves et al., 1999). Those who led traditional Japanese lifestyles or were exposed to Japanese language as a child have lower risks of experiencing cognitive decline.

MENTAL HEALTH ISSUES

Aging is a risk factor for depression (Blazer et al. 1998); epidemiological studies report that 15–27 percent of elders in the United States experience mild forms of depressive symptoms known as subsyndromal depression, which does not meet criteria for a specific depressive syndrome (Lebowitz et al. 1997). Although little research has been reported on mental health status of Japanese American elders, available studies indicate they have higher rates of depressive symptoms than white American elders (Kuo 1984; Yamamoto 1985; Shibusawa & Mui 2001). For example, a study of 131 community-dwelling Japanese American elders found that elders with poor health and poor social support were more likely to experience depressive symptoms compared to those who reported they had good health and friends who gave them emotional support. The results also indicated that Japanese American elders who feared becoming dependent on family members were vulnerable to depression (Shibusawa & Mui 2001).

Japanese American elders prefer to resolve problems on their own before seeking assistance from others, and usually they seek help only after the situation has worsened (Sakauye 1989). Personal and family problems are kept within the family, because, traditionally, preserving family reputation has priority over individual needs. As with other Asian American groups, Japanese Americans generally are reluctant to seek mental health services, perhaps because of culturally fostered shame and stigma against mental illness (Kitano 1976). Japanese, along with other Asian Americans, have higher rates of using psychiatric emergency services than other ethnic groups, as they hesitate to seek mental health treatment until there is a full-blown crisis (Sakauye 1989).

The Japanese Americans' reluctance to acknowledge psychological disorders inhibits elders who are depressed or who have early stages of dementia from receiving appropriate interventions (Fugita et al. 1991). Japanese Americans sixty-five years of age and older have suicide rates almost twice as high as the rate among younger Japanese American populations (Kitano, Shibusawa, & Kitano 1997). Although completed suicide rates among Japanese Americans sixty-five and older are almost equal to those of white elders, the rate among Japanese Americans over seventy-five is higher compared to older white cohorts (Baker 1994). The suicide rate among Japanese American women aged seventy-five to eighty-four is 2.5 times higher than for white women, and among Japanese American men aged eighty-five and older, it is almost three times greater than for white men (Baker 1994).

Nursing home staff, of course, should always be alert to possible depression among all groups of patients. The Geriatric Depression Scale (GDS) is commonly used to assess elders for depressive symptomatology. The Japanese version of the GDS, translated by Niino, Imaizumi, & Kawakami (1991), is available in the United States. Both the English and Japanese versions of this scale were found reliable with a small community sample of Japanese Americans (Mui & Shibusawa 2003).

NURSING HOME VS. FAMILY CARE

Attitudes about nursing home vs. family long-term care among Japanese American elders were surveyed in a community-based epidemiological study in Seattle, Washington, by McCormick and colleagues (1996) who interviewed 1,142 elders aged sixty-five and older of Japanese descent. When elders were asked about the type of care they wanted if they became permanently disabled by dementia or temporarily disabled by hip fracture, 53 percent indicated that they would choose nursing home over family if they had dementia; for hip fracture, however, the majority preferred paid, in-home services (54 percent) and family care (29 percent) over nursing homes (12 percent). Second-generation immigrants (*Nisei*) who were acculturated and not married were generally more likely to be amenable toward nursing homes (McCormick et al. 1996). A study of Japanese Canadians also found that elders would prefer to pay for formal services than burden family members in the event they needed long-term care (Matsuoka 1999).

The rate of institutionalization among Japanese American elderly in 1990 was 1.6 percent (Himes, Hogan, & Eggebeen 1996). This is lower than the overall prevalence of nursing home use among U.S. elders, which is 4 percent at any point in time (Strahan 1997). Institutionalization rates are higher in geographical areas where Japanese American facilities are available. In the Seattle area, for example, where there is a Japanese nursing home, the prevalence of nursing home use at any given time was 5 percent (McCormick et al. 1996).

Although an increasing number of Japanese American elders are willing to receive formal, paid care, elders who only speak Japanese would rather not be helped by non-Japanese service workers (Shibusawa, Ishikawa, & Mui 1999). This reluctance is particularly evident with in-home care; language barriers and a discomfort with non-Japanese persons in their homes inhibit these persons from obtaining in-home help. A shortage of Japanese-speaking home care workers has occurred, as recent immigrants from Japan tend to have high levels of education and do not seek home care jobs. Some elders continue to struggle on their own with no outside services. A serious concern for many Japanese elders who do not speak English is the possibility of entering residential facilities that lack Japanese-speaking staff.

COPING WITH ASSISTANCE FROM OTHERS

Previously self-reliant elders who become frail and must depend on others for care may have psychological problems stemming from the loss of independence (Dunkle 1985; Stoller 1984). As care recipients, elders also have to learn how to relate to caregivers, and they may feel guilty when they are unable to reciprocate the help they receive (Walker & Allen 1991); this, in turn, can lead to depression (Dunkle 1985). Although dependency on family members in old age was a cultural norm in traditional Japanese society, the prospect of becoming dependent on family is a source of distress for most Japanese American elders (Shibusawa & Mui 2001).

The way in which elders handle the stress of having to receive care depends on whether they feel they have any control whatsoever over their lives (Pearlin & Schooler 1978). Elders who believe they can effect change in their environment are less prone to depression (Pruchno et al. 1997; Schlatter et al. 1993), and those who can assert their needs and preferences to the care provider (Coeling & Biordi 2000) experience fewer symptoms of depression than do elders who feel they have no control over their lives (Coeling & Biordi 2000; Wong et al. 1999). Passive ways of coping, on the other hand, in which elders accept problematic situations without taking action, are associated with increased depressive symptoms (Pratt et al. 1985).

Coping styles among Japanese elders are influenced by the conception of the self in Japanese culture. Whereas Western cultures are rooted in individualism, East Asian cultures, including Japanese culture, are based on collectivism (Gudykunst 1997). Individualistic cultures emphasize self-determination and self-reliance, whereas collectivistic cultures stress interdependence, with the needs of the group taking precedence over one's own needs. Japanese tend to emphasize accommodating to the needs of others rather than imposing one's own agenda on them, and they tend to value adapting to the environment over controlling it. The process of enduring and adapting to unfavorable circumstances is known as *gaman*, which translates as "endurance," "perseverance," or "bearing the unbearable" (Tomita 1998). The tolerance for adversity stems from the Buddhist notion of fatalism and the importance of accepting reality.

In Western cultures, in contrast, passive responses, which lack any personal initiative to change stressful situations, are often viewed as a negative coping strategy (Sastry & Ross 1998). Some researchers in the West, therefore, view *gaman* as an act of repression and denial (Itai & McRae 1994), but Japanese view *gaman* as a capacity to endure difficulties posed by the environment, including interpersonal relationships. According to Johnson (1993, p. 89), *gaman* includes "the ability to suppress complaints, conceal discomfort, and demonstrate a tolerance for adverse circumstances." Another word expressing acceptance of conditions one cannot change is *shikataganai*, meaning "things cannot be helped" (Tempo & Saito 1996). This word is recognized even by third-generation immigrants (*Sansei*) who do not speak Japanese.

Therefore, among Japanese elders, one culturally based adaptation strategy is to suppress one's dissatisfaction rather than imposing on the good-will of care providers. When people receive assistance in Japanese society, they are expected to accept the care passively without voicing complaints or asserting their desires. To do so would be a betrayal of the caregiver, a sign that one does not appreciate the assistance. Those receiving care are expected to "*enryo*," which means "hold back" or "restrain" one's own wishes.

Because of the cultural value placed on not burdening others when receiving help, Japanese American elders in nursing homes may feel that they must passively accept assistance without asserting themselves or negotiating for the kind of help they want. In light of these cultural values, caregivers in nursing homes must realize that Japanese elders may not be forthcoming about their needs or wishes, and so providers should take time to establish a trusting relationship that allows elders to become more comfortable in communicating and asserting their needs.

ISSUES WITHIN NURSING HOMES

USE OF RESTRAINTS

The rate of agitated behavior among elderly with dementia in Japanese nursing homes is similar to the overall rate of such behavior in nursing homes in the U.S. (Schreiner et al. 2000). However, nursing homes in Japan differ from those in the United States in how they manage undesirable behavior. Less than 9 percent of residents in Japan are restrained at any time compared to 15–17 percent of residents in nursing homes in the U.S. (Ljunggren, Phillips, & Sgadari 1997). Trunk restraints are used more frequently in the U.S. for residents who are physically dependent or cognitively impaired. Japanese elders and their family members may not be familiar with the use of restraints in nursing homes, so it is important that care providers explain to the elder and the family the reasons for using restraints when they are required.

FOOD PREFERENCES

The Japanese diet, compared to the American diet, is low in fat and total calories but high in salt, and traditionally includes rice, *miso* soup made of fish stock and soybean paste, and pickled vegetables with fish or shellfish (Drewnowski & Popkin 1997; Egusa et. al. 1993). Research comparing second- and third-generation Japanese American women indicated that second-generation women maintained more traditional meals (Kudo, Falciglia, & Couch 2000). It is difficult for Japanese American elders to adjust to food in nursing homes, especially if they have been used to eating rice at every meal. Japanese rice differs from Chinese short-grain rice or Indian basmati rice, as it is stickier in texture when cooked. Precooked Japanese rice is available in small packages which are sold at most Japanese food markets in major urban areas in the U.S. These precooked rice packages can be heated in a microwave oven and are easy for nursing home staff to prepare. Single portions of *miso* soup are also available in packages and are served simply by adding hot water. Low-sodium soy sauce is also available in Japanese food markets for elders whose sodium intake is restricted. Staff may want to encourage family members to provide foods such as precooked rice, *miso* soup, and soy sauce for Japanese elders, as these items will undoubtedly add to their quality of life in nursing homes.

BATHING

Bathing is an important ritual in Japan. Japanese prefer daily tub baths, and bathing, in Japan, is an important service for elders (Schreiner, Yamamoto, & Shiotani 2000). Most day care and skilled nursing home facilities in Japan have elaborate bathing facilities where elders are able to soak in the tub. Although daily baths may not be an option for most nursing homes in the U.S., staff may want to consider allowing extra time for Japanese residents to soak in the tub.

INTERACTION WITH OTHER RESIDENTS

No research data are available for how Japanese American elders interact with other Japanese Americans or residents of other ethnicities in nursing homes. Intragroup differences exist among Japanese Americans, and although Japan is often viewed as a homogenous culture compared to the United States, differences based on class and geographical origin exist. Okinawa-born Japanese, for example, were discriminated against within the Japanese American communities in Hawaii. Because of social-class prejudices, some older, recently arrived Japanese immigrants tend to distinguish themselves from Japanese immigrants who arrived earlier; the former view themselves as more prosperous urbanites whereas earlier Japanese immigrants tended to come from poor, rural areas. Some prejudice also exists among Japanese Americans toward Japanese women known as "war brides," who came to the United States with husbands who were military personnel during the U.S. occupation of Japan following World War II. Now in their seventies, these women were victims of the prejudice in Japan toward any young Japanese woman who dated and married U.S. servicemen following Japan's defeat in the war.

As stated above, there are no studies that compare social interaction between Japanese American elders and other elders in U.S. nursing homes. A cross-national study of social engagement among nursing home residents in Japan, Denmark, Iceland, and the United States indicated that social engagement is low among residents in Japan compared to residents in the other countries (Schroll et al. 1997). According to the study, nursing home residents in Japan functioning poorly in activities of daily living (ADLs) were less likely to be engaged in activities than were their counterparts in Europe and the U.S. This may be the case because staff and family do not push elders to participate in activities. There is a high number of bed-ridden elderly in Japan due to the fact, in part, that values of respecting elders inhibit children and others from forcing elders to do something they do not want to do.

COMMUNICATION AND INTERACTION

The way Japanese Americans interact and communicate is influenced by the conception of self in Japanese culture, which we saw earlier also applies to their coping styles. Research comparing interactions between Japanese-American and Caucasian families in Hawaii has shown that the two groups differ in interactions in terms of power, coalition, closeness, negotiation, clarity of self-disclosure, responsibility, invasiveness, affect, and empathy (Hsu et al. 1985). Researchers have also observed that second-generation Japanese Americans have a different style of interacting than their European American counterparts. According to Miyamoto (1986–87), certain traits, such as being less spontaneous in their interactions, make Japanese Americans feel more comfortable when relating to their own group. The shared history of being an oppressed and marginalized people, especially during and immediately following World War II, may also explain why some Japanese Americans feel more comfortable interacting with one another than with people of other ethnic backgrounds.

INTERACTION BETWEEN STAFF AND RESIDENTS

In a culture where group harmony is valued over individualism, as stated earlier, people are socialized from a young age to be mindful of the impact that the assertion of one's preferences has on another person. Japanese are especially sensitive about not wanting to burden others, especially when the other people are unable to reciprocate for the help that they receive. Japanese American elders, especially women, may refrain from asserting their needs and wishes to the staff. Campbell (1974), in a study of nursing homes in Japan, notes that, compared to the United States, passive dependency is more acceptable to both staff and patients in Japan. According to Campbell, in Japan staff prefers to work with frail elderly, as they are more passive and less demanding, causing fewer interpersonal conflicts. Although patients who endure hardships without voicing complaints are viewed as virtuous in traditional Japanese culture, passive acceptance of care in nursing homes can lead to depression among elders. It is important, therefore, that staff remain aware of depressive symptoms, such as social withdrawal and loss of appetite, when working with Japanese elders who do not communicate their wishes.

Residents capable of engaging in activities may benefit from doing small tasks that the staff finds for them. Hikoyeda and Wallace (2001), in their study of older Japanese Americans in residential care facilities, found that boredom was a significant problem and that some residents created their own work to help pass the time. In nursing homes in Japan, residents are often encouraged to help staff through activities such as folding towels and cleaning tables. Giving residents tasks to help staff may give them a feeling of satisfaction and accomplishment, and also lessen the feelings of obligation which come from not being able to reciprocate for the help they receive.

Interactions between staff and Japanese residents depend on the language preferences of the elders. For example, Japanese American elders like Mrs. Tanaka, who were born in the United States, speak fluent English and may resent being treated as if they were immigrants. It is important to keep in mind that most second-generation European Americans are not asked about their ethnicity or cultural background, and yet people often ask U.S.-born Asian Americans where they are from (that is, what country they immigrated from). On the other hand, staff should pay special attention to the linguistic needs of someone like Mrs. Kimura, a recent immigrant, who is unable to speak English.

Takeo Doi (1988), a Japanese psychoanalyst well known for his work on the Japanese psyche, notes that nonverbal communication is often as important as verbal communication among Japanese. This means that social workers will need to pay careful attention to the nonverbal cues of Japanese residents. For example, when a Japanese resident is invited to go on an outing, the resident may hesitate and reply, "Hmm, I'll need to see, I'm not sure." In most cultures this would probably be interpreted to mean that the resident cannot make up his or her mind. Although that interpretation may also hold in Japanese culture, such a response can also mean that the resident does not want to go but is reluctant to say no for fear of offending the social worker.

Japanese, in general, tend to distinguish between the "private" and "public" domains in their lives; they are very selective about what they will share and will not share with others (Doi 1988). Social workers should respect that Japanese elders do not wish to divulge personal information to people they do not know. This does not mean, however, that social workers cannot gather enough information for a psychosocial intake assessment or engage Japanese elders with life review activities. As with many elders, Japanese elders, too, can benefit therapeutically by sharing their life histories, but social workers need to maintain respect for Japanese elders who may refuse to talk about a particular issue. This means that social workers should not probe when they sense that the elder does not want to comment further on a topic.

Most Japanese Americans who were interned during World War II are usually open toward sharing that they were in a camp, but their comfort level toward sharing painful memories about internment varies. It is also important to remember that external events also can trigger memories of World War II. For many Japanese Americans, the ways in which Arab and Muslim Americans were treated following the 9/11 terrorist attacks reminded them of the horrors they experienced during the days following Japan's attack on Pearl Harbor (Shibusawa 2005). In such cases social workers should take time to listen to Japanese residents who may want to talk about their reactions.

There is no literature on conflicts among nursing home residents that arise from historical events, but social workers will need to be sensitive if an American resident whose background is not Japanese is bitter toward Japanese, and workers should monitor the ways in which such a resident interacts with Japanese residents.

INTERACTION BETWEEN STAFF AND FAMILY MEMBERS

Conflict and communication problems often occur between nursing home staff and family members (Pillemer et al. 1998), sometimes, as a result of discrepancies between staff and family members about the appropriate tasks for each group. Families often feel that the staff does not recognize their expertise and so they feel ignored and invalidated (ibid.), or they feel that they have not been given enough information. Staff turnover can also affect families. Whenever there are changes in staffing, families should be informed beforehand, and new staff members should introduce themselves to family members.

Communication among staff and family members is very important for the psychological well-being of the resident as well as the family. The same type of cultural issues that affect communication between staff and residents also affect the relationship between staff and families. Families may be reluctant to voice their wishes because they do not want to be a burden on the staff. The notion of not wanting to burden staff may be particularly strong among Japanese families. This is because of the cultural value of "*enryo*" in which people are expected to restrain from asserting their needs and wishes so as not to impose themselves on others. Emphasis on politeness may also inhibit families from asking staff for assistance. For example, a family member might not solicit the help of a staff member who appears busy when helping their elder move to the bathroom. Studies indicate that policies that include families as part of the caregiving team lead to highest satisfaction among families (Friedemann, Montgomery, Rice & Farrell 1999). When involving Japanese American families in case conferences, it is important for staff to make sure that the families feel comfortable enough to voice their opinions and wishes.

RECREATIONAL ACTIVITIES

When an elder enters a nursing home, it is important for staff to find out the kinds of activities that have been meaningful to the resident while living in the community. The types of activities among retired, healthy Japanese American elders vary according to gender and levels of acculturation. Second-generation Japanese Americans, born and raised in the U.S., enjoy the same activities as their European American counterparts. For example, recreational programs at a Los Angeles senior citizens center where many residents are second-generation immigrants include swing classes, bridge, and golf. On the other hand, Japanese American elders who grew up in Japan are often involved with traditional Japanese activities such as poetry writing (*haiku, senryu,* or *waka*); calligraphy, water colors (*sumie*), singing (*nagauta*), and playing Japanese musical instruments such as a *shamisen* (guitar-like instrument). It is important to note that involvement in traditional Japanese cultural activities is not taken lightly but typically requires a sustained commitment to learning and mastering a discipline. Thus activities often become what Japanese call *"ikigai,"* "something to live for."

The following are illustrations of a few Japanese American women and their activities. The women were participants in a study conducted by the author and live in a senior citizen's apartment building in a Japanese American community in Los Angeles.

MRS. C.

Mrs. C., an eighty-nine-year-old Japanese American woman, immigrated to the U.S. when she was in her fifties because her daughter had moved there when she married an American. Mrs. C., since retiring from her job as a seamstress, has been taking classes in *senryu*, a form of poetry which consists of a single sentence. She has placed small pieces of paper throughout her apartment so that she can jot notes whenever she has an inspiration for writing a poem. Her *senryu* teacher types her creations so she can keep her collection in an album. The following is one *senryu* written by Mrs. C.: "My friend says, late afternoon, she feels like crying." Mrs. C. explained that she wrote this to express her feelings of loneliness, which she feels acutely when she sees the sunset in the late afternoons. She says, "Loneliness, at my age, comes from not having a homeland. Even if I were to return to Japan there are no reserved seats for me. . . . There is no place for me, so I no longer have a homeland and I feel like crying."

Another poem that expresses her sadness reads: "Old and alone, this small room, the place of comfort."

If Mrs. C. were to enter a nursing home, it would be important for staff to encourage her to continue writing poetry, as it is not only an outlet for her creativity but also provides a way for her to express her emotions.

MRS. J.

Mrs. J., also eighty-nine years old, has been pursuing Japanese calligraphy as a hobby for many years, and her living room is filled with scrolls of her calligraphy. She states that she can forget all her problems when she is engrossed in rubbing the ink-stone to make the ink for her calligraphy. Calligraphy, for Mrs. J., is a form of meditation. She has a ninety-three-year-old sister living in Japan who composes *waka,* another form of Japanese poetry. Whenever her sister sends her latest creations, Mrs. J. chooses the one she likes, writes them in calligraphy, and takes them to her sister when she visits her in Japan. Thus she feels very connected to her sister through their respective activities.

MRS. G.

Mrs. G., who is eighty-seven, likes to collect Japanese sayings on how one should behave in old age. She copies them into a notebook over and over again as a reminder. The sayings consist of wisdom on how not to become a "complainer." One says that "the elderly should only answer when they are asked to speak," that is, the elderly should not try to control others. Mrs. G. also has a framed calligraphy on her wall which was written by the head priest of her Buddhist temple which states: "Be tolerant of others, have a round heart [be mellow and generous], don't get angry, don't be self-centered, and place others first." Mrs. G. has severe physical impairments as a result of the strenuous physical work she was engaged in when employed as a laborer on a large farm in the Midwest.

Traditional art is not the only area of interest for older Japanese Americans. Mrs. D., for example, who is eighty-three, is an avid fan of a Japanese baseball team and looks forward to the daily Japanese sports newspaper. She says that reading the sports paper keeps her mind alert. Mrs. E., who is ninety years old, loves *karaoke* and goes to weekly classes at a senior citizens center where she sings Japanese songs. She also has a *karaoke* machine in her living room so she can practice singing on her own. Clearly having as much continuity as possible between life before and after nursing home admission is very important for residents (Hikoyeda & Wallace 2001). By finding out the different types of activities that residents used to engage in before entering, staff can help encourage residents to continue to pursue their interests as much as possible.

END-OF-LIFE CARE

In traditional Japanese culture, death is viewed as a natural part of the life cycle (Braun & Nichols 1997). In Buddhist households deceased ancestors are remembered daily by placing water for them on the family altar. *Obon*, a festival that takes place in August, is a time when the spirits of the dead are thought to return to life. Buddhist priests visit homes to chant in front of the family altar during *obon*. At the end of the festival, candle-lit paper lanterns are placed in rivers, symbolizing the departure of the spirits to the other world.

Although the deceased are honored through such Buddhist rituals, Japanese generally are reluctant to discuss death in health care settings (Konishi & Davis 1999). Although there is a move toward informed consent in Japan, physicians and family members tend to shield diagnoses of terminal illness from patients (Konishi & Davis 1999). A 1994 survey conducted in Japan indicates that only one in five cancer patients who died had been informed of their diagnosis (Benowitz 1999). Physicians in Japan tend to believe that families rather than patients are the best judge of the patients' ability to handle information about terminal illnesses such as cancer (Akibayashi, Fetters, & Elwyn 1999). When there is no family consent for disclosure, many physicians feel that they should not disclose the diagnosis to the patient. Physicians view "familial consent" as more important than "individual consent."

End-of-life care in the United States, on the other hand, is based on the model of patient autonomy (Kagawa-Singer & Blackhall 2001). Emphasis is placed on the rights of the individual to be informed about their medical condition and treatment options. Individuals are believed to have the right to choose or refuse life-sustaining medical care through advance care directives (Kagawa-Singer & Blackhall 2001).

Recent research indicates that attitudes toward end-of-life care among Japanese Americans depend on their levels of acculturation. Studies in Hawaii report that one-third of the Japanese surveyed had living wills (Braun, Onaka, & Horiuchi 2001). In a 1998 population-based survey, more Japanese, Chinese, and Caucasians than Filipinos and Native Hawaiians supported legalizing physician aid in dying (Braun, Onaka & Horiuchi 2001). These findings were attributed to the fact that the former groups have higher levels of education and income than the latter groups.

A recent California study among 539 English-speaking Japanese Americans and 340 Japanese-speaking Japanese Americans also indicated the association between acculturation and attitudes toward end-of-life care (Matsumura, et al. 2002). English-speaking Japanese Americans preferred disclosure of a terminal prognosis and were more positive than their Japanese-speaking counterparts toward having advance care planning and not using life-sustaining machines. English-speaking Japanese Americans also demonstrated preference for autonomy in decision making while Japanese-speaking Japanese Americans expressed a preference for family-centered decisions in advance care planning. Both groups, however, expressed similar preferences regarding surrogate decision making. Both English- and Japanese-speaking respondents preferred to have family or friends make decisions as a group rather than designate a single individual in the event that they were not able to make decisions about life-sustaining machines. Adjusting one's wishes to the needs of others is also evident in attitudes for medical treatment at the end of life. It is important, therefore, for nursing home staff to be sensitive to Japanese American elders who may not be as forthcoming in articulating their wishes regarding end-of-life care.

CONCLUSION

This chapter has presented key issues in understanding Japanese American elders in nursing homes and their families. Social workers need to keep in mind that Japanese Americans are a culturally diverse group. A large number of Japanese American elders were born and raised in the U.S. and are more acculturated into the dominant culture compared to Japanese elders who immigrated to the U.S. after reaching adulthood and retained more traditional cultural values.

Many residents and their families experience admission to a nursing home as a crisis. As with families from other cultures, placing one's parents in long-term care facilities can be stressful for Japanese American families, as it goes against the cultural values of filial obligation. Social workers should realize that elders and their families may not have had open and direct communication about their reactions toward nursing home placement. Openness and motivation among social workers toward understanding the cultural background and care preferences of Japanese American patients and families will facilitate better psychological well-being and smoother transitions to institutional care.

REFERENCES

Akibayashi, A., Fetters, M. D., Elwyn, T. S. (1999). Family consent, communication, and advance directives for cancer disclosures: A Japanese case and discussion. *Journal of Medical Ethics* 25, 296–301.

Baker, F. M. (1994). Suicide among ethnic minority elderly: A statistical and psychosocial perspective. *Journal of Geriatric Psychiatry* 27, 241–264.

Berdes, C., & Eckert, J. M. (2001). Race relations and caregiving relationships: A qualitative examination of perspectives from residents and nurse's aides in three nursing homes. *Research on Aging* 23 (1), 109–126.

Benowitz, S. (1999). To tell the truth: A cancer diagnosis in other cultures is often a family affair. *Journal of the National Cancer Institute* 91 (22), 1918–1919.

Blazer, D. G., et al. (1998). Symptoms of depression among community-dwelling elderly African American and white older adults. *Psychological Medicine* 28, 1311–1320.

Braun, K. L., & Nichols, R. (1997). Death and dying in four Asian American cultures: A descriptive study. *Death Studies* 21 (4), 327–359.

Braun, K. L., Onaka, A.T., & Horiuchi, B. Y. (2001). Advance directive completion rates and end-of-life preferences in Hawaii. *Journal of the American Geriatrics Society* 49, 1708–1713.

Brooks, C. (2000). In the twilight zone between black and white: Japanese American resettlement and community in Chicago, 1942–1945. *Journal of American History* 86, 1655–1687.

Broom, L., & Kitsuse, J. I. (1973). *The managed casualty: The Japanese-American family in World War II.* Berkeley: University of California Press.

Campbell, R. (1984). Nursing homes and long-term care in Japan. *Pacific Affairs* 57, 78–89.

Ching, J. W. J., et al. (1995). Perception of family values and roles among Japanese Americans: Clinical considerations. *American Journal of Orthopsychiatry* 65, 216–224.

Coeling, H., & Biordi, D. (2000). The relationship between work strategies used by informal caregivers and care receivers and clinical outcomes. *Journal of Applied Gerontology* 19 (3), 264–283.

Curb, D. J., et al. (1996). Hypertension in elderly Japanese Americans and adult native Hawaiians. *Public Health Reports* 111 (Supplement 2), 53–55.

Department of Health and Human Services (1997). Health People 2010: Progress review: Asian American and Pacific Islanders, Retrieved September 1, 2003, from http://www.healthypeople.gov/data/PROGRVW/asians.

Doi, T. (1988). The anatomy of self: The individual versus society. English translation by Mark Harbison. Tokyo: Kodansha International.

Drewnowski, A., & Popkin, B. M. (1997). The nutrition transition: New trends in the global diet. *Nutrition Reviews* 55 (2), 31–43.

Dunkle, R. (1985). Comparing the depression of elders in two types of caregiving arrangements. *Family Relations* 34, 235–240.

Egusa G., et al. (1993). Westernized food habits and concentrations of serum lipids in the Japanese. *Atherosclerosis* 100 (2), 249–255.

Elo, I. T. (1997). Adult mortality among Asian Americans and Pacific Islanders: A review of the evidence. In K. S. Markides & M. R. Miranda (Eds.), *Minorities, aging and health*, pp. 41–78. Thousand Oaks, Calif.: Sage.

Friedemann, M-L., et al. (1999). Family involvement in the nursing home. *Western Journal of Nursing Research* 21 (4), 549–567.

Fugita, S., et al. (1991). Japanese Americans. In N. Mokuau (Ed.), *Handbook of social services for Asian and Pacific Islanders*, pp. 61–96. New York: Greenwood.

Fujimoto, W. Y., et al. (1987). Prevalence of diabetes mellitus and impaired glucose tolerance among second-generation Japanese American men. *Diabetes* 36, 721–729.

Galanti, G-A. (2001). Japanese Americans and self-care. *Western Journal of Medicine* 174 (3), 208–209.

Graves, A. B., et al. (1999). Cognitive decline and Japanese culture in a cohort of older Japanese Americans in King County, WA: The Kame Project. *Journals of Gerontology, Social Sciences* 54, S154–S161.

Gudykunst, W. (1997). Cultural variability in communication. *Communication Research* 24 (4), 327–341.

Hikoyeda, N., & Wallace, S. P. (2001). Do ethnic-specific long-term care facilities improve resident quality of life? Findings from the Japanese American community. *Journal of Gerontological Social Work* 36 (1/2), 83–106.

Himes, C. L., Hogan, D. P., & Eggebeen, D. J. (1996). Living arrangements of minority elders. *Journals of Gerontology, Social Sciences* 51 (1), 542–548.

Hospitals a Pillar to Japanese Americans. (1998). *Los Angeles Times*, February 1.

Hsu, J., et al. (1985). Family interaction patterns among Japanese-American and Caucasian families in Hawaii. *American Journal of Psychiatry* 142 (5), 577–581.

Itai, G., & McRae, C. (1994). Counseling older Japanese American clients: An overview and observations. *Journal of Counseling and Development* 72 (4), 373–378.

Johnson, F. A. (1993). *Dependency and Japanese socialization: Psychoanalytic and anthropological investigations into Amae*. New York: New York University Press.

Johnson, F. A., & Marsella, A. J. (1978). Differential attitudes toward verbal behavior in students of Japanese and European ancestry. *Genetic Psychology Monographs* 97, 43–76.

Kagawa-Singer, M., & Blackhall, L. J. (2001). Negotiating cross-cultural issues at the end of life: "You got to go where he lives." *Journal of the American Medical Association* 286 (23), 2993–3001.

Kamo, Y., & Zhou, M. (1994). Living arrangement of elderly Chinese and Japanese in the United States. *Journal of Marriage and the Family* 544–558.

Kiefer, C. (1974). Lessons from the Issei. In J. Gubrium (Ed.), *Late life communities and environmental policy*, pp.167–197. Springfield, Ill.: Charles C Thomas.

Kinoshita, Y., & Kiefer, C. W. (1992). *Refuge of the honored: Social organization in a Japanese retirement community*. Berkeley: University of California Press.

Kitano, H. H. L. (1976). *Japanese Americans: The evolution of a subculture*. 2nd ed. Englewood Cliffs, N.J.: Prentice Hall.

Kitano, H. H. L. (1988). The Japanese American family. In C. H. Mindel, R. W. Habenstein, & R. Wright Jr (Eds.), *Ethnic families in America: Patterns and validations*, 3rd ed. New York: Elsevier.

Kitano, H. H. L. (1993). *Generation and Identity: The Japanese American*. Needham Heights, Mass.: Ginn.

Kitano, H., & Daniels, R. (1987). *Asian Americans: Emerging minorities*. Englewood Cliffs, N.J.: Prentice Hall.

Kitano, H., Shibusawa, T., & Kitano, K. J. (1997). Asian American elderly mental health. In K. S. Markeides & M. Miranda (Eds.), *Minorities, aging and health*, pp. 295–324. Thousand Oaks, Calif.: Sage.

Konishi, E., & Davis, A. J. (1999). Japanese nurses' perceptions about disclosure of information at the patients' end of life. *Nursing and Health Sciences* 1, 179–187.

Kudo, Y., Falciglia, G. A., & Couch, S. C. (2000). Evolution of meal patterns and food choices of Japanese-American females born in the United States. *European Journal of Clinical Nutrition* 54 (8), 665–670.

Kuo, W. H. (1984). Prevalence of depression among Asian Americans. *Journal of Nervous and Mental Disease* 172 (8), 449–457.

Lebowitz, B. D., et al. (1997). Diagnosis and treatment of depression in late life: Consensus statement update, *Journal of the American Medical Association* 278(14), 1186–1190.

Lee, S. M. (1998). Asian Americans: Diverse and growing. *Population Bulletin* 53, 2–40.

Lee, S. M., & Yamanaka, K. (1990). Patterns of Asian American intermarriage and marital assimilation. *Journal of Comparative Family Studies* 21, 287–305.

Ljunggren, G., Phillips, C. D., & Sgadari, A. (1997). Comparisons of restraint use in nursing homes in eight countries. *Age and Ageing* 26, 43–47.

Mass, A. (1991). Psychological effects of the camps on the Japanese Americans. In R. Daniels, S. C. Taylor, & H. H. L. Kitano (Eds.), *Japanese Americans: From relocation to redress*, pp. 159–162. Seattle: University of Washington Press.

Matsumura, S., et al. (2002). Acculturation and attitudes toward end-of-life care: A cross-cultural survey of Japanese Americans and Japanese. *Journal of General Internal Medicine* 17, 531–539.

Matsuoka, A. (1999). Preferred care in later life among Japanese Canadians. *Journal of Multicultural Social Work* 7, 127–148.

McCormick, U. J., et al. (1996). Attitudes toward use of nursing homes and home care in older Japanese-Americans. *Journal of the American Geriatrics Society* 44, 769–777.

Miyamoto, F. (1986–87). Problems of interpersonal style among the Nisei. *Amerasia Journal* 13, 29–45.

Mui, A., & Shibusawa, T. (2003). Japanese American elders and the Geriatric Depression Scale. *Clinical Gerontologist* 26, (3/4), 91–104.

Nagata, D. (1993). *Legacy of silence: Exploring the long-term effects of the Japanese American internment*. New York: Plenum.

Niino, N., Imaizumi, T., & Kawakami, N. (1991). A Japanese translation of the geriatric depression scale. *Clinical Gerontologist* 10 (3), 85–87.

Nishi, S. M. (1995). Japanese Americans. In P. G. Min (Ed.), *Asian Americans: Contemporary issues and trends*, pp. 95–133. Thousand Oaks, Calif.: Sage.

Osako, M. (1979). Aging and family among Japanese Americans: The role of ethnic tradition in the adjustment to old age. *The Gerontologist* 19, 448–455.

Pearlin, L., & Schooler, K. (1978). The structure of coping. *Journal of Health and Social Behavior* 19, 2–21.

Pillemer, K., et al. (1998). Building bridges between families and nursing home staff. *The Gerontologist* 38 (4), 499–503.

Pratt, C., Schmall, V., & Wright, S. & Cleland, M. (1985). Burden and coping strategies of caregivers to Alzheimer's patients. *Family Relations* 34, 27–33.

Pruchno, R., Burant, C., & Peters, N. (1997). Understanding the well-being of care receivers. *The Gerontologist* 37 (1), 102–109.

Reed D. M., et al. (1983). Social networks and coronary heart disease among Japanese men in Hawaii. *American Journal of Epidemiology* 117, 384–396.

Reed, D. M., et al. (1998). Predictors of healthy aging in men with high life expectancies. *American Journal of Public Health* 88 (10), 1463–1468.

Root, M. P. P. (1996). The multiracial experience: Racial borders as a significant frontier in race relations. In M. P. P. Root (Ed.), *The multiracial experience: Racial borders as the new frontier*. Thousand Oaks, Calif.: Sage.

Sakauye, K. M. (1989). Ethnic variations in family support of the frail elderly. In M. Z. Goldstein (Ed.), *Family involvement in treatment of the frail elderly*, pp. 65–106. Washington, D.C.: American Psychiatric Press.

Sastry, J., & Ross, C. (1998). Asian ethnicity and the sense of personal control. *Social Psychology Quarterly* 61(2), 101–120.

Schlatter, A., et al. (1993). Depression and life satisfaction in the elderly: The development of an interview schedule. *Journal of MARC Research* 1, 27–42.

Schreiner, A. S., Yamamoto, E., & Shiotani, H. (2000). Agitated behavior in elderly nursing home residents with dementia in Japan. *Journal of Gerontology* 55B (3), P180–P186.

Schroll, M., et al. (1997). An international study of social engagement among nursing home residents. *Age and Ageing* 26, 55–59.

Shibusawa, T. (2005). Japanese families. In M. McGoldrick, J. K. Pearce, & J. Giordano (Eds.), *Ethnicity and family therapy*, 3rd ed. New York: Guilford.

Shibusawa, T., Ishikawa, H., & Mui, A. C. (1999). Help-seeking attitudes among Japanese American older adults. Paper presented at the Fifty-second Annual Scientific Program of the Gerontological Society of America, November, San Francisco, California.

Shibusawa, T., & Mui, A. C. (2001). Stress, coping and depression among Japanese American elders. *Journal of Gerontological Social Work* 36 (1/2), 63–81.

Spaid, W., & Barusch, A. (1994). Emotional closeness and caregiver burden in the marital relationship. *Journal of Gerontological Social Work* 21 (3/4), 197–211.

Strahan, G. W. (1997). *An overview of nursing homes and their current residents: Data from the 1995 National Nursing Home Survey. Advance data from Vital and Health Statistics* (Publication no. 280). Hyattsville, Md.: National Center for Health Statistics.

Stoller, E. (1984). Self-assessments of health by the elderly: The impact of informal assistance. *Journal of Health and Social Behavior* 25, 260–270.

Tanabe, M. K. G. (n.d.). Health and health care of Japanese-American elders. Retrieved May 25, 2005, from http://www.stanford.edu/group/ethnoger/japanese.html.

Tanjasiri, S. P., Wallace, S. P., & Shibata, K. (1995). Picture imperfect: Hidden problems among Asian Pacific Islander elders. *The Gerontologist* 35, 753–760.

Tempo, P. M., & Saito, A. (1996). Techniques of working with Japanese American families. In G. Yeo & D. Gallager-Thompson (Eds.), *Ethnicity and the dementias*, pp. 89–108. Bristol, Pa.: Taylor & Francis.

Tomita, S. K. (1998). The consequences of belonging: Conflict management techniques among Japanese Americans. *Journal of Elder Abuse & Neglect* 9, 41–68.

U.S. Census Bureau (2000). *Census 2000 Profile*. Washington, D.C.: U.S. Government Printing Office.

Walker, A., & Allen, K. (1991). Relationships between caregiving daughters and their elderly mothers. *The Gerontologist* 31 (3), 389–396.

Wong, S., et al. (1999). Perceived control, self-reinforcement, and depression among Asian American and Caucasian American elders. *Journal of Applied Gerontology* 18 (1), 46–62.

Yamamoto, J., Rhee, S., & Chang, D. (1994). Psychiatric disorders among elderly Koreans in the United States. *Community Mental Health Journal* 30 (1), 17–26.

Yoo, D. K. (2000). *Growing up Nisei: Race, generation, and culture among Japanese Americans of California, 1924–49.* Urbana: University of Chicago Press.

RESOURCES

Organizations and Websites

Japanese American Citizen's League. www.jacl.org.
Japanese American National Museum. www.janm.org.
Japanese American Service Committee. www.jasc-chicago.org.
Japanese Historical Society of Northern California. www.nikkeiheritage.org.
Keiro facilities in Southern California. www.keiro.org/KSP/facility.html.
Kimochi, San Franciso, California. www.kimochi-inc.org.
Little Tokyo Service Center—Caregiver Support Group. www.ltsc.org.
Yu-Ai Kai/Japanese Community Senior Service. www.yuaikai.org.

Japanese American Nursing Facilities

Japanese American Community Pioneer Center, Los Angeles, California.
Keiro Retirement Home. Los Angeles, California.
Kimochi, San Francisco, California.
Little Tokyo Towers, Los Angeles, California.
Los Angeles Keiro.
Nikkei Manor, Programs for Japanese American Elders, Seattle, Washington.
Nikkei Service Center, Central California Nikkei Foundation, Fresno, California.
San Jose Keiro.
Seattle Keiro.
Seinan Senior Citizen's Center, Los Angeles, California.

Readings

Fujita, S. S., & Fernandez, M. (2004). *Altered lives, enduring community: Japanese Americans remember their World War II incarceration.* Seattle: University of Washington Press.

Houston, J. W. (1973). *Farewell to Manzanaar: A true story of Japanese American experience during and after the World War II internment.* New York: Bantam Books.

Ichioka, Y. (1988). *The Issei: The world of first-generation Japanese immigrants, 1885–1924.* New York: Free Press.

Kikumura, A. (2002). *Encyclopedia of Japanese descendants in the Americas: An illustrated history of the Nikkei.* Walnut Creek, Calif.: AltaMira.

Kitano, H. H. L. (1993). *Generation and identity: The Japanese American.* Needham Heights, Mass: Ginn.

Matsumoto, V. (1993). *Farming the home place: A Japanese American community in California, 1919–1982.* Ithaca, N.Y.: Cornell University Press.

Niiya, B. (Ed.). (2000). *Encyclopedia of Japanese American history: An A-to-Z reference from 1868 to the present.* New York: Facts on File.

Uchida, Y. (1982). *Desert exile: The uprooting of a Japanese American family.* Seattle: University of Washington Press.

Yamamoto, H. (1981). *Seventeen syllables and other stories.* Latham, N.Y.: Kitchen Table—Women of Color Press.

Yamauchi, W. (1994). *Songs my mother taught me: Stories, plays and memoir.* New York: Feminist Press at the City University of New York.

Yoo, D. K. (2000). *Growing up Nisei: Race, generation, and culture among Japanese Americans of California 1924–1949.* Urbana: University of Chicago Press.

6

Korean American Elders

Su-Jeong Park and Suk-Young Kang

Ms. Suh is an eighty-year-old Korean Catholic widow who was transferred to a nursing home from another nursing home. Her admitting diagnosis was cardiovascular accident (CVA) with hemiparesis and hypertension (HTN). Ms. Suh has a sixth-grade education and spent her entire life as a homemaker. She immigrated to the United States in 1975, after her husband's death, and has five sons and one daughter living in Korea, New York, and Chicago. When she first came to the U.S., she lived with her daughter's family for several years and helped with the cooking and cleaning, and babysat for her grandchildren. She subsequently moved out of her daughter's home and lived with a Korean roommate until she was admitted to a nursing home after a stroke.

Ms. Suh has expressed somatic complaints since admission. She has asked to see a primary physician numerous times because of somatic complaints including chronic headache, abdominal pain, chest pain, and sleep disturbance. The primary physician prescribed pain medication, but Ms. Suh still complains of medical problems. The nursing supervisor on the unit referred Ms. Suh for a psychiatric screening. Ms. Suh was evaluated in the Korean language by a Korean American psychiatrist and was diagnosed with major depression. The Korean American psychiatrist recommended antidepressant medication and individual psychotherapy.

One day the Korean-speaking social worker was called to the unit, as Ms. Suh was firmly refusing to take the prescribed antidepressant medication, stating, "There is no reason to take this medication because I am not crazy. What I need is pain medication to alleviate my chronic headache and abdominal pain." The social worker approached Ms. Suh to offer individual counseling for her depressive symptoms. When she asked Ms. Suh how she was feeling, she answered, "I'm fine. I don't have any particular problems except chronic headache and abdominal pain."

When asked whether she was experiencing *han* (unhappiness or grudges) or *hwabyung* (culturally sanctioned expression of depression and anxiety), Ms. Suh admitted to these ailments, stating, "Who doesn't have *han* or *hwabyung* at my age." Ms. Suh was told that she would be seen by a Korean American psychiatrist with whom she could communicate in Korean. She became extremely agitated, saying, "Why do I need a psychiatrist? What for? I'm fine, and I don't want any help from anybody." When the Korean American psychiatrist approached Ms. Suh to engage in conversation, she strongly resisted and his attempt was not successful.

Symptoms of depression and other emotional problems, for many Korean American elders, are often masked by strong somatic symptoms; not only does this represent a more socially acceptable way to express a psychological disturbance (Chun, Enomoto, & Sue 1996; Kim 1985; Lee, Lei, & Sue 2001) but somatic illness is also more culturally acceptable among Koreans (Mui 1996; Pang 1996). Because of the stigma associated with mental illness, psychological distress expressed through the body rather than the mind is more acceptable (Chun et al. 1996; Gaw 1993; Lee et al. 2001; Pang 1994, 1996). Common somatic symptoms related to Korean culture include frequent sighs, tightness in the chest, headaches, body aches, insomnia, epigastric lumps, panic, fatigue, chills, and fever (Pang 1995). The somatization of psychiatric disorders in Korean American elders is demonstrated by the ailment *hwabyung,* the expression of psychiatric disorders, primarily depression and anxiety that is culturally recognized and accepted (Chun et al. 1996; Lee et al. 2001; Pang 1990, 1995). *Han,* the expression of unhappiness or grudges, is another indicator of mental illness associated with passive frustrations and hostility resulting from disappointment in one's life (Pang 1996). *Han* is culturally understood to be the result of significant others or oneself behaving in an oppressive, disloyal, or negligent manner. Common symptoms related to *han* include insomnia, sad facial expressions, self-pity, and self-deprecation.

In contrast to the traditional Western emphasis on self-disclosure and the expression of individual feelings, Asian cultures, including Korean culture, stress implicit meanings over verbal communication (Chin 1993; Kim & Kim 1997; Pang 1996). Clearly the strong somatic tendency in many Korean American elders is a direct result of their negative attitudes toward mental illness and their customary suppression of verbal and nonverbal expression (Kim 1985; Pang 1996). It is therefore essential that social workers and other service providers are sensitive to the unspoken needs and emotional responses of Korean American nursing home residents, with the understanding that physical complaints may mask psychological disturbances. The information presented in this chapter provides a general framework of Korean history and cultural traditions, but as with people belonging to every ethnic and racial group, each Korean American resident and relative must be regarded as an individual. The important differences between traditional Korean values and mainstream values in the United States are summarized in Table 6.1.

With increased life expectancy and an increase in the population of elderly Korean American immigrants, culturally sensitive nursing home care for this population is critically important. Like the elderly of many other ethnic and racial groups, Korean American elders need diverse health, personal,

TABLE 6.1 Differences Between Korean Traditional Values and American Mainstream Values

Korean Traditional Values	American Mainstream Values
Family Values	
Family-oriented	Individual-oriented
Interdependency	Autonomy and independence
Vertical, authoritarian structure	Horizontal, democratic structure
Respect for parents and elders, family loyalty and filial piety duty, obedience, acceptance	Individual self-determination, own happiness, freedom of choice and independence
Family discipline via shame and punishment	Discipline relies on school and other agencies
Life Philosophy	
Family/kinship bonds, collectivism	Individualism, pragmatism
Success through self-discipline and will	Fulfilling one's potential
Sense of stoicism and fatalism	Sense of optimism and opportunism
Reciprocity and obligation	Avoidance of obligation to family
Status conscious and face-saving	Self-realization; do your own thing
Holistic living in harmony with nature	Control and conquer nature
Communication Style	
Subtle, nonverbal, body language	Emphasis on verbal language
Control of feelings	Free expression of feelings
Flowery, indirect expression	Direct, explicit expression
No eye-to-eye contact	Eye contact is important
Honorific language	Equality in language
Self-effacing	Self-promoting
No physical contact or hugging in public	Hugging and kissing in public

Source: L. I. Kim & G. S. Kim (1997). *Korean American immigrants and their children* (San Francisco: San Francisco Study Center), p. 20. Adapted with permission.

and social services for assistance in daily living because of chronic disabilities resulting from physical or mental conditions. However, Korean American elders are less likely to use nursing homes, primarily because of their cultural values and beliefs.

It is hoped that the information provided in this chapter will assure a comprehensive, culturally sensitive approach to social work assessment and interventions for Korean American nursing home residents and their relatives and effective work with interdisciplinary teams.

HISTORICAL DEVELOPMENT OF KOREAN CULTURE AND KOREAN STATES

GEOGRAPHIC LOCATION

Korea, established in the Korean peninsula approximately five thousand years ago, is attached to the northeastern region of China and the far eastern region of Russia. The Korean peninsula was occupied by Japan from 1910 to 1945 and, after World War II, was divided into two separate states, South Korea and North Korea, the former occupied by the United States and the latter by the former Soviet Union. To the west across the West Sea, or Yellow Sea, the states face China, and to the east and south across the East Sea is Japan. The geographic and political circumstances of Korea have forced the Korean governments to maintain a careful balance in their relationships with China, Japan, Russia, and the United States. Meanwhile, Koreans have maintained a homogeneous culture that includes their own language, their own foods, and a way of life that differs from that of their neighbors, China and Japan.

MIGRATION HISTORY AND CURRENT ISSUES

More than six thousand miles separates South Korea from the United States, and yet many Koreans have chosen to migrate to the U.S. because of the ongoing relationship between that nation and South Korea, especially since World War II (Min 1996). Park (1997) has identified five factors that have influenced Korean immigration to the United States since 1965: (1) the division of Korea into North and South Korea after World War II; (2) the U.S. government's ongoing political, military, and economic involvement in the Korean peninsula; (3) the growth of the new middle class in South Korea; (4) the advance of a new international division of labor and the status of South

Korea in this new situation; and (5) changed immigration policies on the part of both U.S. and South Korean governments.

The following three sections examine the major immigration waves of Koreans to the United States (Min 2000; Shin 1998).

Labor Immigration to Hawaii: 1903–1924

More than seven thousand Koreans, mostly men between the ages of twenty and thirty, came to work in the sugar plantations in Honolulu, Hawaii, between 1903 and 1905, and the majority were laborers, ex-soldiers, students, and political refugees, but pressure from the Japanese government put an end to this early labor migration in the summer of 1905 (Min 2000).

After the Gentlemen's Agreement was signed between the United States and Japan in 1907, only Korean "picture brides," seventeen years old on average, could be admitted to the U.S. between 1910 and 1924. From 1924 until the end of World War II, U.S. immigration law severely limited immigration, and, except for several hundred students, practically no Korean immigrants came to the U.S. (Hurh & Kim 1984; Min 1996). The series of Asian Exclusion Acts barred immigrants from citizenship and property ownership, and, in 1924, amendments to the National Origins Act declared Japanese (which included Koreans at that time) ineligible for citizenship and prohibited them from entering the U.S. Thus the Korean immigration to the United States that began with the labor immigration to Hawaii was discontinued until the end of World War II.

Post–Korean War Immigration: 1950–1964

After the end of World War II immigration resumed, and by the time the national origins quota system was abolished in 1965, 14,027 Koreans had immigrated to the U.S. These can be divided into three categories: 6,423 Korean wives of U.S. servicemen stationed in Korea, 5,348 war orphans, and professional workers (Hurh & Kim 1984). The McCarren-Walter Act of 1952 abolished the 1917 Asia Barred Zone and allowed an annual quota of 100 immigrants from each of the Pacific and Asian countries. In addition to this act, the War Brides Act of 1945 allowed veterans to bring spouses and children above the quota numbers (Min 2000).

The Largest Immigration: 1965–the Present

Large-scale Korean immigration began only after the passage of the U.S. Immigration and Naturalization Act of 1965, the Hart-Cellar Act, which abolished the national origins quota system. In 1962 an overseas emigration law was passed by the South Korean government to encourage emigration in order to control population, lower unemployment, earn foreign exchange, and obtain knowledge of advanced technology. This immigration cohort, primarily college-trained professionals from the urban middle-class of Korean society, is generally better educated than the previous two groups (I. Kim, as cited in Park 1997). There were exceptions, however, including Ms. Suh, who immigrated within this cohort but had not been educated beyond sixth grade.

Lack of economic opportunities, social and political insecurity owing to the military dictatorship, and the difficulty of sending children to higher educational institutions in South Korea pushed many Koreans to immigrate to the United States in the 1970s and the early 1980s (Min 2000). Many college-educated South Koreans chose immigration in order to resolve their unemployment problems in the 1970s and the early 1980s (Min 1996).

The majority of Korean American older adults immigrated after the 1965 Immigration and Naturalization Act became effective in 1968 in order to join their adult children who came to the U.S. after 1965. Because the immigration process can last several years, many Korean American elders joined their children in the 1970s. Some were born in the current North Korean area before the Korean War (1950–53) and then fled from the communist regime to South Korea, subsequently migrating to the U.S. According to the 2000 Census, 94 percent of Korean-Americans sixty-five years of age and older were not born in the U.S. (Korean American Coalition 2003).

KOREAN ADOPTEES

Approximately one hundred thousand Korean children have been adopted by families in the United States since 1953 (Huh 1997). Although there is no reliable information about the exact number of Korean adoptees, many are now approaching their fifties and sixties, and more research about this population is needed.

OTHER IMMIGRATION ROUTES

Some Korean Americans have come to the U.S. through Germany, South Vietnam, and the Middle East, and many immigrated after working as miners, construction and transportation workers, sailors, and nurses in other countries. By 1990, the total number of immigrants of Korean ancestry to the U.S. who had come from Latin American nations, including Argentina, Brazil, and Paraguay, reached forty thousand, and some emigrated because of economic and political instability in the South American nations where they lived (Park 1997).

DEMOGRAPHIC CHARACTERISTICS

The 2000 Census (U.S. Census Bureau 2001) reported a population of 1,076,872 Korean Americans, an increase of 35 percent over the 1990 Census figure of 797,304. The 1990 U.S. Census figure indicated a 125 percent increase over the 1980 Census figure of 354,593. The largest percentage increase was seen between 1970 and 1980, when the number of Koreans increased from 70,510 to 354,593. This is attributed to the liberalized immigration policy following enactment of the 1965 U.S. Immigration Law and South Korea's relaxed emigration policy beginning in 1962. Korean Americans aged sixty-five and older are underrepresented compared to the rest of the U.S. population in the same age bracket, as shown in Table 6.2 (U.S. Bureau of the Census 2001).

GEOGRAPHIC DISTRIBUTION

Korean Americans are urban dwellers, with 96 percent residing in cities and only 4 percent in rural areas (U.S. Census Bureau 2000). Korean immigrants tend to settle where people from their country already reside, and this provides opportunities for newcomers to learn about life in the U.S. from relatives, friends, and acquaintances who have already immigrated. Korean American elders with language barriers may stay in close contact or live in a Korean community, whereas Korean immigrants with school-age children frequently move to a white, middle-class, suburban neighborhood after the initial acculturation period (Min 2000).

TABLE 6.2 Age Distribution of Korean Americans and Total U.S. Population: 2000

Age	Korean Americans	U.S. Population
Under 5	5.4 %	6.8 %
5–19	22.1 %	21.8 %
20–44	44.5 %	37.5 %
45–64	21.8 %	21.9 %
65 or older	6.2 %	12.0 %

Source: Census 2000 Brief (2001). http://www.census.gov/prod/2001pubs/c2kbr01–12.pdf; Korean American Coalition-Census Information Center in partnership with the Center for Korean American and Korean Studies, California State University, Los Angeles. http://www.calstatela.edu/centers/ckaks/census/31303_table1.pdf.

EDUCATIONAL ATTAINMENT

According to results of a study in the Chicago area, 40 percent of Korean American elders over sixty years of age were high school graduates compared to 9 percent of Korean elders in South Korea (Yoh and Bell 1987). A recent study in the New York City area showed that 81 percent of Korean American elders are high school graduates. However, only 3 percent of Korean American elders have a college degree (Cross 2003).

PHYSICAL, COGNITIVE, AND PSYCHOLOGICAL HEALTH

PHYSICAL HEALTH: CHRONIC HEALTH CONDITIONS

The prevalence of chronic health conditions varies by race and ethnicity in the older population. One recent study reports that in New York City the most prevalent medical conditions among Asian American elders are arthritis, high blood pressure, high cholesterol, cataracts, and diabetes (Mui 2003). Mui's study indicates that when compared to the general elderly population, Asian American elders report higher rates of cataracts, hypertension, and diabetes. Mui also found that women are more likely to have osteoporosis, anemia, and arthritis than men. Compared to other Asian American elders, Korean American elders in New York City are more likely to have arthritis, high blood pressure, and osteoporosis (Mui 2003). Several studies report that Korean American elders are more likely to report having arthritis, hypertension, heart disease, and stroke than non-Hispanic white persons or people who are Hispanic (Lee, Yeo, & Gallagher-Thompson 1993; Mui 2001).

Lee and associates (1993) indicate that Korean American elders show a prevalence of diabetes that is four times the rate of older Americans in general in the U.S. This study indicates that, compared to white elders, Korean American elders have lower prevalence of heart disease, stroke, and all risk factors including high blood pressure, high levels of cholesterol, current smoking status, and physical inactivity. However, the study shows a significantly higher prevalence of diabetes compared to other risk factors. Korean American elderly women are more likely to report having arthritis but less likely to report having heart disease compared to Korean American elderly men. Korean American men are also more likely to have had cancer compared to Korean American women (ibid.).

One study shows that there are major differences in patterns of health risk between Korean elders in Korea and Korean American elders (Shin, Shin, & Blanchette 2002). According to this study, circulatory disease, including hypertension and coronary heart disease, and cancer are the two major health problems of Korean elders in Korea. On the other hand, Korean American elders report a higher prevalence of diabetes than Korean elders in Korea. They also report a high risk of hypertension and cardiovascular disease.

ATTITUDES REGARDING DEMENTIA

Dementia is a syndrome of cognitive loss that is sufficient to interfere with functioning in occupational or social activities, and there are several types of dementia. The essential features of dementia include not only multiple cognitive deficits but also a broad range of behavioral disturbances including agitation, sleep disturbances, and others (Beaulieu 2002). Figures on the prevalence of dementia among Korean American elders are largely unavailable, as many families may hide the illness from the community (Chee & Levkoff 2001).

Most Korean American elders and their relatives consider dementia or Alzheimer's disease to be a normal aging process rather than disease (Chee & Levkoff 2001; Jin, Ryan, & Anas 2001; Lee & Sung 1998; Youn et al. 1999). One study indicates, however, that memory impairment is considered to be caused by lack of ability and is viewed as worrisome (Bieman-Copland & Ryan 1998). Several studies indicate that most Korean Americans think senile dementia is physically based and caused by lack of stamina, malnutrition, poor blood circulation, or some other reason (Jin, Ryan, & Anas 2001; Lee & Sung 1998; Youn et al. 1999).

Within Korean culture, dementia and its symptoms in elders are categorized in several ways. First, dementia is understood as a biomedical label, a physiologically based cognitive illness. In the biomedical model, dementia is understood as *chi-mae,* which translates as *"Alzheimer's disease"* or *poong,* which roughly translates as "stroke." The term *chi-mae* is commonly used to refer to cognitive impairment in elders. Second, dementia is also labeled by the folk idiom *noh-mang,* which means "old and crazy." It also describes the aberrant behaviors of demented elders. The term, *noh-mang* is a stigmatizing term that has negative connotations. Moreover, *noh-mang* can be used to denote people whose behavior is beyond the acceptable social norms and to signify a lack of respect for the elder's cognitive impairment and related aberrant behaviors.

Among these terms, *noh-mang* and *chi-mae* are commonly used by Korean American nursing home residents and their families. Korean American families commonly use the term *chi-mae* as a diagnosis of dementia for Korean American elders. However, *noh-mang,* the negative term for dementia, is commonly used among alert Korean American nursing home residents. It is

easily observed that alert residents, lacking an understanding of the diagnosis, stigmatize those with dementia and tend to avoid interacting with demented Korean American nursing home residents. Social workers and other
health care professionals should work toward decreasing the stigma surrounding the condition by providing residents and families with education
and resources. It is also important to create interventions and programs for
residents with dementia, provide support groups for family members, and
support Korean American relatives' efforts to cope with dementia and related
behavior problems.

DEPRESSION

Despite an increase in the population of elderly Korean American immigrants, few researchers have studied their mental health status. Pang (1996)
suggests that there is relatively little evidence that elderly Korean American
immigrants have received mental health services in the community or that
they use antidepressants. The case study of Ms. Suh, above, provides insight
as to why Korean Americans resist mental health services. One study shows
that older Korean Americans and older whites are at similar risk for depressive symptoms (Yamamoto, Rhee, & Chang 1994); another suggests that
depressive symptoms in elderly Korean Americans are more prevalent than
in elderly Chinese Americans (Mui 2001). Mui's study also demonstrates that
older Korean women are more vulnerable to depressive symptoms than older
Korean men. Other studies suggest that elderly Korean Americans are vulnerable to psychological distress in the form of depressive symptoms due to
stresses associated with immigration, acculturation, poor health, social isolation and language barriers (Burnette & Mui 1996; Kiefer et al. 1985; Lee, Crittenden, & Yu 1996; Mui 1996, 2001; Yamamoto, Rhee, & Chang 1994).

Depression is a major mental illness among Korean American elders
largely because of the stressful transition to a new environment, language
barriers, physical illness, and lack of family support (Pang 1994; Yamamoto,
Rhee, & Chang 1994). Symptoms of depression often go unrecognized, undiagnosed, and untreated because of cultural factors (Pang 1995), including
the tendency among this population to internalize emotions instead of
expressing them publicly (Chun, Enomoto, & Sue 1996; Lee, Lei, & Sue 2001;
Pang 1996). Mental illness and emotional problems are generally stigma-
tized and perceived as deviant and harmful behavior (Choi 2001; Pang 1996),
which inhibits Korean Americans from seeking professional help (Cho 1998;
Choi 2001).

Korean Americans have difficulty establishing a therapeutic relationship
with health professionals, as they generally depend on themselves for emo-

tional care (Kim 1985; Pang 1996). They view mental illness as a transitory cognitive state that can be overcome through personal determination (Pang 1996). Korean Americans also believe that one can avoid depression by being religious and flexible and by keeping busy and talking with friends and family (Hyun 2001; Kim 1985; Pang 1994, 1996). In addition, their deep sense of shame and stigma regarding mental illness impedes seeking professional help until their illness becomes more severe and serious (Choi 2001; Kim 1985).

One of the social worker's major goals in working with Korean American nursing home residents is for mental health issues to be addressed effectively by the interdisciplinary team with careful attention to the unique cultural attitudes and beliefs toward mental illness. This was an important aspect of the social worker's interventions in her work with Ms. Suh. Social workers assisting Korean American nursing home residents need to provide culturally appropriate mental health treatments and interventions and educate interdisciplinary team members about culturally appropriate approaches to provision of services.

CULTURAL CHARACTERISTICS AND NURSING HOME PLACEMENT

FAMILY RELATIONSHIPS

Korean culture recognizes that the hierarchy of authority within the family and society are determined by gender, generation, age, and class. Although it seems that this tradition may have changed, it remains an influential force on the thinking and behavior of Korean Americans (Kim 1996). Among older couples and more traditional Korean American families, the division of rights and responsibilities between genders still favors males. It is not uncommon, for example, for an unemployed husband to expect his wife to prepare family meals after returning from her work. This example may not be as applicable to younger Korean Americans, but older adults may maintain these inequalities in relationships (Kim 1996).

Korean American elders who came to the U.S. in their old age have been disadvantaged in that they usually do not have the financial assets to legitimize their higher status in family relations. They were unable to provide financially for the family, as they could not find jobs in the new land. Often, moreover, their knowledge and experiences appeared to be irrelevant to providing advice to their children on how to succeed in the U.S. The language barrier and lack of transportation often resulted in dependence on their adult children (Kauh 1999), and this dependency often caused them to lose their role as providers for their offspring. Korean American elders, therefore, may exercise little power and be granted less status than they received in South Korea (Kauh 1999).

Ms. Suh helped her daughter with housekeeping and babysitting for many years, and Korean grandparents frequently care for grandchildren and do the family's housework because their adult children need to work outside the home. But even though this assistance contributes to the Korean American family economically, Korean American elders generally cannot exercise authority and power within their families. Many also accept the fact that their children cannot perform their traditional roles because of the living situation in the U.S. (Kauh 1999).

Min (1998) suggests that there are two groups of Korean American elders living in the U.S.: the "invited elderly" who immigrated to the U.S. in their mid-fifties to mid-sixties at the invitation of adult children already settled in this country; and "immigrated elderly," those who immigrated to the U.S. independently, probably were employed following immigration, and reached retirement age in the United States.

Most Korean American elders in the U.S. are the "invited elderly" (Kim & Kim 2001). Their numbers are likely to decrease due to a reduction in Korean immigration overall over the years and two 1996 laws: the Personal Responsibility and Work Opportunity Reconciliation Act (PL 104–193), which limits elderly people without citizenship access to public assistance programs, and the Illegal Immigration Reform and Immigration Responsibility Act (PL 104–208), which stipulated that adult children who sponsor relatives must support their non-naturalized parents.

FILIAL PIETY

In East Asia people's behavior is shaped by Confucianism, the dominant belief system. It was introduced from China to Korea by the first century, along with Taoism and Buddhism (Kim & Kim 1997). These three ideas have coexisted and influenced Korean people spiritually, but Confucianism became the dominant political and social ideology from the Chosun dynasty (1392–1910) to the present.

Filial piety has been an institutionalized norm over a long period of time in Korea, China, Japan, and other Asian societies; influenced by Confucianism, it regulates intergenerational relationships. Adult children are obliged to give their elderly parents emotional and financial support at any cost (Ishii-Kuntz 1997; Kim, Kim, & Hurh 1991), and thus this norm plays a key role in selection of the primary caregivers for Korean American elderly. The oldest son is responsible for his elderly parents physically and financially, as he is the person who receives most of the family inheritance. Even if he does not live in the same household, he is required to provide assistance to his parents with all available resources. In Korea, if an elderly woman or a widower becomes frail, the oldest son's wife usually becomes the primary caregiver. Sometimes the wife provides care for her elderly husband (Youn et al. 1999).

Traditionally, filial piety obligates children only to support the parents of a son, which is the basis of the traditional patrilineal and patrilocal extended family system in Korea. Thus families that have no son adopt a son from near family kin to carry on the family name. In a patrilocal family system, a married son and his family are expected to reside with his parents or live under their strong authority. In return, the eldest son has primogeniture, a right to inherit a greater portion of the wealth from the parents, so it is natural for the eldest son to have the greatest power in the decision-making process concerning family issues (Kim & Kim 2001).

This norm has been weakened, however, in Korean American families in the U.S. Most husbands and most wives in Korean American families are employed to support their family, and thus fewer daughters-in-law are available to provide care among Korean Americans than among Koreans. Children in many families may feel guilty because of conflicts between traditional Korean values and realities in the U.S.

Korean sons traditionally are supposed to provide all support for the parents, but the changed economic circumstances following immigration to the U.S. often leaves sons unable to be the sole provider for their parents. Daughters may also be providers for their own parents in addition to their parents-in-law. In most Korean American immigrant families, both husbands and wives are employed in order to contribute to the family income. As noted above, the "invited elderly" in Korean American families often do not have enough resources to sustain the traditional family system (Kim & Kim 2001). All these factors have modified the partrilineal and primogeniture family system in the U.S. to a conjugal family system, a nuclear family with an independent residence where the husband's and wife's kin lines are equally important (Kim & Kim 2001).

There is a gap now between the traditional expectations of Korean American "invited elders" and the financial capacity of Korean American adult children to meet those expectations. After a period of co-residence with adult children, Korean American "invited elders" may try to move out and live independently, perhaps with U.S. government support such as government-subsidized apartments for older adults, Supplementary Security Income (SSI), Food Stamps, and Medicaid. In the case study that began this chapter, Ms. Suh had moved out of her daughter's home because her daughter's family needed space for her grandchildren. She received SSI, Food Stamps, and Medicaid, and she had the financial capacity to live independently.

Social workers counseling Korean American families with invited elderly members who may need nursing home care need to consider the modified family system during the decision making process. Social workers may have to engage many family members in the process because it may be impossible to bring in only one decision maker from the family.

Yoo and Sung (1997) have suggested that Korean American elders wish to live independently because they prefer privacy and freedom rather than a troubled relationship with their children. They suggested that public welfare programs, income, and education were associated with Korean American elders' independent residence. A study by Yoh and Bell (1987) indicates that a prior pattern of shared residence by parents and adult children in South Korea has shifted to a pattern of accepting the prospect of separate living arrangements by the generations residing in the U.S.

SOCIAL NETWORKS OF KOREAN AMERICANS

Most Korean Americans develop informal social ties primarily with other Korean Americans, regardless of socioeconomic status, geographic location, or the size or concentration of the local Korean population (Kim 1988). Korean American churches are the most important organizations in the community in terms of size, influence, and financial resources (Kim & Yu 1996). The church is a place where elders can meet with friends and adult children who are not living in the same household.

More than 60 percent of Korean American elders in the U.S. are Protestant (Yoh & Bell 1987; Mui 2001; Yoo & Sung 1997; Yu et al. 1988), whereas in South Korea only 12 percent of elders reported themselves as Protestant (Yoh & Bell 1987). A high proportion of Korean American immigrants may be Protestant prior to their migration (Min 2000).

FOOD

Quandt (1999) pointed out that food plays an important role as social "glue" among Korean Americans. Thus the gift of food is viewed by Korean American nursing home residents as providing not only nutritional sustenance but also social meaning. The process of eating together or giving and receiving Korean food reinforces social relations and group harmony. Korean American nursing home residents may also value this process as a way to maintain reciprocity in social relations and to create a sense of camaraderie with other residents.

Korean American nursing home residents have been observed to frequently exchange food, and food sharing is clearly valued by most elders, regardless of ethnicity (Quandt et al.). Sharing and exchanging food helps them feel engaged with other residents. Many Korean American nursing home residents believe that food sharing is part of generalized reciprocity. When members of the younger generations of their family regularly bring them Korean food, they are often willing to share Korean food with other Korean American nursing home residents during meals. At times there is also direct food reciprocity, where returning food or other items is equivalent to a gift. Moreover, instead of specific reciprocity, generalized reciprocity appears to be the rule or obligation, with little need to repay a food gift with the same item.

ATTITUDES TOWARD DEATH

Culture is the most important factor related to attitudes about death, and elders from different cultures tend to react differently to death and dying (Schumaker, Warren, & Groth-Marnat 1991). Some studies indicate that, whereas some cultures fear death, others regard it as a normal part of life (Schumaker et al. 1991; Stroebe et al. 1992; Westman & Canter 1985). Studies reflect that Asian cultures are found to report a lower level of death-related anxiety than other cultures (Schumaker et al. 1991; Westman & Canter 1985).

As in other Asian cultures, Korean American elders perceive death according to the philosophical or religious thinking of Buddhism, Confucianism, or Christianity (Wu, Tang, & Kwok 2002). For example, reincarnation in Buddhism is a well-accepted belief among Korean American elders who consider death to be a continuous and integral part of life, not separate from life or an end. Some Korean American elders believe that their present life will determine their afterlife.

On the other hand, Korean American elders may also consider death as unfortunate, and they may believe that merely talking about death is bad luck. Therefore, direct discussion of death may elicit negative cognitive and emotional reactions toward specific death-related issues, such as pain in dying and having a terminal illness.

NURSING HOME PLACEMENT AND ADJUSTMENT

ADMISSION DECISIONS

Admission to a nursing home is often an emotionally difficult time for Korean American elders, not only because they are unfamiliar with nursing homes but also because of their negative image of them. Korean Americans consider a nursing home to be a "homeless shelter for the elderly," a place for elderly people who have no children or were abandoned by their children. Korean Americans view institutionalization of the elderly as conflicting with traditional values, and there are many emotional issues for Korean American nursing home residents that include high expectations of filial responsibility and family solidarity.

Studies indicate that most Korean American elders are either unaware of community-based, long-term care services or have never used them. As with their attitudes about nursing homes, this is because their culture is rooted in filial piety wherein care provided for the elderly by family has been accepted as a normative duty (Chi 1989; Kim 1991; Park 1983).

Family members, especially the first son and daughter-in-law, are expected to be the major supporters of the ill elderly, and it is considered culturally desirable for frail parents to live with a married son (Hong & Ham 1992; Kim 1991; Mui 1996). The obligation of filial piety in caring for frail parents is still felt strongly, and it has been assumed that filial piety plays an important role in motivating family members to care for the elderly (Kim 1991). Therefore nursing home placement is an extremely stressful and shameful transition for Korean American elders. Children with a strong obligation of filial piety may feel guilty for placing their parents in a nursing home.

Ethical issues may arise in the admission process, as the children often make the placement decision without consulting or involving their parents in any way (Idziak 2002). Therefore social workers and other professional caregivers have the responsibility to discuss options with capable older adults in order to identify which option is the older adult's preference and in her or his best interest medically and feasible in terms of family and community supports.

MR. CHUNG

Mr. Chung is a seventy-three-year-old married man and a Korean Baptist who was admitted to a nursing home from the hospital. His major diagnosis is cardiovascular accident (CVA) with right-side hemiparesis. He received intensive occupational and physical therapy for a few months after admission. With intensive therapy, he was able to perform his activities of daily living (ADLs) independently, with minimal assistance. One day he approached the social worker and requested that he be discharged, stating that he had not even known that he had been placed in a nursing home: "My family told me a lie that this is a hospital. If I knew that this is a nursing home, I wouldn't be here." And he added, "I asked my family [his wife and daughter] to take me home, but they insisted that I have to stay here because I'm sick." The social worker contacted his family, but they strongly refused to take him home because of the primary caregiver's own advancing age and physical problems. The social worker discussed this with the resident, but he continued to express his strong wishes to go home, insisting, "I don't understand why I'm here. If I go home, my family will take care of me." Indeed, according to the primary physician, Mr. Chung was able to go home anytime. The social worker had a meeting with Mr. Chung and his family to discuss options related to discharge planning.

It is extremely important for Korean American residents to be active participants in the decision-making process about nursing home placement and to be given accurate information about their conditions and need for placement. Mr. Chung had a negative attitude about nursing home placement and was sent to a nursing home against his wishes. In this case, reconciliation needed to be achieved between Mr. Chung's desire to return to the community and his family's ability to provide only limited care for him. One of the social worker's major roles is to help clarify and respect the resident's wishes and choices, and if the resident is discharged, to educate family members about options including assisted living and community and social supports that could ease the obligations or burdens on relatives.

AUTONOMY AND RESIDENT RIGHTS

In terms of residents' rights in medical care and treatment, "A Resident's Bill of Rights" clearly states that residents have the right to obtain complete medical information, such as diagnosis, treatment, and prognosis that they can reasonably be expected to understand (Idziak 2002). In Western culture, individual rights is a prominent value, and a resident may accept and discuss informed consent, disclosure of diagnosis, prognosis, and the realistic assessment of the efficacy of medical care (Meleis & Jonsen 1983). Such autonomy in medical care and treatment may allow a resident to participate in making choices about viable medical treatments on his or her own (Idziak 2002). Several studies indicate, however, that autonomy in medical care and treatment may not be universally accepted (Idziak 2002; Meleis & Jonsen 1983), and that conflicts can arise between health care providers, residents, and family members whose cultures differ from the mainstream regarding autonomy in medical care.

MR. SONG

Mr. Song is a seventy-four-year-old Korean, Catholic, married man who was admitted to a nursing home with diagnoses of depressive disorder and esophageal cancer. He received intensive radiation therapy and recovered completely. Two years later he was again sent to the hospital for diagnostic tests, as blood was discovered in his stools. The test indicated that he had colon cancer. His physician told his wife and son about his new onset of cancer and recommended chemotherapy or surgery as viable treatments. The physician asked the son how his father should be approached with this news, and even asked the son to be a translator to discuss treatment options. But the son strongly insisted that his father not be informed about the new onset of cancer, stating, "We want to keep my father as comfortable as possible until he dies. He suffered from severe pain and side effects due to radiation therapy when he had esophageal cancer. We don't want him to go through another invasive treatment, such as chemotherapy or surgery." Although the physician approached the family several times, they reacted in the same way and even demanded that the physician not discuss anything with the father. The physician believed, however, that the family members were not acting fairly by keeping information from Mr. Song about his current medical condition. Because it was Mr. Song's life, the physician believed that the decision should be solely Mr. Song's and not his relatives'.

This case illustrates how conflicts may arise between health care providers and family members whose culture has a different set of beliefs and values regarding residents' autonomy and medical treatments. Most Asians, including Koreans, believe that being truthful with a resident about acute illness and medical treatments may harmfully affect the resident (Blackhall et al. 1995; Muller & Desmond 1992). Being openly truthful may be considered dangerous and rude, and may even be seen as signifying the loss of hope. Thus withholding the truth from a resident is valued. One study indicates that Korean Americans might best be described as "family-centered" in that the family expects that only they will be told of the resident's diagnosis and prognosis, and they alone will make decisions about medical treatments (Blackhall et al. 1995).

In Mr. Song's case, the social worker and health care providers need to show respect for the relatives' and residents' beliefs and even be willing to compromise. In this process, one of the social worker's key roles is to help clarify both the resident's and the relatives' wishes and choices about medical treatments and explain this to the interdisciplinary team, as well as to educate the family about the positive aspects of telling the resident the truth and respecting the resident's autonomy.

ADVANCE DIRECTIVES

Ideally, the process of developing advance directives results from ongoing discussions between the resident, family, and staff (Cohen-Mansfield 2002).

However, Korean Americans rarely discuss future treatment wishes or even advance directives, including "Do Not Resuscitate" orders (DNR) or a "Health Care Proxy," before admission to a nursing home.

One study found that an individual's attitudes and decisions about advance directive preferences and end-of-life issues are influenced by ethnicity, cultural beliefs, gender, and educational level (Vaughn, Kiyasu, & McCormick 2000). For Korean American nursing home residents, cultural beliefs and norms such as filial piety are dominant and may be reflected in the decision-making process regarding advance directive preferences. Based on Korean cultural beliefs, a DNR order could be regarded as giving up on life or a disregard for elders (ibid.). Some Korean American elders who strongly believe in the importance of preserving life view a DNR order as suicide or the passive killing of a resident. These beliefs support the efforts that families make to prolong the lives of their elders. Korean Americans who fear death or regard advance directives as stigmatizing are usually reluctant to discuss advance directive preferences and make decisions in advance. Some Korean American nursing home residents leave decision making about advance directives solely to the family.

Although Korean Americans generally exhibit these cultural norms and beliefs, each resident must be viewed as a unique individual who has retained her or his cultural identity. A major struggle for social workers, then, is to uphold the principles of advance directives, and yet be sensitive to Korean Americans' unique cultural beliefs and unfamiliarity with advance directives. Social workers should try to understand the views of residents and their relatives, but also help Korean Americans and their relatives understand advance directives and alleviate their biases by providing education and facilitating conversations about end-of-life issues.

RELIGION

Many studies indicate that religion can be beneficial to mental health (Chang, Noonan & Tennstedt 1998; Ellison 1991; Matthews, Larson, & Barry 1993; Pang 1996; Pargament 1998; Picot et al. 1997; Stuckey 2001). King and Dein (1998), however, view religion as intensifying emotional stress instead of reducing it.

Several studies indicate that most Korean American elders living in the community have a religious affiliation, including Buddhism, Catholicism, or Protestantism (Moon, Lubben, & Villa 1998; Pang 1996; Park 1989). Many Korean American nursing home residents identify with these same religions and practice their faith at the facility. Some Korean American residents may consider religious activity to be the primary source of social contact with the community and opportunities to socialize with other residents, as well as providing coping strategies for adjusting to a nursing home environment. Social workers and other staff should help residents continue to practice their religious beliefs and request that local religious organizations provide services in the nursing home regularly or otherwise facilitate participation of residents in their religious and social activities.

RECREATIONAL ACTIVITIES AND INTERESTS

Korean American residents struggle to fit into the mainstream culture at a nursing home, and they may participate in recreational activities with people from other ethnic groups at their birthday parties and mainstream holiday celebrations, and in English classes. Several studies indicate that recreational activities help immigrant groups gain familiarity with a new culture and strengthen their own cultures and identities (Kelly 1996; Kim, Kleiber, & Kropf 2001; Kleiber 1999). Recreational activities can also help develop community, social interaction, and relationships in new environments (Stokowski 1994).

Generally, Korean American nursing home residents want to maintain traditional Korean activities, such as celebrations of Korean holidays and participation in Korean social gatherings with other residents. Such activities should be developed to strengthen cultural connections and values and provide opportunities to retain ethnic identity. At the same time, social workers and other staff should encourage Korean American residents to participate in recreational activities reflecting U.S. culture to learn more about, and be familiar with, mainstream culture. Recreational activities, for Korean American elders, are used to experience a shift in emotional atmosphere, termed *Ki-Bun-Chun-Whan,* and to offer opportunities for self- development. They can help these elders re-create their sense of "being Korean" and provide a sense of security from participation in the Korean community and sharing the same culture, values, and traditions (Kim, Kleiber, & Kropf 2001). A kind of special interpersonal bond, called *Jeong,* can make them feel close together and reconnected to their sense of "being Korean" (ibid.).

Social interaction can be strengthened through singing Korean folk songs and listening to music; Korean television programs and videotapes may become central to daily recreational activities, and Korean American residents also may have informal gatherings based on gender or religious background.

COMMUNICATION BETWEEN RESIDENTS AND STAFF

The acquisition of English-language skills is ranked as the highest priority among Korean immigrants in the U.S., but it is also the most difficult task (Kim 1988). Although they may learn English from classes offered in the

Korean American community, there may be few opportunities to use and practice English in daily life (Min 2000). Given this reality, it is not surprising that first-generation immigrant communication among Korean Americans is almost exclusively in Korean and that Korean American elders rarely speak or understand English. The Ethnic Elderly Needs Assessment Survey of Asian Americans in Chicago reported that 84.1 percent of 196 Korean American participants spoke English poorly or not at all, and 82.6 percent of 195 participants read English poorly or not at all (Yu et al. 1988).

Poor communication skills and language barriers impede communication with other nursing home residents and contribute to the difficulties Korean American residents have in adjusting. The inability to communicate may increase their psychological distress and unfamiliarity with services. Language barriers may also prevent Korean American nursing home residents from seeking medical and psychological services effectively. Social workers and other staff need to use appropriate approaches to communicate by involving a staff translator, professional interpreter, community service provider, or family members. One of the main advantages of using family members is that staff can respond to a resident's needs immediately when there is no staff available who can communicate with the resident in Korean. There are risks in using relatives as translators, however, including breaches of confidentiality, embarrassing the resident, and an inaccurate or inappropriate translation.

Approaches for improving communication include pictures or a written communication board in both Korean and English, nonverbal techniques such as gestures, and Korean/English classes for Korean-speaking residents and for staff and residents who do not speak Korean. For Korean American nursing home residents who do not speak English, culturally appropriate approaches that include non-verbal techniques may result in improved communication between residents and staff.

Elders in the Korean culture are regarded with a great deal of respect that is communicated in numerous ways. Korean American elders are called "grandparents" rather than by either their first or last names. They believe that handing a person an object with a single hand is a show of disrespect and so it is important for staff to use two hands when handing an elder an object. Nonverbal communication and commonly used gestures are also interpreted differently by Korean American nursing home residents. Korean American elders, for example, consider that pointing the index finger or giving the thumbs-up sign reflect bad manners or defiance.

ROOMMATES AND ROOM CHANGES

Rooms are obviously important personal spaces, as they provide individuals with privacy, control, and a sense of personal identity (Cooper 1984; Miles &

Sachs 1990). Rooms in nursing homes constitute the equivalent function of "homes," with personal meanings, so that assignment of roommates and changing roommates are challenging problems in daily living in nursing homes (Idziak 2000). This may be even more challenging for Korean American residents, as they may be living with someone from a different culture who speaks another language. They may request a roommate change in order to be with a resident with the same culture and language or for other reasons, but Korean American residents and their relatives tend to be cautious about discussing roommate issues or conflicts, partially because Koreans traditionally respect the maintenance of harmonious relationships with other people.

SEXUALITY AMONG KOREAN AMERICAN RESIDENTS

Sexuality is a major aspect of physical and emotional intimacy that is a significant life issue for older adults (Knowlton 2000; Zeiss & Kasl-Godley 2001). Sexuality can be defined as "any combination of sexual behavior, sexual activity, emotional intimacy, or sense of sexual identity" (Hillman 2000, pp. 5–6). Several studies indicate that, although sexual activity decreases with age, many elderly people are still sexually active (Hillman 2000; Knowlton 2000; Richardson & Lazur 1995; Zeiss & Kasl-Godley 2001). Although sexuality is an important issue for older adults, their sexual needs are generally stereotyped, misunderstood, or ignored (Schlesinger 1996). Expressions of physical intimacy, moreover, are widely viewed as abnormal or inappropriate behaviors in the elderly (Miles & Parker 1999). Professionals may react to residents' sexual behaviors by projecting their own beliefs and values (Sarisky 2002; Schlesinger 1996). They may be judgmental or reprimand residents.

Relatively little is known about Korean American nursing home residents' sexuality and related issues. Because of cultural factors, they are unlikely to talk about their sexual needs and experiences as most have been raised with prevailing Korean cultural stereotypes about sexuality and sexual activity. Family members may have negative attitudes regarding sexual behaviors and implicitly or explicitly discourage or deny their existence. Among Korean American women of all ages, being overly curious, concerned, or knowledgeable about one's body and greater sexual knowledge or expression may be viewed as inappropriate.

To address sexuality and manage sexual behaviors in a nursing home, an educational in-service training for staff should be created and developed. According to Fairchild, Carrino, and Ramirez (1996), in-service training should have three objectives for staff, including dispelling myths and stereotypes and presenting information about sexual expression in old age, modifying negative responses to resident sexual behavior and learning to help residents manage sexual relationships, and developing empathy for the resident through role playing. Other interventions include improving the resident's privacy; encouraging alternative forms of sexual expression to meet sexual needs; and providing counseling, education, and acknowledgment of the importance of sexuality for the quality of life.

In dealing with sexuality at a nursing home, social workers must help ensure that residents' rights are respected. Moreover, social workers need to assist in ensuring that sexual needs of residents are addressed in a sensitive, safe, and respectful manner that promotes a good quality of life rather than taking away more rights from residents.

CONCLUSIONS AND RECOMMENDATIONS

Social workers and other health care providers need to understand the unique circumstances of Korean American nursing home residents, as well as the uniqueness of each individual, and work in culturally appropriate ways to support a positive quality of life. The following six interventions are especially important.

1. Residents need to participate in the decision-making process regarding nursing home placement. They should have opportunities to discuss the possible need for placement and the options for the best care. Considering that Korean American elders and their families have limited knowledge and negative attitudes regarding nursing homes, social workers need to provide supportive and educational services to help them understand the concept of a nursing home.

2. Korean American residents, as in the case of Mrs. Suh, are unlikely to recognize mental health problems or seek help from professionals. Many internalize their mental health problems and tend to mask them by complaining of physical or psychosomatic symptoms. Therefore, it is important for social workers and health care professionals to assess Korean American residents' psychological functioning and help-seeking behaviors from the perspective of their Korean cultural background. Developing an understanding of how mental health issues are perceived and manifested among Korean American elders allows social workers and other health care providers to offer culturally appropriate clinical interventions.

3. Most Korean American nursing home residents do not speak English. Although they seek help from staff, they frequently encounter service providers who do not belong to or understand their culture and language.

Social workers and other health care providers must attempt to find ways to communicate appropriately and effectively by using a translator, nonverbal techniques such as a Korean-American picture or written communication board, or providing Korean-English classes for both staff and Korean American residents.

4. To support the psychosocial well-being of Korean American nursing home residents, it is important to provide culturally familiar social and recreational activities and food preferences to strengthen cultural connectedness and maintain ethnic identity. Psychosocial well-being is also supported by intergenerational activities that help residents feel important and connected through interactions with grandchildren. Programs that allow residents to learn and connect to American culture and people belonging to other ethnic groups are also valuable, and staff should encourage Korean American residents to participate in a Resident Council as a vehicle to exercise their rights, express their needs, and protect their interests.

5. In-service staff training should be encouraged in order to educate staff about the importance of considering cultural uniqueness and other relevant factors in providing culturally competent services to Korean American residents and their relatives. Interdisciplinary staff needs to learn about cultural norms and values regarding mental health and illness, nonverbal and verbal communication, family dynamics, food preferences, and other areas, as the need arises. Education also should be offered to residents and relatives to help them understand the systems and services at a nursing home, and to explain ways that relatives may participate, when appropriate, in the care of residents.

6. Social workers and health care professionals need to work with residents to develop support systems that include relatives, religious organizations, and community-based Korean American associations. This can help residents to adjust to an institutional setting, develop meaningful social relationships with other residents, and enhance their experiences at the nursing home.

REFERENCES

Beaulieu, E. (2002). *A guide for nursing home social workers.* New York: Springer.

Bieman-Copland, S., & Ryan, E. (1998). Age biased beliefs about memory successes and failures. *Journal of Gerontology: Psychological Sciences* 53B, 105–118.

Blackhall, L., et al. (1995). Ethnicity and attitudes toward patient autonomy. *Journal of the American Medical Association* 274/10 (September), 820–825.

Burnette, D., & Mui, A. (1996). Psychological well-being of three cohorts of older American women who live alone. *Journal of Women and Aging* 8 (1), 63–80.

Chang, B., Noonan, A., & Tennstedt, S. (1998). The role of religion/spirituality in coping with caregiving for disabled elders. *The Gerontologist* 38, 463–470.

Chee, Y., & Levkoff, S. (2001). Culture and dementia: Accounts by family caregivers and health professionals for dementia-affected elders in South Korea. *Journal of Cross-Cultural Gerontology* 16, 111–125.

Chi, K. (1989). *The Foundation of spiritual history of Korean people (Han- Minjok-ui jungshin-chuk ki'cho)*. Kyunggido, Korea: Center for Korean Studies.

Chin, L. (1993). Toward a psychology of difference: Psychotherapy for a culturally diverse population. In J. Lau Chin, V. De La Cancela, & Y. Jenkins (Eds.), *Diversity in psychotherapy: The politics of race, ethnicity, and gender*, pp. 69–92. London: Praeger.

Cho, P. (1998). Awareness and utilization: A comment. *The Gerontologist* 38 (3), 317–319.

Choi, N. (2001). Diversity within diversity: Research and social work practice issues with Asian American elders. *Journal of Human Behavior in the Social Environment* 3 (3/4), 301–319.

Chun, C., Enomoto, K., & Sue, S. (1996). Health care issues among Asian Americans: Implications of somatization. In P. Kato & T. Mann (Eds.), *Handbook of diversity issues in health psychology*, pp. 347–365. New York: Plenum.

Cohen-Mansfield, J. (2002). Development of a framework to encourage addressing advance directives when resources are limited. *Journal of Aging and Health* 14 (1), 24–41.

Cooper, K. (1984). Territorial behavior among the institutionalized: A nursing perspective. *Journal of Psychosocial Nursing and Mental Health Services* 22, 6–11.

Cross, P. (2003). A demographic and economic profile. In *Asian American Elders in New York City: A study of health, social needs, quality of life, and quality of care*, pp. 12–27. New York: Asian American Federation of New York, Brookdale Center on Aging, Hunter College.

Ellison, C. (1991). Religious involvement and subjective well-being. *Journal of Health and Social Behavior* 32 (1), 80–99.

Fairchild, S., Carrino, G., & Ramirez, M. (1996). Social workers' perceptions of staff attitudes toward resident sexuality in a random sample of New York State nursing homes: A pilot study. *Journal of Gerontological Social Work* 26 (1/2), 153–169.

Gaw, A. (1993). Psychiatric care of Chinese Americans. In A. C. Gaw (Ed.), *Culture, ethnicity and mental illness*, pp. 245–280. Washington, D.C.: American Psychiatric Press.

Hillman, J. (2000). *Clinical perspectives on elderly sexuality*. New York: Kluwer Academic/Plenum.

Huh, N. (1997). Korean children's ethnic identity formation and understanding of adoption. Unpublished doctoral dissertation, State University of New York at Albany.

Hurh, W., & Kim, K. (1984). *Korean immigrants in America: A structural analysis of ethnic confinement and adhesive adaptation*. Rutherford, N.J.: Fairleigh Dickinson University Press.

Hyun, K. (2001). Is an independent self a requisite for Asian immigrants' psychological well-being in the U.S.? The case of Korean Americans. *Journal of Human Behavior in the Social Environment* 3 (3/4), 179–200.

Idziak, J. (2002). *Ethical dilemmas in long-term care*. 2nd ed. Dubuque, Iowa: Simon & Kolz.

Ishii-Kuntz, M. (1997). Intergenerational relationships among Chinese, Japanese, and Korean Americans. *Family Relations* 46 (1), 23–32.

Jin, Y., Ryan, E., & Anas, A. (2001). Korean beliefs about everyday memory and aging for self and others. *International Journal of Aging and Human Development* 52 (2), 103–113.

Kauh, T. (1999). Changing status and roles of older Korean immigrants in the United States. *International Journal of Aging and Human Development* 49 (3), 213–229.

Kelly, J. (1996). *Leisure*. Needham Heights, Mass.: Allyn & Bacon.

Kiefer, C., et al. (1985). Adjustment problems of Korean American elderly. *The Gerontologist* 25 (5), 477–481.

Kim, B. (1988). The language situation of Korean American. In S. McKay & S. Wong, (Eds.), *Language diversity problem or resource? A social and educational perspective on language minorities in the United States*, pp. 252–275. Boston: Heinle and Heinle.

Kim, B. (1996). Korean families. In M. McGoldrick, J. Gordano, & J. Pearce (Eds.), *Ethnicity and family therapy*, pp. 281–294. New York: Guilford.

Kim, E., and Yu, E. (1996). *East to the United States: Korean American life stories*. New York: New Press.

Kim, E., Kleiber, D., & Kropf, N. (2001). Leisure activities, ethnic preservation, and cultural preservation of older Korean-Americans. In N. Choi, (Ed.), *Social work practice with the Asian American elderly*, pp. 107–130. New York: Haworth Social Work Practice Press.

Kim, K. (1991). *Psychoanalytic interpretation of Korean traditional culture: Myths, shamanism, and religious experience*. Seoul: Gyo Mun Sa.

Kim, K., Kim, S., & Hurh, W. (1991). Filial piety and intergenerational relationship in Korean immigrant families. *International Journal of Aging and Human Development* 33 (3), 233–245.

Kim, L., & Kim, G. (1997). *Korean American immigrants and their children*. San Francisco: Many Cultures.

Kim, S. (1985). Family therapy for Asian Americans: A strategic-structural framework. *Psychotherapy* 22/2 (summer), 342–348.

Kim, S., & Kim, K. C. (2001). Intimacy at a distance, Korean American style: Invited Korean elderly and their married children. In L. K. Olson, (Ed.), *Age through ethnic lenses*, pp. 45–58. New York: Rowman & Littlefield.

King, M., & Dein, S. (1998). The spiritual variable in psychiatric research. *Psychological Medicine* 28, 1259–1262.

Kleiber, D. (1999). *Leisure experience and human development*. New York: Basic Books.

Knowlton, L. (2000). Sexuality and aging. *Psychiatric Times* 17 (January) [online]. Available at http://www.mhsource.com/pt/p000159.html.

Koenig, H. (1994). *Aging and god: Spiritual pathways to mental health in midlife and later years*. New York: Hayworth.

Korean American Coalition-Census Information Center in Partnership with the Center for Korean American and Korean Studies (2003). Census Tables, Korean population in U.S. California State University, Los Angeles. Available at http://www.calstatela.edu/centers/ckaks/census_tables.html.

Lee, J., Lei, A., & Sue, S. (2001). The current state of mental health research on Asian Americans. *Journal of Human Behavior in the Social Environment* 3 (3/4), 159–177.

Lee, J., Yeo, G., & Gallagher-Thompson, D. (1993). Cardiovascular disease risk factors and attitudes towards prevention among Korean-American elders. *Journal of Cross-Cultural Gerontology* 8 (1), 17–33.

Lee, M., Crittenden, K., & Yu, E. (1996). Social support and depression among elderly Korean immigrants in the United States. *International Journal of Aging and Development* 42 (4), 313–327.

Lee, Y., & Sung, K. (1998). Cultural influences on caregiving burden: Cases of Koreans and Americans. *International Journal of Aging and Human Development* 46, 125–141.

Loo, C., Tong, B., & True, R. (1989). A bitter bean: Mental health status and attitudes in Chinatown. *Journal of Community Psychology* 17, 283–296.

Matthews, D., Larson, D., & Barry, C. (1993). *The faith factor: An annotated bibliography of clinical research on spiritual subjects.* Rockville, Md.: National Institute for Healthcare Research.

Meleis, A., & Jonsen, A. (1983). Ethical crises and cultural differences. *Western Journal of Medicine* 138/6 (June), 889–893.

Miles, S., & Parker, K. (1999). Sexuality in the nursing home: Iatrogenic loneliness. *Generations* (spring), 36–43.

Miles, S., & Sachs, G. (1990). Intimate strangers: Roommates in nursing homes. In R. A. Kane, & A. L. Caplan (Eds.), *Everyday ethics: Resolving dilemmas in nursing home life,* pp. 90–99. New York: Springer.

Min, P. (1996). *Caught in the middle: Korean merchants in America's multiethnic cities.* Berkeley: University of California Press.

Min, P. (1998). *Change and conflicts: Korean immigrant families in New York.* Boston: Allyn & Bacon.

Min, P. (2000). Korean Americans' language use. In S. McKay, & S. Wong (Eds.), *New immigrants in the United States,* pp. 306–332. Cambridge: Cambridge University Press.

Moon, A., Lubben, J., & Villa, V. (1998). Awareness and utilization of community long-term care services by elderly Korean and non-Hispanic white Americans. *The Gerontologist* 38 (3), 309–316.

Mui, A. (1996). Depression among elderly Chinese immigrants: An exploratory study. *Social Work* 41 (6), 577–696.

Mui, A. (2001). Stress, coping, and depression among elderly Korean immigrants. *Journal of Human Behavior in the Social Environment* 3 (3/4), 281–299.

Mui, A. (2003). Physical health, mental health and quality of life. In *Asian American elders in New York City: A study of health, social needs, quality of life, and quality of care,* pp. 28–46. New York: Asian American Federation of New York.

Mui, A., Choi, N., & Monk, A. (1998). *Long-term care and ethnicity.* Westport, Conn.: Greenwood.

Muller, J., & Desmond, B. (1992). Ethical dilemmas in a cross-cultural context: A Chinese example. *Western Journal of Medicine* 157/3 (September), 323–327.

Pang, K. (1990). Hwabyung: the construction of a Korean popular illness among Korean elderly immigrant women in the United States. *Culture, Medicine and Psychiatry* 14 (4), 495–512.

Pang, K. (1994). Understanding depression among elderly Korean immigrants through their folk illness. *Medical Anthropological Quarterly* 8 (2), 209–216.

Pang, K. (1995). A cross-cultural understanding of depression among elderly Korean immigrants: Prevalence, symptoms and diagnosis. *Clinical Gerontologist* 15 (4), 3–20.

Pang, K. (1996). Self-care strategy of elderly Korean immigrants in the Washington, D.C. Metropolitan Area. *Journal of Cross Cultural Gerontology* 11, 229–254.

Pargament, K. (1998). *The psychology of religion and coping: Theory, research, practice.* New York: Guilford.

Park, C. (1983). Historical review of Korean Confucianism. In *Main currents of Korean thoughts,* pp. 26–82. Korean National Commission for UNESCO, Seoul: Si-sa-yong-o-sa.

Park, K. (1989). Korean elderly in Queens. Paper presented at the Sixth Annual Conference of the Asian-American Studies. Hunter College, City University of New York.

Park, K. (1997). *The Korean American dream: Immigrants and small business in New York City.* Ithaca: Cornell University Press.

Picot, S., et al. (1997). Religiosity and perceived rewards of black and white caregivers. *The Gerontologist* 37, 89–101.

Quandt, S. (1999). Hunger and food security among older adults in a rural community. *Human Organization* 58, 28–35.

Quandt, S., et al. (2001). The social and nutritional meaning of food sharing among older rural adults. *Journal of Aging Studies* 15, 145–62.

Richardson, J., & Lazur, A. (1995). Sexuality in the nursing home patient. *American Family Physician* 51 (1), 121–124.

Sarisky, J. (2002). Sexuality and elderly people in long-term care facilities. *Aging* (May), 4–6.

Schlesinger, B. (1996). The sexless years or sex rediscovered. *Journal of Gerontological Social Work* 26 (1/2): 117–131.

Schumaker, J., Warren, W., & Groth-Marnat, G. (1991). Death anxiety in Japan and Australia. *Journal of Social Psychology* 131 (4), 511–518.

Shin, S. (1998). Paibu dollar please! Bilingual Korean American children in New York City. Unpublished dissertation. University of Michigan, Ann Arbor.

Shin, K., Shin, C., & Blanchette, P. (2002). Health and health care of Korean-American elders. Retrieved January 18, 2002 from http://www.stanford.edu/group/ethnoger/korean.html.

Snowden, L., & Cheung, F. (1990). Use of inpatient mental health services by members of ethnic minority groups. *American Psychologist* 45, 347–355.

Stokowski, P. (1994). *Leisure in society: A network structural perspective.* New York: Mansell.

Stroebe, M., et al. (1992). Broken hearts or broken bonds: Love and death in historical perspective. *American Psychologist* 47, 1205–1212.

Stuckey, J. (2001). Blessed assurance: The role of religion and spirituality in Alzheimer's disease caregiving and other significant life events. *Journal of Aging Studies* 15, 69–84.

U.S. Census Bureau (1992). *1990 Census of Population, General Population Characteristics, United States, 1990 CP-1–1.* Table 48. Available at http://www.census.gov/prod/cen1990/cp1/cp-1–1.pdf.

U.S. Census Bureau (2000). *Census 2000 Summary File 2 (SF2).* Washington, D.C.: U.S. Government Printing Office.

U.S. Census Bureau (2001). *Profile of General Demographic Characteristics.* Washington, D.C.: U.S. Government Printing Office.

Vaughn, G., Kiyasu, E., & McCormick, W. (2000). Advance directive preferences among subpopulations of Asian nursing home residents in the Pacific Northwest. *Journal of the American Geriatrics Society* 48 (5), 554–557.

Westman, A., & Canter, F. (1985). Fear of death and the concept of extended self. *Psychological Reports* 56 (2), 419–425.

Wu, A., Tang, C., and Kwok, T. (2002). Death anxiety among Chinese elderly people in Hong Kong. *Journal of Aging and Health* 14 (1), 42–56.

Yamamoto, J., Rhee, S., & Chang, D. (1994). Psychiatric disorders among elderly Koreans in the United States. *Community Mental Health Journal* 30 (1), 17–27.

Yoh, J., & Bell, W. (1987). Korean elders in the United States: Intergenerational relations and living arrangements. *The Gerontologist* 27 (1), 66–71.

Yoo, S., & Sung, K. (1997). Elderly Korean's tendency to live independently from their adult children: Adaptation to cultural differences in America. *Journal of Cross-Cultural Gerontology* 12, 225–244.

Youn, G., et al. (1999). Differences in familism values and caregiving outcomes among Korean, Korean American, and White American dementia caregivers. *Psychology and Aging* 14 (3), 355–364.

Yu, E., et al. (1988). Final report: ethnic elderly needs assessment. Pacific/Asian American Mental Health Research Center, University of Illinois at Chicago.

Zeiss, A., & Kasl-Godley, J. (2001). Sexuality in older adults' relationships. *Generations* 25/2 (summer), 18–25.

RESOURCES

Organizations and Websites

Centennial Committee of Korean Immigration to the United States. http://www.korean centennial.org/.
Korean American Coalition-Census Information Center. http://www.calstatela.edu/centers/ ckaks/census_tables.html.
Korean American Historical Society. http://www.kahs.org/links.html.
Korean American Museum. http://www.kamuseum.org/.

Additional Readings

Chin, S. (1991). Korean birthday rituals. *Journal of Cross-Cultural Gerontology* 6 (2), 145–152.
Frank, G., et al. (1998). A discourse of relationships in bioethics: Patient autonomy and end-of-life decision making among elderly Korean Americans. *Medical Anthropology Quarterly* 12 (4), 403–423.
Park, J., & Kwon, Y. (1990). Modification of the Mini-Mental State Examination for use in the elderly in a non-Western society. Part 1, Development of Korean version of Mini-Mental State Examination. *International Journal of Geriatric Psychiatry* 5 (6), 381–387.
Pourat, N., et al. (1999). Predictors of use of traditional Korean healers among elderly Koreans in Los Angeles. *The Gerontologist* 39 (6), 711–719.

7

Mexican American Elders

Yvette Solis-Longoria

MRS. NAVARRO

Mrs. Navarro is an eighty-six-year-old, first-generation Mexican American female admitted to a nursing home for rehabilitation after a fall that caused a hip fracture. She was referred to the social worker because the rehab team was concerned about her slow progress toward achieving the goal to return home. The nursing staff reports that she has periods of crying, nighttime restlessness, and poor appetite, and her relatives argue among themselves about discharge plans. The staff is struggling to find the best way to work with multiple family members and maintain confidentiality.

Mrs. Navarro has been widowed for thirty-eight years and has four children. Two sons live in town, and one lives about three hours away, and her daughter lives about one block away. Mrs. Navarro's younger sister and niece have lived next door to Mrs. Navarro for almost forty-five years. Mrs. Navarro was diagnosed with vascular dementia three years ago and requires assistance with her Instrumental Activities of Daily Living (IADLs), such as managing finances, maintaining her home, shopping, and preparing meals, but she manages her ADLs, for example, bathing, dressing, toileting, eating, and transferring. The family is uncertain about Mrs. Navarro's ability to return home, and her family has begun to consider whether her stay should be long-term. But they are concerned about the cost and had thought that Medicare would pay for the services. The nursing home is across town from Mrs. Navarro's neighborhood, making visits difficult and stressful for her children, who all work. Mrs. Navarro misses her sister, and her sister is upset that the children want Mrs. Navarro to live with her and the niece. The sister who normally visited Mrs. Navarro daily has been unable to visit, as she lacks transportation. The social worker will need to address all these issues that are affecting Mrs. Navarro's rehab progress and discharge planning.

MR. CAMPOS

Mr. Campos is a seventy-six-year-old second-generation Mexican American married male admitted to the nursing home for rehabilitation after a cerebral vascular accident (CVA) left him with left-sided weakness. The nursing staff reports that he does not allow the staff to assist with his ADLs, and when Mrs. Campos tried to transfer her husband from his bed to a chair, both almost sustained injuries. Mr. Campos has a feeding tube for nutrition, as he has difficulty swallowing as a result of the CVA and has in place an order for NPO (Latin: *Nil per Os* [nothing by mouth]). He has been referred to the social worker because he resists physical and occupational therapy; staff also reports that his family is impeding progress in rehab as they prevent him from exercising, feeling that the movements are painful. The family has been bringing snacks, despite the NPO order. Mr. Campos is only supposed to eat in the presence of the speech pathologist, and the snacks put him at risk for aspiration.

He has five children, three who live in the city where the nursing home is located and two who live out of state and do not agree with discharge plans to return Mr. Campos home. He has become incontinent of bowel and bladder, ambulates only by means of a wheelchair and with assistance, and requires a two-person transfer. Mrs. Campos visits every day for most of the day and is becoming increasingly difficult with staff, as she does not want her husband out of bed very long. It is apparent that family members have unrealistic expectations of his potential to return home without twenty-four-hour care, and there are limited resources to provide this care at home.

Mr. Campos is angry with his family, continually asks them when he will go home, and does not want to participate in therapy. The children who reside out of town feel he needs to remain long-term, as they have visited and do not believe that their mother can manage his care at home. The children in town, however, plan on the daughter moving in with her parents to help with the caregiving. Because of his income, Mr. Campos does not qualify for primary home care provider services through Medicaid or the Community Based Alternative (CBA) program that assists long-term care residents who return to the community. The interdisciplinary team believes that the family is unable to develop a realistic plan for Mr. Campos upon the completion of his rehabilitation, and they are conferring with the social worker regarding the discharge process.

Mrs. Navarro and Mr. Campos are both Mexican American elders, but they exhibit important differences, such as a different primary language (Table 7.1). The staff's inability to speak a resident's primary language, of course, can have significant implications for communication not only with staff but

TABLE 7.1 Comparison of Mrs. Navarro and Mr. Campos

	Mrs. Navarro	**Mr. Campos**
Nativity	Born in Mexico	Born in U.S.
Primary language	Spanish	English
Cultural identification	Mexican American	Mexican American
World War II	Lived in rural Texas	Lived in San Antonio, Texas
Food Preference	Blend of Mexican and American	Blend of Mexican and American
Generational category	Immigrant	Second generation

also with other residents. The experiences of staff who worked with these two residents illustrate many of the important issues discussed here, and are referred to throughout the chapter. Readers will learn how elders and their social support networks can benefit from social work interventions to assist them in coping with nursing home experiences.

Long-term care services have traditionally been used mostly by Anglo-American elders, but recently there has been an upward trend in the admissions of minority elders. Culturally competent and sensitive practices will be more critical in the future, as more Mexican Americans reach later adulthood and need information about, and access to, long-term care options (Torres-Gil 1990).

This chapter focuses on Mexican American nursing home residents, specifically on their unique cultural values, worldviews, and family structure.

MEXICAN AMERICANS IN THE U.S.: HISTORICAL BACKGROUND

The American Southwest became part of the United States in 1848, when Mexico was defeated in the U.S-Mexican War. Therefore, Mexican culture in the southwestern states joined with Anglo culture by force, as Mexicans at that time did not migrate to the United States but were absorbed in the regions that are now California, Arizona, New Mexico, Texas, Utah, Nevada, and parts of Colorado, Wyoming, Oklahoma, and Kansas. The Treaty of Guadalupe Hidalgo established property and civil rights for Mexicans who were living in these newly formed territories at that time. The treaty was to guarantee U.S. citizenship but not necessarily protection of their property (de la Torre & Estrada 2001).

As described by Falicov (2005), "Complementarity of economic needs between Mexico and the United States has resulted in a historical roller coaster, with periods when the United States recruits workers, encourages relocation, and legalizes migration, and periods of avoidance, when immigration is discouraged, made illegal, and punished with repatriation" (p. 229). Immigration from Mexico has resulted from political upheaval, insecure economic conditions, and industrial and agricultural growth in the southwestern U.S. From 1910 to 1920 laborers were recruited to work on ranches, farms, and in factories. During the Great Depression in the 1930s, many Mexican Americans were deported to Mexico partly because of employment limitations and resentment by American citizens.

Employment opportunities improved in the 1940s because of World War II, increasing the immigration of Mexicans to obtain employment as laborers; thus neighborhoods—*urban ghettos* or *barrios*—were created. Keefe and Padilla (1987, p. 9) define a *barrio* as an urban residential area with at least a 40 percent Mexican American makeup.

In 1942 the Bracero Agreement established a U.S. government program that increased the use of temporary farm workers from Mexico for twenty-two years and contributed to prosperity for U.S. landowners. Many workers remained illegally after the end of the program, primarily because they had established families while working on the farms. Others had available resources and support to become U.S. citizens. During this period of U.S. expansion, many Mexican American elders experienced dramatic changes from being landowners to becoming farmhands on what was once their land. Mexican Americans faced housing discrimination, low wages, and employment discrimination that allowed little progress for many who remained and are now elder U.S. citizens (Markides & Mindel 1987). Angel and Angel (1998) estimate that almost 50 percent of Mexican Americans over sixty-five years of age residing in the U.S. were born in Mexico.

DEMOGRAPHIC CHARACTERISTICS

The 2000 U.S. Census reported 20,640,711 Mexican Americans out of a total of 35.3 million Hispanics residing in the U.S. The population of Mexican Americans increased from 13.5 million in 1990 to 20.6 million in 2000. The Census indicated that Mexican Americans are concentrated in California, Texas, Nevada, and Colorado. Mexican American elders, *ancianos,* represent a diverse ethnic group concentrated in California, Texas, Arizona, and Florida (Lecca et al. 1998). For many generations families of most Mexican American elders have lived in regions of the U.S. that once belonged to Mexico.

Among Hispanics, Mexican Americans had the lowest average family income in 1999—$30,735—with approximately half their elderly living near or below the poverty level. They are likely to receive Social Security benefits as a sole source of income, with almost nonexistent secondary retirement bene-fits. About 44 percent of Mexican Americans have a high school diploma or higher. Approximately 60 percent of Hispanic elders have lower than a ninth-grade education compared to 19.4 percent of non-Hispanic elders. About 16 percent have a high school diploma compared to 34 percent, and 3 percent of non-Hispanic elders have a bachelor's degree compared to 9 percent of non-Hispanic elders nationally (U.S. Census Bureau 2000). Mexican Ameri-cans have a median age of 24.2; as a whole the Hispanic population is youth-ful, with a median age of 25.9 compared to the median age of 35.3 for the total U.S. population. It is estimated that Hispanic elders over age sixty-five will comprise 14.1 percent of the total Hispanic population by 2020 (ibid.).

THE FAMILY

Family members provide a strong presence and support in times of hard-ships and celebrations. *Familismo*, a commonly held belief among traditional Mexican American elderly, promotes the well-being of family over meeting individual needs. It is a collectivistic viewpoint that emphasizes cohesion and cooperation. The family interdependence of *familismo* "involves extended family members sharing the nurturing and disciplining of children, finan-cial responsibility, companionship for lonely or isolated members, and prob-lem solving. . . . The process of separation/individuation, so highly regarded in American culture, is deemphasized in favor of close family ties, indepen-dent of age, gender, or social class" (Falicov 2005, pp. 213–214). Many Mexi-can American families are large and multigenerational, and some of the elders live with their children and grandchildren.

Fictive kin relationships are also important in the family composition (Keefe and Padilla 1987). Through the ceremony of baptism, important ex-tended family members are often created who are significant family figures. These include *compadres* and *comadres* (companions) and *padrinos* and *madri-nas* (godparents). The relationship of *compadrazo* that develops between the child's parents and godparents (sponsors) can be long-lasting and significant to the family. Godparents influence family well-being and decision making throughout life and may or may not be blood-related.

The Mexican American family is an important socioeconomic resource, with clear roles and responsibilities. Social workers often discover that family members share their incomes to better provide for the family's economic needs. During times of hardship, the close-knit relationships emerge for the family's survival. It is traditionally believed that family will provide child care and elder care (Resendez & Vargas 1997). There is a strong expectation of "filial piety," a moral obligation of children to provide care for their aging parents, and the youngest daughter often has the responsibility of becoming the caregiver for her parents. If the daughter's behavior does not meet this expectation, she may be considered disrespectful (Falicov 1996). It is important for social workers to understand that some family caregivers may hide their stress from the relative they are helping so as not to show disrespect for the role given them. They may not seek support because they fear being viewed as unsuccessful in the caregiving role. Furthermore, while there is a cultural expectation of filial piety, some elders who experience role change from provider to receiver feel demoralized and feel they have lost their value or purpose as a member of the family.

Many Mexican American families have a history of family members migrating to the U.S. at different times, with prolonged separations. Reincorporation of family members can be traumatic, and these experiences can affect relationships within families. Obtaining a "migration narrative" can be a useful approach to understanding a family's cultural and migratory experiences (Falicov 2005). Potential areas to explore include length of residence in the U.S., sequence of immigration of family members, family members who have not yet immigrated, stresses and knowledge learned in Mexico and the U.S., and strengths and resources (Falicov 2005, p. 231). This exploration should occur with sensitivity to feelings of vulnerability that undocumented immigrants may have.

HEALTH ISSUES

PHYSICAL HEALTH

Torres-Gil (1990) reports that, among Mexican American elders, a decline in physical health is a major concern and fear, as they are faced with chronic illnesses such as hypertension, diabetes mellitus, arthritis, cardiovascular disease, high cholesterol, pneumonia, influenza, infectious and parasitic diseases, tuberculosis, and gallstone disease. A particular concern is the high rate of non-insulin dependent diabetes in older adults; one research study found that mortality from diabetes was five times greater for Mexican American elders than for non–Mexican American elders (Angel & Angel 1998). Mexican American elders are also twice as likely to have one limitation in ADLs and IADLs compared to non–Mexican American elders (Talamantes, Lawler, & Espino 1995).

The onset of health problems in Mexican American elders frequently begins at a younger age than in other groups, often around age fifty-seven

(Becerra & Shaw 1984). Potential explanations include the young age at which they begin work, as well as their experiences as manual laborers on farms, in construction, and in factories, often working under extreme environmental conditions resulting in the likelihood of a short work life and a future with physical disabilities (Torres 1999; Markides et al. 1999; Ruiz 1995). Markides and Mindel (1987) describe a feeling among some Mexican American elders that they will live a short life as a result of past hardships, described as a "psychological death."

Some Mexican American elders suffer from culturally related health conditions that health professionals frequently do not recognize. For example, many experience *susto* (fear), *un ataque* (fainting), *fatiga* (shortness of breath), or *dolor de riñones* (back pain). Health professionals may erroneously dismiss such complaints and not address them as valid health conditions (Lecca et al. 1998).

The use of *curanderos* (folk healers) and *espiritismo* (spiritualism) should also be considered in assessing Mexican American elders and their approaches to treating illness. The use of such folk medicine interventions is relevant to understanding and respecting the decision-making process in elders, and folk practices may need to be adapted for nursing home use (Applewhite 1995). It should not be assumed, however, that all Mexican American elders use folk approaches to treatment; this practice is rooted in the traditional values and cultural experiences of some Mexican Americans but not others, and it is important to understand that many people use both *curanderismo* and modern medical approaches. The underutilization of health and mental health services may not always be the result of using folk medicine but may follow from the high costs of medical care and lack of medical insurance (Mayers 1989).

A study found that 9.8 percent of 2,734 elderly Mexican Americans used herbal medicine within the two weeks prior to their interview, and the most commonly used herbs were chamomile and mint (Loera et al. 2001). The most closely associated characteristics with using these remedies were female gender, having been born in Mexico, older than seventy-five years of age, living alone, and experiencing financial strain. Increased use of herbal medicines was also associated with arthritis, urinary incontinence, asthma, and hip fracture in this sample.

MENTAL HEALTH

Criticisms by professionals of mental health attitudes and treatment among Mexican Americans have resulted from historical accounts that focus on folk aspects of mental health rather than more significant psychosocial aspects

(Markides & Mindel 1987; Weaver 1973; Applewhite 1995). Weaver (1973) presented two commonly held viewpoints of Mexican American elders: that illness, whether physical or mental, is a matter of chance, and one can do little about it; and that supernatural forces are involved and remedies are unavailable from doctors but must come from a folk healer or from prayer. A frequently held belief is that mental health ailments are "God's will" and must be endured, as they are untreatable by human beings.

Mental health aliments are often attributed to *espiritismo* (spiritual forces), which cannot be addressed outside the culture nor understood by service providers. Specific mental health ailments identified among the Mexican American elderly such as *mal de ojo* (evil eye), *son nérvios* (being nervous), *está sufreyendo* (suffering), *susto* (being scared), and fear of *un ataque de nérvios* (uncontrollable crying, screaming, verbal or physical aggression or suicidal gestures) may be described (Yee 1997). Because of close-knit family support systems, mental health services may not be explored until the needs become unmanageable. Among undocumented immigrants, use of mental health services is discouraged by the fear that their illegal status will be detected (Falicov 2005).

Results of one of the first large-scale studies of Mexican American elders (EPESE) indicated that this group has a higher prevalence of disabilities than non–Mexican American elders in performing ADLs, as well as a greater prevalence of depressive symptoms. Possible explanations are that many of these elders experience the onset of disabilities at younger ages, with decreased overall independence, and, because of their harsh lives, they are less acculturated than other Hispanic American elders in their age cohort. Some are newly migrated, have limited financial resources, and work histories as laborers or domestic workers (Markides et al. 1999). Many have feelings of resentment and disappointment about the need for care and believe that family should provide the care. There may be feelings of inadequacy because of the inability to contribute to meeting family needs, resulting in depression and anxiety (Torres 1999).

Mexican American elders experiencing mental health problems are more likely than younger family members to be accepted and provided for within the family out of respect for their age and roles within the family (Abramson, Trejo, & Lai 2002). There may be underlying feelings of embarrassment within the family so that outsiders are not allowed to know about the mental or emotional aliments of family members out of respect for this relative. The onset of a physical disability affecting the ability to work or maintain certain roles within the family may cause elders to be depressed and have feelings of worthlessness which may not be discussed out of respect for elders and to avoid embarrassment.

There has been very limited research about dementia or cognitive impairment among members of racial and ethnic minority groups. It is estimated that Mexican American elders are twice as likely to develop Alzheimer's disease by age ninety compared to non–Mexican American elders (Espino & Lewis 1998). As noted earlier, some families conceal the elder family member with a cognitive impairment to protect the family from shame and embarrassment in the community, and other families may believe that the impairment is "God's will" and cannot be changed. It is important that long-term care service providers show respect for and familiarity with key cultural concepts pertaining to Mexican patients with dementia (Espino et al. 2001).

Yee (1997) estimates that as many as 25 percent of older adults will have some level of cognitive impairment, and therefore nursing home placement will be increasingly needed. When assessing cognitive impairment and identifying available options for Mexican American individuals and families in addressing this problem, social workers need to consider the influence of educational levels, language skills, financial concerns, communication skills, medical history, living conditions, and family support networks. Many impediments arise to accurate assessment of the mental status of Mexican elders. Families may report that the elderly family member is nervous, or they may believe that the impairment is a normal part of aging, instead of identifying dementia as an illness. Social workers should develop "culture fair" verses "culture free" tools for assessing cognitive impairment, (Arguelles & Lowenstein 1997; Kane 2000), and they should be aware that inaccurate Spanish translations may lead to false impairment scores on standardized cognitive assessment instruments such as the Mini Mental Status Examination (Folstein, Folstein, & McHugh 1975).

Because Mexican American families often provide care at home, elders with cognitive impairment may be isolated from available treatments and thus deteriorate faster (Ortiz & Fitten 2000). Not making use of available services may lead to increased physical and cognitive deterioration and overburden already strained family support networks, making nursing home admission a crisis and more problematic. When elders are kept at home longer than is viable, nursing home admission may need to take place quickly, without the full understanding and support of all parties involved, creating greater stress in an already difficult process.

Cox and Monk (1993) examined the widespread belief that Mexican American families do not need nursing home care, because they have large family support networks for caregiving. This belief ignores the realities of the lack of community resources available to families, longer life expectancy, and employment obligations of family members that prohibit twenty-four-hour caregiving at home.

Social workers can educate Mexican American elders and their significant others, as well as interdisciplinary staff, about Alzheimer's disease and other dementias, conditions often frightening and misunderstood. Bell and Troxel (2001) offer a straightforward approach to meeting educational and training needs: they emphasize that, in order to promote culturally sensitive treatment, elders with dementia should be treated as individuals with consideration for how their environment affects their daily life.

VIEWS ABOUT AGING

The aging processes of Mexican American and non–Mexican American elders are generally similar. They continually adapt to physical and cognitive deterioration, and many have decreased income and inadequate support from society. Although they have the same basic human needs as non–Mexican American elders, the needs of many Mexican American elders are intensified as a result of their specific life experiences, which generally increase their chances of aging with severe disabilities (Maldonado 1980). Maldonado identified three types of experiences relevant to understanding Mexican American elders: (1) migration history and level of acculturation; (2) the ability to survive racism and discrimination, and the lack of employment opportunities, along with limited living arrangements, educational opportunities, and resources, all of which may adversely affect the aging process; and (3) adaptation to increasing social changes in their environment, and reaching old age only to realize that their lifelong belief of being taken care of by their family may not be a possibility.

Most Mexican American elders share certain characteristics: they speak Spanish, belong to the Catholic faith, and have strong family values. Traditionally Mexican American elders are respected and remain vital to family decision making. Maldonado (1980) noted that "the Mexican American elderly are a product of their history and drive for survival. A history that includes Mexicanized culture foundations, overt discrimination, and accelerated social change" (p. 29). Traditional values also include *jerarquismo,* a respect for authority or hierarchy, and *personalismo,* the development of trust and mutual respect in a relationship. *Espiritismo* is the belief that good and bad spirits affect a sense of wellness; a focusing on present needs is known as *presentismo.* First-generation Mexican American elders bring the culture and traditions of Mexico to the U.S., including the belief that families should be responsible for care of their elders, a practice that spans generations.

Becerra and Shaw (1984) explain urbanization as a difficult process for Mexican American elders, primarily because it broke up established support networks, roles, and relationships. Acculturation varies among Mexican American elders and should be assessed individually to best understand its impact on an older individual. This will allow a more thorough understanding of values, viewpoints, and experiences affecting aging. The Spanish language influences acculturation, as Mexican American elders may prefer to use Spanish as their primary language and are criticized for not also speaking English well. Maintaining the Spanish language and close-knit communities are strengths that Mexican American elders use to cope with aging and societal changes. Falicov (2005) cautions that "a therapist who quickly becomes an agent of adaptation to the new culture may create more rather than less emotional distress. . . . Promoting acculturation goals may also in effect 'impose' values without awareness of cultural biases as, for example, when the therapist supports the 'Americanized' second generation against 'old-fashioned' parents" (p. 231).

PREFERENCES FOR ELDER CARE

Although Mexican American families strongly believe that "older adults should be cared for within the nurturing environment of the family" (Green 2000, p. 171), this does not mean that Mexican American older adults always want to live with their families. Purdy and Arguello (1992) examined living preferences of Mexican American elderly and found a desire to live alone, independent of but near their family. Findings have also suggested that outside assistance for elder care is preferred over living with and placing additional burdens on their families, but elder caregiving is viewed as the responsibility and preference of Mexican American families.

Less acculturated elders have continued to strongly believe in family responsibility for caregiving, whereas more acculturated elders may consider a nursing home over family if they are cognitively impaired (Johnson et al. 1997). The communities that many Mexican American elders have lived in or moved away from may have been isolated from Anglo-American culture, thereby preserving the family role in elder caregiving, with limited exposure to nursing home services (Resendez & Vargas 1997). Although some caregivers feel the effects of caregiver burden, they may not acknowledge this in describing their feelings (John & McMillian 1998).

COPING WITH CARE RECEIVING

Later adulthood is a difficult life stage in and of itself, particularly as one becomes frail and dependent on others for assistance. Compounding the challenges of the aging process, admission to a nursing home is the initial exposure for many to a living arrangement where they are being cared for by strangers (Brody 1977; Lustbader 2001). The manner in which one copes with this new experience will depend on prior life experiences and one's history of coping with stressful situations, as well as the resident's attitudes and beliefs (Brody 1977). In Mr. Campos's case, the social worker was able to explain to staff that he resisted bathing because he was bathed by a male orderly; he was not comfortable with bathing in the presence of a male, regardless of the man's nurse status, and preferred care by female members of the staff whom he believed showed him more respect.

As stated earlier, some commonly valued attitudes and behaviors among Mexican American elders, such as *personalismo, respeto,* and *simpático,* are integral to their coping with institutionalization. In Cox and Dooley's (1996) study, respondents reported that they wanted to maintain a peaceful situation in the family, so they accepted nursing home placement as the only option for maintaining a sense of *simpático* for the family. Others reported that acceptance of non-family caregiving was very disappointing, and that they had failed to raise their children to respect their elders. The notion that "it is God's will" conveyed a sense of acceptance and making the best of the situation.

Some elders have a genuine concern for the caregiver and need to offer gratitude for the care given. Much has been documented about the strong cohesive Mexican American family support system and its value in elder caregiving; for some elders, however, the care is accepted more easily if it is reciprocal. The elder may want the opportunity to give to the family unit and not just receive (Angel et al. 1996). The opportunity to fulfill and maintain relationships is important to Mexican American elders in nursing homes; residents isolated from family and friends may have a more difficult time (Cox & Dooly 1996). In Mrs. Navarro's case, the social worker understood that Mrs. Navarro had eaten breakfast and lunch with her sister, Josie, every day for more than twenty-five years. When the nursing home and the family arranged for the sisters to eat together again, Mrs. Navarro began to eat more food.

ISSUES WITHIN NURSING HOMES

COMMUNICATION

Social workers and other staff providing services to Mexican American residents and their relatives should use the language the resident prefers and understands best. Social workers who do not speak Spanish fluently enough to provide services in this language should understand that more than a translation is required to establish a professional relationship with the resident. Translators may be useful for converting written materials or documents so that elders or significant others understand them, but when feelings need to be conveyed, the social workers should brief the interpreter in advance of the session to alert that person to how the resident may be feeling so that the interpreter can convey the resident's feelings and understand the resident's need for empathy (Alexander 2004).

Nursing home social workers need to understand the use of interpreters versus translators and the communication that social work requires in this setting. The use of interpreters versus translators may depend on availability and the situation in which the social worker and elder are engaged. Sue and Sue (1990) suggest that, if an interpreter or a translator will be used, it is important to meet in advance to discuss the purpose and situation in order for accurate interpretation or translation to take place. Appropriate preparation by the social worker can foster respectfulness toward the resident and family. It is also important to note the discomfort that residents and their relatives may feel upon hearing one's name pronounced almost beyond recognition, which may also be seen as a sign of disrespect (Yee 1997).

The use of non–social work staff who may speak the language also needs careful consideration in order to address issues of confidentiality and documentation. It is important that confidentiality remains central to all parties involved. The social worker will need to document the use of a translator or interpreter in the medical record and may need to add this as a requirement in the treatment plan. Alexander (2004) points out that using a family member, including a child, is discouraged, as the elder may believe that certain subjects should not be discussed with family.

INTERACTION WITH STAFF AND FAMILY

Mexican American elders generally do not arrive for admission to the nursing home alone but are accompanied by many significant family members. As discussed previously, *personalismo, respeto,* and *simpático* are important values to guide communication and behavior with Mexican American nursing home residents and their relatives (Falicov 1996). Falicov (2005) advises that,

> Manifesting real interest in the client, rather than gaining data via referral sheets or obtaining many behavioral details about a problem, is essential, given

the Mexican American emphasis on *personalismo,* or building personal relationships. Similarly, a therapist who suggests an explicit contract about the number of sessions or treatment goals may be too task-oriented rather than person-oriented. (p. 237)

Staff may feel challenged if a large number of visitors and relatives are involved with the resident. Social workers should help staff identify all family members who need access to information that is generally given only to the responsible party listed in the medical record. The decision to supply information needs to be based on the importance of the elder's relationship with both distant as well as close relatives.

It became apparent in Mrs. Navarro's situation that her sister was very important to her, and that Josie's inability to visit impeded Mrs. Navarro's progress. The social worker helped Josie complete an application for transportation services offered through the city that would enable her to visit. In Mr. Campos's situation, the social worker collaborated with the interdisciplinary team to facilitate daily visits by Mrs. Campos as part of her husband's routine in order to enhance his recovery and meet her need to provide care. In both these cases, residents and relatives would benefit if staff encouraged visits at times that fit conveniently into their schedules. Some nursing homes have "no set visitation hours" so that significant others may gain a sense of partnership with the nursing home as a caregiver.

If caregiving was performed at home prior to admission, then some Mexican American families may have difficulty letting go of their roles or duties. The nursing home staff may need support from the social worker to involve significant others in daily care such as helping at mealtimes or with bathing.

Lustbader (2001) discusses cultural changes that have been made in some nursing homes such as the Pioneer Network (Barken 1999) and the Eden Alternative (Thomas 1994), which focus on the dignity and individuality of the resident. Social workers who can embrace such philosophies are better equipped to foster a culturally sensitive atmosphere for the elderly, their families, and the staff. Rehabilitation in such a system begins with a psychosocial assessment to identify the needs and strengths that the resident and family have that can assist them in coping with the situation and also promote a trusting relationship with the staff. Social workers should consult with the interdisciplinary team to increase the team's understanding of the elder's needs, as well as ensure that recovery and coping are promoted by family involvement and that staff does not direct judgmental attitudes and behaviors toward the resident or family. Social work intervention can provide an opportunity for elders and their families to grieve the loss of their role as primary caregiver. Intervention focuses on a relationship with *confianza* (trust) and *respeto* (respect) allowing for *personalismo* and integration of the family into the caregiving process.

Social workers may find it useful to strengthen their relations with significant family members by frequently contacting them. Nursing home care planning conferences traditionally occur on specific days at times that may conflict with family schedules. Social workers may adapt the care plan process to assure that those family members who are significant to the elder are included, particularly with the participation of the certified nurse assistant involved in direct care. It is important that social workers engage the family in the rehabilitation process, clearly explaining expectations with sensitivity to family needs, as was done in Mrs. Navarro's case. Families will need support and encouragement to learn new roles, and at the same time social workers will need to encourage staff to be tolerant of the family's involvement in care.

It is not uncommon for a nursing home to offer short-term rehabilitation services, paid for by Medicare, in which discharge planning is crucial to the recovery process. Social workers can be more effective with discharge planning by assessing, early in the rehabilitation process, where the elder will reside and who the primary caregiver will be, and by consulting with the interdisciplinary team regarding the need for physical accommodations in housing arrangements, assistive devices, and need for referrals and support during the discharge process. The rehabilitation team may include the primary physician, registered nurse, licensed vocational nurse, certified nurse assistant, physical, occupational and speech therapists, dietician, chaplain, activity coordinator, geriatric psychiatrist, and licensed social worker. The interdisciplinary team will assist elders and their families in understanding the rehab goal of promoting the highest level of functional independence. Some Mexican American families may view rehab treatments as disrespectful to the elder, as the treatments can be painful and will emphasize the elder's limitations. Relatives may also resent the rehab experience, as their inability to provide direct care may make them feel ashamed.

Often this is the first experience with a nursing home for Mexican American elders and their relatives. It may be helpful for social workers to explore available resources with the resident and relatives along with planning options for addressing short- and long-term needs. It is critical to explain the role of social workers in contrast to the other interdisciplinary team members, and to maintain a collection of culture-specific community resources that can promote positive relationships with long-term caregivers in the community.

Cultural sensitivity begins with the willingness of long-term care organizations to understand the changing nursing home population, with its variations in age, ethnic and racial composition, and family expectations. Adopting and promoting a philosophy of individuality and "home" gives residents, families, and staff the opportunity to personalize the environment and provide comfort during this life transition. An implication of Kolb's (2003) study of ethnically and racially diverse nursing home residents and their relatives and friends was that "staff behaviors that communicate care and empathy to residents and their caregiving relatives are especially helpful," and she suggested that their significance to Latina/o caregivers might reflect cultural values of *familismo* and *personalismo* (pp. 166–167). Becerra and Shaw (1984) describe how Mexican American families define a positive caregiving relationship as a respectful, two-way relationship between the elder and direct care staff. Mexican American elders in a nursing home value the *dignidad, delicadeza,* and *comprensión* (dignity, gentleness, and understanding) with which staff treats them (Odell & Stafford 1992).

FOOD PREFERENCES

Food preferences, like other preferences, should not be generalized with regard to Mexican American elders. Food preferences are influenced by life experiences, income, education, geographical area, acculturation level, and traditions. Many Mexican American elders are accustomed to a diet that reflects pre-Columbian, Spanish, French, and, most recently, U.S. culture. Mexican American foods have traditionally included complex carbohydrates, predominately corn and corn products, rice, beans, and breads. Protein may come from eggs, beans, fish, shellfish, and meat of all types—beef, pork, chicken, and goat. A common cooking method is frying, and so the diet is high in fat but low in calcium, iron, vitamin A, folacin, and vitamin C (American Dietetic Association 1989). Dietary changes between generations of Mexican Americans is resulting in healthy nutritional changes, including increased consumption of dairy products, less fatty meats, and decreasing use of lard and Mexican creams. However, income generally continues to dictate the food choices families make; change is occurring and healthier foods are eaten, but these foods are often more expensive.

The families of Mr. Campos and Mrs. Navarro could be supportive after nursing home placement by preparing and bringing traditional dishes such as *arroz con pollo* (chicken with rice), *calavasa* (squash and pork), and *frijoles a la charra* (a bean soup), all of which may improve the resident's appetite. Staff can ask relatives for recipes to incorporate into the menu. An important consideration is the social aspect of meals; families eating together and conversing can enhance the well-being of the elder and relatives as they adjust to the nursing home. Ongoing educational outreach into Mexican American communities can also promote healthy cooking alternatives without losing residents' customary, unique cultural cuisine (Caudle 1993).

RECREATIONAL ACTIVITIES

The emphasis on activities in nursing homes generally derives from an Anglo-American culture of birthday parties and Bible study, with limited consideration of cultural and recreational variations (Thomas 1996). Because of their strong work ethic and the little importance they may give to hobbies such as crafts, reading, or exercise, Mexican American elders may not view retirement as a positive life event. For many, leisure activity was a luxury they could not afford throughout their earlier lives. However, this reality can provide opportunities for the nursing home staff to develop a sense of community in activity planning with elders (Facio 1996).

Continuation of participation in meaningful activities is important and may include creating artwork, participating in the resident council, going on outings to familiar neighborhoods, watching *novellas* (Spanish soap operas) on TV, cooking and planning celebrations with staff, and participating in activities, such as poetry writing, that require personal privacy. Andrade and Korte (1993) explore the use of reminiscence group work that may have positive effects on the transition of Mexican American elders into the nursing home. The sharing of stories, *dichos* (riddles), and *cuentos* (storytelling) at family social gatherings is familiar among Mexican American elders. The establishment of a men's-only group, or a women's-only group, may be a useful approach to customary socialization and discussion of politics, past work experiences, and family traditions.

For some female elders, life experiences may include belonging to social clubs and attending dances at neighborhood senior centers. Other traditional activities that can be developed in nursing homes include *bunco* and *lotería* (Mexican bingo) games. Staff can explore whether local church groups have members who will volunteer to provide the nursing home with these games.

In San Antonio, Texas, social clubs comprised mostly of Mexican Americans raise funds for local neighborhood needs or work together with religious organizations to secure donations or scholarships. For some elders, maintaining membership in these groups after admission to a nursing home is important to self-esteem, identity, and a sense of contributing to the community. Involvement in a religious organization may also serve as a form of leisure activity, and continuing to attend one's local worship service of choice may be important for promoting a sense of well-being (Facio 1996). Establishing partnerships with such groups may be beneficial to the nursing home as a whole as a resource for activity programs, volunteers, and fund-raising. Groups may sponsor bimonthly dances, donate prizes for *lotería*, facilitate games within the nursing home, or offer transportation to worship services or club meetings (Torres 1999). Damron-Rodriguez (1998) observes that "social activities in senior centers and residential facilities that center around Halloween or St. Patrick's Day may totally lack meaning for the ethnic elder. A life without meaningful cultural ritual and ceremony, substituted with Valentine's Day parties or Bingo, may add a sense of despair rather than integrity" (p. 63).

END-OF-LIFE ISSUES

Some elderly Mexican Americans see death from the standpoint of *Fé* (spirituality) as a coping mechanism, viewing death as a natural part of life and dependent on God's will (Talamantes, Gomez, & Braun 2000) . Some have the fatalistic outlook that individuals have little influence and ability to intervene in what has been predetermined (Markides & Mindel 1987). These values imply that individuals do not have the right to make decisions about death, dying, or the withholding of treatment. Discussion of advance directives may depend on the level of acculturation, income, and age of family members. Thus social workers may experience barriers in discussing advance directives because of the religious and cultural values of Mexican American residents and their relatives. The issue of resuscitation wishes may also be a difficult topic to explore, as some elders and their families may feel that only God has the right to make this decision. Mexican American elders may prefer to have cardiopulmonary resuscitation (CPR) initiated and be considered to have full-code status. Another cultural belief is that a terminal diagnosis or certain treatment options may not be discussed with elders so that they can maintain a positive attitude and continue to have hope.

Research with focus groups of consumers and providers in Michigan and Arizona determined that attitudes toward palliative care in terminal illness were intertwined with culturally based beliefs about the role of family in caregiving and religious and spiritual beliefs (Gelfand et al. 2001). Relatives also may be embarrassed by use of hospice care, as it can be seen to reflect the inability of relatives to provide care.

Important rituals around death include planning a mass in honor of the person's death, taking food or a gift to the grave on *Día de los Muertos* (Day of the dead), or building an altar for offerings of the person's favorite things in life. Often poetry written about the individual may be read, and this may best convey what the person meant to others. Holding a vigil is a common practice in which family and friends offer support to the elder in the dying process. Families may have candles burning in constant remembrance of the deceased individual. These rituals serve to honor the person and bring the family together for support, mourning, maintaining relationships, and celebration (Talamantes, Gomez, & Braun 2000).

SOCIAL WORK PRACTICE CONSIDERATIONS

Admission to a nursing home is the last resort for many families and a difficult transition for elders and their significant others. Brody (1977) estimated that the most difficult and crucial time for residents coping with nursing home placement generally lasts about three months following admission. Considering the information presented earlier in this chapter, what can be done to assist with the transition process for Mexican American elders? It is critical to understand that each Mexican American elder and each of their relatives is a unique individual within a broad cultural group of Mexican Americans, and expectations about behavior during the transitional period should not be generalized. Fandetti and Goldmeier (1988) note that, to avoid generalizations, "ethnicity should be seen as an emergent property rather than a static, unchanging phenomenon" (p. 172). A resident's culture should be assessed from the viewpoint of the person's life experiences, significant relationships, and other aspects of the individual. Reminiscence has been used effectively to help Mexican Americans address certain subjects in old age including, but not limited to, ego syntonic issues, experiences with racism, and processes of cultural change (Zuniga 1989). Learning about the lifelong experiences of elders through reminiscence helps social workers understand changes and diversity in the elders' experiences.

SOCIAL WORK VALUES AND ETHICS

Social work ethics and values support recognition and validation of individual differences, and practice consistent with these values is essential in work with Mexican American elders and their relatives, as well as work in helping members of interdisciplinary teams to individualize care. Social work practice in the nursing home has developed significantly with the passage of the federal Omnibus Reconciliation Act (OBRA), which emphasizes the dignity and self-determination of all institutionalized individuals. Passed in 1987 and enacted in 1990, OBRA brought significant changes in addressing residents' psychosocial needs. Nursing homes with 120 beds or more would now have to employ a full-time, licensed social worker to address this new standard (Haulotte and Purvis 1996).

The National Association of Social Workers (NASW) *Code of Ethics* (2004) includes two principles to guide social workers in adhering to culturally competent practice with Mexican American nursing home residents and their families: (1) recognize the dignity and worth of the person, and understand cultural and ethnic differences; and (2) work for social justice, with sensitivity toward the effects of oppressive hardships and respect for cultural diversity (Crewe 2004).

Applewhite (1998) has identified several relevant core values that relate specifically to social work practice with Mexican American elders:

- Value cultural diversity and cultural integrity with a genuine and open appreciation of inter and intra group differences among elderly Latinos.
- Value the social and historical contributions of elderly Latinos to their culture, community, and broader society.
- Respect the help seeking behavior of Latino elders
- Value the cultural resources and natural support system utilized by elderly Latinos in problem solving.
- Value the strength of the nuclear and extended family and fictive kin, and the role the elder Latinos assume in this family constellation.
- Respect the traditional beliefs, folk methods, and spiritual roles of elderly Latinos in the folk healing process.
- Value culture and ethnicity as interactive and emergent forces in later life among elderly Latino cohorts.
- Validate the experiences, both positive and negative, of elderly Latinos from a social, cultural, historical, political, and spiritual perspective. (pp. 7–8)

These values follow the concepts in the NASW *Code of Ethics* and OBRA, and offer a foundation for understanding culturally competent social work practice.

To educate social workers who are entering the field of caring for the elderly and increase their understanding of cultural competence, Davis (2003) offers a life course perspective or "life ways" framework. The "life ways" perspective values the reality that within all ethnic groups there remains individuality that the elder brings from his or her life experiences. This is particularly relevant to elderly Mexican Americans who strongly value relationships formed with others. Davis's model seeks to teach social workers to view elder clients from the perspective of a teaching role, allowing for a therapeutic relationship to develop through the fundamental social work skills of active listening, reflecting, and exploring the individual's life story. At times social workers rely solely on written material about specific ethnic groups, which often leads to generalizations or assumptions that fail to result in needed services.

CULTURE CHANGE IN NURSING HOMES

The culture changes that some nursing homes are undergoing give social workers the opportunity to advocate practices that promote self-determination, the feeling of being needed and valued, and respect and dignity in aging for all nursing home residents. Social workers must continue to strive for the elimination of loneliness, helplessness, and boredom that so many older adults and staff of nursing homes experience (Thomas 1996). The Eden Alternative and Pioneering movements propose instrumental changes in how nursing homes treat residents, using approaches that are consistent with social work values. These initiatives are consistent with the Mexican American value of *personalismo*, which requires relationships of mutual trust and respect, knowing who the caregivers are, and consistency in staffing. Cross-training of non-nursing staff in ADL needs increases the staff's familiarity with residents and promotes relationships.

THE NURSING HOME CAREGIVERS

Nursing homes face critical challenges in promoting quality of life for Mexican American elders and at the same time meeting higher regulatory standards, tighter financial strains, and the difficulty of finding a qualified, caring workforce. Current workforce trends may have a positive effect on Mexican American elderly, as minority women are increasingly filling the positions of nursing aides (Bonder, Martin, & Miracle 2001, Callahan 2000). Some observers suggest that the strong caregiving role that many Mexican American women are raised with encourages them to pursue nursing careers or enter other helping professions to fulfill a caregiving need (Beckett & Dungee-Anderson 2000). Mexican Americans are estimated to occupy nearly one-third of nursing assistant positions, which historically entail low pay, little recognition, and hard physical and emotional work, conditions that lead to dramatic shortages in a workforce of vulnerable minority women (DuBois, Yavno, & Stanford 2001).

Social workers can promote staff awareness, sensitivity, and skill development, and also support career ladders for certified nursing assistants as well as the training of staff to care for residents with dementia. Mexican American elders who hear their familiar language and see familiar faces can derive much comfort in their transition to a nursing home. Social workers' participation in interdisciplinary diversity training can enhance staff understanding of residents' and staff needs and dispel generalizations about Mexican American elders and Mexican American staff.

UNDERUTILIZATION OF LONG-TERM CARE

A widespread belief, according to Facio (1996), is that Mexican American families provide all necessary care for elders, and thus there is no need for nursing home services. This strongly held belief, often taught even within Mexican American families and society, reinforces the idea of "the good daughter" or "the good son" who takes care of her or his elder parent at home. Markides, Martin, & Gomez (1983), however, discuss the increasing level of care needed by elders as physical and mental deterioration occur and resources are used up, underlining that the "romantic" notion of "taking care of our own" is unrealistic. There is a lack of time, knowledge, training, and financial means necessary for long-term caregiving at home. Because of the misperception that Mexican American families can manage cognitive impairment, behavioral problems, immobility, and incontinence, society has failed to realize that nursing home caregiving often is the only option available to families, and that additional services may be desired (Angel et al. 1996).

A number of issues influence underutilization. Mexican American elders may feel uneasy about living in a predominately Anglo-American culture (Angel & Angel 1997). Another stressor may be the limited availability of facilities close to the family network, and possible lack of transportation that would allow visitation and support maintenance of relationships. Mexican American families may have limited knowledge of how nursing home care is paid for, and they often lack access to a Medicaid caseworker, especially if they live in a rural community. Medicaid must pay for nursing home care for residents belonging to a great many ethnic and racial groups because of the exorbitant costs, but there are a limited number of certified Medicaid beds, and these beds may not be in long-term care available near the family. Prior to admission, Mexican American elders may combine their income with the family's to support the family's needs, which means that admission to a facility under Medicaid would mean loss of income for the family. This may create emotional distress for the elder who knows that his or her family needs the income; the decision to enter a nursing home would thus contradict the cultural norm of *familismo*.

Contradictory values and beliefs about the family's caregiving responsibility and feelings of burdening the family may cause Mexican American elders to "[suffer] in silence," as they do not want to cause additional stress for the family (Conward & Hernandez 1992, p. 83). Fears of discrimination, substandard care, and limited family support are other concerns of Mexican American elders (Johnson et al. 1997). Discrimination, whether real or imagined, may prohibit the use of caregiving options. Greater awareness and enforcement of civil rights may be necessary in the admission practices of nursing homes (Lacayo 1993; Torres 1999). Relatives may also feel ashamed when they realize they can no longer provide necessary care and seek nursing home placement (Espino et al. 1998).

In a youth oriented-culture, Mexican American young adults are pursuing education, finding employment, moving away from traditionally close-knit Mexican American communities, and leaving behind aging family members and traditional caregiving beliefs (Green & Monahan 1984). Younger adults are exposed to more information, and, as they become more socioeconomically secure, they become aware of the availability of long-term care resources for their aging family members. According to several authors, societal changes that are weakening the Mexican American family's ability to provide elder care include longer life expectancy, lower fertility, women in the work force, fewer two-parent families, and mobility of children away from their aging relatives (Becerra & Shaw 1984; Angel et al. 2004)

IMPLICATIONS FOR POLICY AND EDUCATION

The future caregiving needs of Mexican American elders and their families will depend greatly on changes in today's long-term care practices. Nursing home care is often the option of last resort for elders and families, and policy should reflect such personal choice with emphasis on caregiver resources in the community. The idea of providing funding to relatives who want to attempt home care and may need support, including financial help to offset the caregiver's inability to work, needs to be diligently pursued. Torres-Gil (1999) and Espino (1993) call for the expansion of community-based services that allow families the option of keeping a relative at home.

The assumption that Mexican American families do not need to use nursing home services because relatives will provide all necessary assistance may have resulted in limited service development, creating a disservice to many in need. The employment of professional staff that is both bilingual and bicultural is important, as well as encouraging leisure activities and traditions that may result in more Mexican Americans feeling welcome as consumers (Angel & Angel 1997). A grass-roots educational plan for the community is needed to provide resource and referral information on all aspects of caregiving, health care, financial supports, and long-term care planning such as nursing home placement. This plan can empower elders and their significant others by informing them of services that include respite, home health, in-home provider programs, day care, nursing homes, senior centers, and accessible urban and rural transportation. Policy makers need to develop tax credits for in-home family caregivers, expanded disability transportation services, and intergenerational housing options to promote a sense of community and family which is crucial to many Mexican American elders. Funding for long-term care organizations that provide child care or living quarters for employees at the facilities all promote family friendly work policies and benefit residents.

In the areas of education and research, Williams and Torrez (1998) criticize previous writings and studies regarding Mexican American elders, suggesting that these support stereotyping or even confusion about this group. Research has reflected the viewpoints of Anglo-American researchers, and generalizations have been made from information gathered in rural communities or that relies on Anglo, middle-class elder males as subjects. Research on support systems that Mexican Americans use may begin to address one societal assumption about the concept of *familism*: mistaking a family's underutilization of care services as a family's "informed" choice to provide the care. Community caregiving resource development for Mexican American families cannot be based on societal assumptions. Research and education efforts could also provide an accurate understanding of the differences, rather than similarities, in the role of family in elder caregiving in Mexico and in Mexican American families. Research is needed that explores how various subgroups within the Mexican American population cope with nursing home life, taking into account acculturation, assimilation, education, income, values, and familial relationships.

CONCLUSION

Latina/o elders in the U.S. are estimated to reach 16 percent of the older adult population by 2050, compared to 4 percent in 1990 (Queiro-Tajalli 2000). Social workers need to be prepared to educate providers and consumers of long-term care services about cultural and ethnic sensitivity. Nursing homes are experiencing changes in two primary areas: who will the future residents be; and (2) who will make up the workforce necessary to meet the increasing need for long-term care.

This chapter provides information about Mexican American elders and emphasized that each elder lives her or his life based on a unique combination of regional, historical, political, socioeconomic, and migration histories that make up the Mexican American culture. Mexican American elders bring diverse work histories and family traditions, strengths that help them cope in this stage of life. These elders are a heterogeneous group of people with similarities and differences. The promotion of a sense of residents' *bienestar*, or well-being, a connection to a community, and individuality remain crucial while meeting regulatory standards to provide good quality of life to all people who live in nursing homes.

REFERENCES

Abramson, A. T., Trejo, L., Lai, D. W. L. (2002). Culture and mental health: Providing appropriate services for a diverse older population." *Generations* 26 (1), 21–27.

Alexander, T. (2004). Lost in translation. Presented at the Twenty-fourth Annual C. J. Collins Symposium, Our Lady of the Lake University, San Antonio, Texas.

Andrade, P. A., & Korte, A. O. (1993). En aquellos tiempos: A reminiscence group with the Hispanic elderly. *Journal of Gerontological Social Work* 20 (3–4), 25–42.

Angel, J. L., et al. (1996). Nativity, declining health, and preferences in living arrangements among elderly Mexican Americans: Implications for long-term care. *The Gerontologist 36*, (4), 464- 473.

Angel, J. L., et al. (2004). Can family still cope? Social support and health as determinates of nursing home use in the older Mexican-origin population. *Journal of Aging and Health* 16 (3), 338–354.

Angel, J. L., & Angel, R. J. (1998). Aging trends—Mexican Americans in the southwestern USA. *Journal of Cross-Cultural Gerontology* 13, 281–290.

Angel, R. J., & Angel, J. L. (1997). *Who Will Care for Us? Aging and Long-Term Care in Multicultural America.* New York: New York University Press.

Applewhite, S. L. (1995). Curanderismo: Demystifying the health beliefs and practices of elderly Mexican Americans. *Health and Social Work* 20 (4), 247-253.

Applewhite, S. L. (1998). Culturally competent practice with elderly Latinos. In M. Delgado (Ed.), *Latino elders and the twenty-first century: Issues and challenges for culturally competent research and practice*, pp. 1–15. New York: Haworth.

Arguelles, T., & Loewnstein, D. (1997). Research say *si* to development of culturally appropriate cognitive assessment tools. *Generations* 21 (1), 30–31.

Barkan, B. (1981). The Live Oak regenerative community: Reconnnecting culture within the long-term care environment. *Aging Magazine* 2 (7), 321–322.

Ballesteros, O. A., & Ballesteros, M. (1992). *"Viejo el sol y todavilla brilla" Mexican sayings: The treasure of a people.* Austin, Tex.: Eakin.

Becerra, R. M., & Shaw, D. (1984). *The Hispanic elderly: A research guide.* Lanham, Md.: University Press of America.

Beckett, J. O., & Dungee-Anderson, D. (2000). Older persons of color: Asian/Pacific Islander Americans, African Americans, Hispanic Americans, and American Indians. In R. L. Schneider, N. P. Kropf, & A. J. Kisor (Eds.), *Gerontological social work: Knowledge, service settings, and special populations*, pp. 257–301. Belmont, Calif.: Wadsworth.

Bell, V., & Troxel, D. (2001). *The Best Friends staff: Building a culture of care in Alzheimer's programs.* Baltimore, Md.: Health Professionals Press.

Bonder, B., Martin, L., & Miracle, A. (2001). Achieving cultural competence: The challenge for clients and healthcare workers in a multicultural society. *Generations* 25 (1), 35–42.

Brody, E. (1977). *Long-term care of older people: A practical guide.* New York: Human Sciences Press.

Callahan, J. J., Jr. (2000). Policy perspectives on workforce issues and care of older people. *Generations* 25 (1), 12–16.

Caudle, P. (1993). Providing culturally sensitive health care to Hispanic clients. *Nurse Practitioner* 18 (12), 40–51.

Conward, T., & Hernandez, G. G. (1992). Ethical issues in health care delivery to elderly people: Specific focus on black Americans and Hispanics. In F. Safford and G. Krell (Eds.), *Gerontology for health professionals: A practice guide*, pp. 96–112. Washington, D.C.: NASW Press.

Cox, C., & Monk, A. (1993). Hispanic culture and Alzheimer's patients. *Health & Social Work* 18 (2), 92–100.

Cox, E. O., & Dooley, A. C. (1996). Care receivers' perception of their role in the care process. *Journal of Gerontological Social Work* 26 (1/2), 133–152.

Crewe, S. E. (2004). Ethnogerontology: Preparing culturally competent social workers for the diverse facing of aging. *Journal of Gerontological Social Work* 43 (4), 45–58.

Damron-Rodriguez, J. (1998). Respecting ethnic elders: A perspective for care providers. *Journal of Gerontological Social Work* 29 (2/3), 53–72.

Davis, M. (2003). Life course perspectives: Life ways. Presented at The Conference: Multicultural Awareness in Working with Older Adults and Their Families. National Association of Social Workers Texas Committee on Aging and the University of Texas at Austin School of Social Work and the CSWE SAGE Project, Austin, Texas.

de la Torre, A., & Estrada, A. (2001). *Mexican Americans and health*. Tucson: University of Arizonia Press.

Delgado, M. (1998). *Latino elders and the twenty-first century: Issues and challenges for culturally competent research and practice*. New York: Haworth.

Du Bois, B. C., Yavno, C.H., & Stanford, P. E. (2001). Care options for older Mexican Americans: Issues affecting health and long-term care service needs. In L.K. Olson (Ed.), *Age through ethnic lenses*, pp. 71–85. Oxford: Rowman & Littlefield.

Espino, D. V. (1993). Hispanic elderly and long-term care: Implications for ethnically sensitive services. In C. M. Barresi and D. E. Stull (Eds.), *Ethnic elderly and long-term care*, pp. 101–112. New York: Springer.

Espino, D., & Lewis, R. (1998). Dementia in older minority populations. *Journal of Geriatric Psychiatry* 6, S19–S25.

Espino, D., et al. (1988). Hispanic and Non-Hispanic elderly on admission to the nursing home: A pilot study. *The Gerontologist* 28 (6), 821–824.

Espino, D., et al. (2001). Mexican American elders with dementia in long term care. *Clinical Gerontologist* 23 (3–4), 83–96.

Facio, E. (1996). *Understanding older Chicanas*. Thousand Oaks, Calif.: Sage.

Falicov, C. (1996). Mexican families. In M. McGoldrick, J. Giordano, & J. Pearce (Eds.), *Ethnicity and family therapy*, pp. 169–182. New York: Guilford.

Falicov, C. (2005). Mexican families. In M. McGoldrick, J. Giordano, & N. Garcia-Preto (Eds.), *Ethnicity and family therapy*, pp. 229–241. New York: Guilford.

Fandetti, D. V., & Goldmeier, J. (1988). Social workers as cultural mediators in health care settings. *Health & Social Work* 13 (3), 171–179.

Folstein, M. F., Folstein, S. E., & McHugh, P. R. (1975). Mini-mental status: A practical method for grading the mental state of patients for the clinician. *Journal of Psychiatric Research* 12, 189–198.

Gelfand, D., et al. (2001). Mexicans and care for the terminally ill: Family, hospice, and the church. *American Journal of Hospice and Palliative Care* 18 (6), 391–396.

Green, R. (2000). *Social work with the aged and their families*. Hawthorne, N.Y.: Aldine De Gruyter.

Green,V. R., & Monahan, D. J. (1984). Comparative utilization of community based long term care services by Hispanic and Anglo elderly in a case management system. *Journal of Gerontoloogy* 39 (6), 730–735.

Haulotte, S. M., & Purvis, P. (1996). Claiming your space: How to earn acceptance and explain your role. In J. Mc Neil (Ed.), *Guidelines for nursing home social workers*, pp. 15–30 (IQILTHC series Report 96–4). San Marcos: School of Health Professionals, Southwest Texas State University.

John, R., & McMillian, B. (1998). Exploring caregiving burden among Mexican Americans: Cultural prescriptions, family dilemmas. *Journal of Aging and Ethnicity* 1 (2), 93–111.

John, R., Resendiz, J., & De Vargas, L. (1997). Beyond familism? Familism as explicit motive for eldercare among Mexican American caregivers. *Journal of Cross Cultural Gerontology* 12, 145–162.

Johnson, R. A., et al. (1997). Residential preferences and eldercare views of Hispanic elders. *Journal of Cross Cultural Gerontology* 12, 91–107.

Kane, M. N. (2000). Ethnoculturally-sensitive practice and Alzheimer's disease. *American Journal of Alzheimer's Disease* 15 (2), 80–86.

Keefe, S., & A. M. Padilla (1987). *Chicano ethnicity*. Alburquerque: University of New Mexico Press.

Kolb, P. (2003). *Caring for our elders: Multicultural experiences with nursing home placement*. New York: Columbia University Press.

Lacayo, C. G. (1993). Hispanic elderly: Policy issues in long-term care. In C.M. Barresi & D.E. Stull (Eds.), *Ethnic elderly and long-term care*, pp. 223–234. New York: Springer.

Lecca, P. J., et al. (1998). *Cultural competency in health, social, and human services*. New York: Garland.

Loera, J., et al. (2001). Use of herbal medicine by older Mexican Americans. *Journals of Gerontology*, series A, *Biological Sciences and Medical Sciences* 56A (11), M714–M718.

Lustbader, W. (2001). The pioneer challenge: A radical change in the culture of nursing homes. In L. S. Noelker & Z. Harel (Eds.), *Linking quality of long-term care and quality of life*, pp.185–203. New York: Springer.

Maldonado, D. (1980). The ethnic minority elderly: The case of the Mexican American. In R. Wright (Ed.), *Black/Chicano elderly: Service delivery within a cultural context*, pp. 29–30. Arlington: Graduate School of Social Work, University of Texas.

Markides, K. S., Martin, H. W., & Gomez, E. (1996). Older Mexican Americans: A study in an urban barrio. In E. Facio (Ed.), *Understanding older Chicanas*, pp. 61–76. Thousand Oaks, Calif.: Sage.

Markides, K. S., & Mindel, C. H. (1987). *Aging and ethnicity*. Newbury Park, Calif.: Sage.

Markides, K. S., et al. (1999). The health of Mexican American elderly: Selected findings from the Hispanic EPESE. In M. L. Wykle & A. B. Ford (Eds.), *Serving minority elders in the 21st century*, pp.72–90. New York: Springer.

Mayers, R. (1989). Use of folk medicine by elderly Mexican-American women. *Journal of Drug Issues* 19 (2), 283–295.

Odell, C. R., & Safford, F. (1992). Working with traditional and nontraditional families of the elderly. In F. Safford & G. Krell (Eds.), *Gerontology for health professionals: A practice guide*, pp. 80–95. Washington D.C.: NASW Press.

Ortiz, F., & Fitten, L. J. (2000). Barriers to healthcare access for cognitively impaired older Hispanics. *Alzheimer's Disease and Associated Disorders* 14 (3), 141–150.

Purdy, J. K., & Arguello, D.(1992). Hispanic familism in caretaking of older adults: Is it functional? *Journal of Gerontological Social Work* 19 (2), 29–43.

Queiro-Tajalli, I. (2000). Social work intervention with special populations. In R. R. Greene (Ed.), *Social work with the aged and their families*, pp. 161–175. New York: Aldine De Gruyter.

Ruiz, D. S. (1995). A demographic and epidemiologic profile of the ethnic elderly. In D. K.

Padgett (Ed.), *Handbook on ethnicity, aging, and mental health,* pp. 3–17. Westport, Conn.: Greenwood.

Stone, R. I., & Yamada, Y. (1998). Ethics and the frontline long-term care worker: A challenge for the 21st century. *Generations* 22 (3), 45–51.

Sue, D. W., & Sue, D. (1990). *Counseling the culturally different: Theory and practice.* New York: Wiley.

Talamantes, M. A., Gomez, C., & Braun, K. (2000). Advance directives and end-of-life care: The Hispanic perspective. In K. L. Braun, J. H. Pietsch, & P. L. Blanchette (Eds.), *Cultural issues in end-of-life decision making,* pp. 83–99. Thousand Oaks, Calif.: Sage.

Talamantes, M. A., Lowler, W. R., & Espino, D. V. (1995). *Hispanic American elders: Caregiving norms surrounding dying and the use of hospice services: Hospice care and cultural diversity.* New York: Haworth.

Thomas, W. (1996). *Life worth living. How someone you love can still enjoy life in the nursing home. The Eden Alternative in action.* Acton, Mass.: Vander Wyk & Burnham.

Torres, S. (1999). Barriers to mental-health-care access faced by Hispanic elderly. In M. L. Wykle & A. B. Ford (Eds.), *Serving minority elders in the 21st century,* pp. 200–218. New York: Springer.

Torres-Gil, F. (1990). Aging in Hispanic America. In Research Papers Presented at Minority Affairs Initiative Empowerment Conferences. Washington D.C.: AARP.

U.S. Census Bureau (2000). *Census 2000 Profile.* Washington, D.C.: U.S. Government Printing Office.

Williams, N., & Torrez, D. J. (1998). Grandparenthood among Hispanics. In M. E. Szinovacz (Ed.), *Handbook on grandparenthood,* pp. 87–96.Westport, Conn.: Greenwood.

Yee, D. L. (1997). Can long-term care assessments be culturally responsive? *Generations* 21 (1), 25–29.

Zuniga, M. (1989). Mexican-American elderly and reminiscence: Interventions. *Journal of Gerontological Social Work* 14 (3–4), 61–73.

RESOURCES

Organizations and Websites

Ethnic Elders Care Network. www.ecarnet@yahoo.com.
National Alliance for Hispanic Health. http://www.alliance@hispanichealth.org.
National Center for Cultural Competency. http://gucchd.georgetown.edu/nccc/index.html.
National Council of La Raza Headquarters. www.nclr.org/ (202) 289–1380.
San Antonio Hispanic Chamber of Commerce. www.sahcc.org.
Su Familia—National Hispanic Family Health Helpline. 1–866–783–2645.

Additional Readings

De Mente, B. L. (1996). *NTC's dictionary of Mexican Cultural code words.* Lincolnwood, Ill.: NTC.

Montejano, D. (1987). *Anglos and Mexicans in the making of Texas, 1836–1986.* Austin: University of Texas Press.

Rosales, R. (2000). *The illusion of inclusion: The untold political story of San Antonio.* Austin: University of Texas Press.

Skerry, P. (1993). *Mexican Americans: The ambivalent minority.* Cambridge, Mass.: Harvard University Press.

8

Puerto Rican Elders

María Cuadrado

Mrs. Rodriguez, the third in a family of six siblings, came to New York City as a newly-wed in 1942. She was then twenty, and, like many Puerto Rican females arriving at the time, began as a piece worker at the factory where her older sister had been working since arriving the previous year. She worked there for two years, until she had her first son; two daughters and two sons followed every two years, for a total of five. As a mother, Mrs. Rodriguez stayed home taking care of her children, but she also took sewing jobs to help with expenses. Her husband, eight years her senior, worked first as a packer and later as a shipping manager in the same factory.

The couple raised their children in New York City. One son died in Vietnam, and the other two sons married; one stayed in New York and the other moved to Philadelphia. The younger daughter married and resided in New York City until moving with her family to Puerto Rico, where, as a child, she had spent many summers with her aunt. Mrs. Rodriguez's older daughter married and gave birth to three children in New York. As the older daughter and the one living closest, she became her parents' support, helping her mother take care of her father through two years of illness and later becoming her mother's caregiver.

Siblings, as well as aunts, uncles, and friends in New York and Puerto Rico, all had something to say or quietly disapproved when the older daughter began to raise the problem of mother's behavior and the possibility that she might need nursing home care. Only her brother, who lived in New York and saw the difficulties his sister was experiencing, understood that she was reaching her limit. Her sister in Puerto Rico had offered to take their mother to give her sister a rest, but their mother would always insist on returning to New York. This is what she had done when the daughter in Puerto Rico had taken her to live with her after their father died. The brothers explained that their work and family responsibilities made it impossible for them to take care of their mother. After much back and forth, in which no one could find a better way to manage mother's behavior, the siblings became more accepting of the reality, although they were unhappy with having to accept the need for placement.

On admission day the neatly dressed Mrs. Rodriguez seemed slightly restless but comfortable with the social worker who spoke with her in Spanish. Her daughter nervously tried to answer some questions asked of her mother, until the social worker explained that she needed to hear her mother's answers. When asked how old she was, Mrs. Rodriguez answered that she was forty-seven. To the social worker's remark about how well dressed and nice she looked, Mrs. Rodriguez replied that she always dressed nicely and also made sure that her children looked nice. She added that she also enjoyed cooking for them and made sure they ate well. Mrs. Rodriguez could not tell what day it was or when she was born, but she knew her daughter, granddaughter, and son-in-law, who had accompanied her to the nursing home. When asked if she knew why she was there, Mrs. Rodriguez explained that she had come to visit her daughter's friend. Her daughter's look said it all; she had not told her mother that she was coming to live in the nursing home. Almost in tears, her daughter explained that she had not said anything to her mother about coming to live in the facility; she did not want to upset her. The social worker must now consider how she is going to help the daughter explain to her mother the real reason for being there. She would also need to help Mrs. Rodriguez accept placement, and help both mother and daughter adjust to the separation.

Cultural expectations regarding family responsibilities play a major role in the interaction and feelings of family members prior to a family member's admission to a nursing home. They also affect the prospective resident's feelings toward admission, and the interaction between family members and between family and the resident after placement. Kolb (2003), reporting on the experiences of some of the residents admitted to Acacia Nursing Home, explained that Puerto Rican family members often had not discussed admission with the prospective resident before admission day. That is confirmed by my experience conducting admissions at a Brooklyn nursing home.

Reasons why Puerto Ricans avoid the issue may be explained by the complex nature of feelings involved in the admission decision. Although nursing home placement is generally sought only after caregivers have passed their level of endurance, after physical, emotional, and financial resources have been exhausted, the decision to place is usually arrived at with heavy guilt. Guilt is accompanied by a sense of failure and disappointment at not having met expectations, their own and those of the care recipient, family, and community. Compounding guilt and disappointment are the desire to keep a loved one close as long as possible, respect for the loved one and fear of hurting his or her feelings, the belief that no one can provide care as well, and the image of nursing homes as "dead-end places for discards." Denial, unwillingness to face the reality of the mental or physical deterioration that forces placement, also enters into the mix of feelings leading caregivers to refrain from addressing the issue with the person needing placement.

It is very likely, therefore, that persons considering placement have not discussed the issue with others in the family. Caregivers may fear judgment or may wish to safeguard themselves from the possibility that those who have not assumed major responsibilities for providing care may exert pressure to force them to continue beyond their capacity to meet the demands of caregiving.

This chapter should assist social workers to more effectively relate to Puerto Rican nursing home residents and their families by increasing their understanding of their clients' cultural background. It presents a synopsis of the history of Puerto Ricans in the United States, discusses cultural issues as they impact the interaction of residents and their families with nursing home staff and the environment, and considers implications of these background factors for social work intervention in nursing home facilities.

These cultural matters are generally not covered in the literature. Puerto Rican issues are usually subsumed under Hispanic or Latino topics, and the role and functions of social workers in nursing home facilities is minimally addressed. Much of this chapter is based on the author's ten years' experience as director of social services at a nursing home where 93 percent of residents were Puerto Rican.

In reading this chapter, it is important to remember that knowledge of a culture should not be used to create generalizations or prejudgments of individuals based on their ethnic or racial identity, for no population is homogeneous. Instead, the chapter intends to provide a starting point from which to develop an attitude of respect, insight, and appreciation for the value of another's culture in order to facilitate interaction leading to a more accurate assessment of and interventions for the individual.

DEMOGRAPHIC CHARACTERISTICS

SIZE AND LOCATION OF THE POPULATION

The Puerto Rican population in the mainland United States has been steadily increasing in the past decade, with 3.4 million counted in the 2000 U.S. census, an increase of 24.9 percent from the 2.7 million in 1990. The Puerto Rican population remains concentrated in the Northeast, with 60.9 percent residing mainly in New York, New Jersey, and Pennsylvania. In recent years, however, a significant number have been leaving New York City, where up to 80 percent of the population resided through past decades. Whether or not their home island's population is included, Puerto Ricans comprise the second largest Latino/Hispanic group in the U.S. Mexicans rank first with 20.6 million and Cubans third with 1.2 million. An additional 10 million Hispanics/Latinos from the Caribbean and Central and South America reside in the United States (Zalaquett 2004).

The U.S. Census 2000 found that 22.3 percent of stateside Puerto Ricans live in the South, with Florida, home to six hundred thousand, supplanting New Jersey as the state with the second largest concentration of Puerto Ricans. As indicated above, the Northeast, with 60.9 percent, continues to have the highest number of Puerto Ricans, whereas the lowest number resides throughout the Midwest (9.6 percent) and the West (7.2 percent). Regardless of the geographic region, 57 percent reside in urban areas (Puerto Rican Legal Defense and Education Fund [PRLDEF] 2004). The 2000 census also identified 3.6 million Puerto Ricans living on the home island. They, too, are U.S. citizens, free to move back and forth between Puerto Rico and any of the states. Interestingly, in contrast to those on the mainland, a higher number on the island, 71.2 percent, reside in cities (Abacci Atlas, 2004).

AGE OF THE POPULATION

Stateside Puerto Ricans are younger than the U.S. population at large with a median age of 29 compared to 35.6. They are also younger than Puerto Ricans on the island, where the median age is 32.1. In contrast to Mexicans, however, stateside Puerto Ricans are older; the median age for Mexicans is 24.7. And Cubans, with a median age of 42.7, are older than all the above, including the non-Latino U.S. population.

Regarding older adult cohorts, 6.6 percent of stateside Puerto Ricans are sixty-five years of age and older, which is almost half the proportion of older adults in the general population. At 11.2 percent, the number of Puerto Rican older adults on the home island comes closer to that of the U.S. general population. Considering other major Latino groups, Mexicans Americans, with 4 percent, have the lowest proportion in the aging category, and Cubans, with 22.6 percent, have the highest in contrast to other Latinos and the general U.S. population (PRLDEF, Latino Datanota 2004).

EDUCATIONAL LEVEL

Stateside Puerto Ricans lag behind the general population in educational achievement; 66.8 percent has completed high school compared to 84.4 percent of the total U.S. population. Fourteen percent of stateside Puerto Ricans has achieved a college degree or higher, whereas 26.7 percent of the general population has completed higher education. The educational comparison of stateside and island Puerto Ricans presents a mixed picture: fewer on the island, 59.9 percent, have graduated from high school, but a higher number than those in the states, 15.8 percent, completed a college degree or higher (PRLDEF 2004).

SOCIOECONOMIC STATUS

Among stateside Puerto Ricans, in 2000, the median household income was "$28, 738, with 18.2 percent earning incomes over $50,000 annually, while 24.2 percent were living below the poverty level. The higher income levels are attributed to the 19.5 percent of the population working in management and professional employment" (PRLDEF Latino Data Center, *Latino Data-nota*, May 2004). Compared to those on the home island, stateside Puerto Ricans enjoy better economic conditions. The median household income on the island is $14,412; only 5.3 percent of the population earns $50,000 or higher; and 44.6 percent are at the poverty level and unemployment is 12.7 percent (PRLDEF 2004)

These socioeconomic realities are important to keep in mind when working with Puerto Rican nursing home residents and their families. Low socioeconomic status means limited resources throughout one's life to meet housing, nutrition and health care needs. Physically it leads to diseases resulting from poor diet, unhealthy living conditions, and lack of preventive health care and prompt medical attention. Mentally and emotionally, it results in accumulated stress as the individual throughout life attempts to resolve problems and needs with scarce resources and the stigma of minority status.

Low socioeconomic status also translates into lack of personal resources to pay for assistance that supports informal caregiving for older adults living in the community. Support providing respite or other assistance reduces the caregiver's burden and may allow the care recipient to remain in the community. Lack of resources also limits access to alternatives to nursing home placement such as supportive housing, assisted living, and medical or social adult day care. Although Medicaid pays for adult medical day care, the number of such programs is limited, and those with limited resources may not be aware of such services. Home care is paid for by Medicaid as well, but the number of hours it covers often does not meet the need of those who manage to access the services. In short, the ability of persons to take advantage of these and other services is linked to their knowledge of services and procedures to obtain them, but this ability is often determined by socioeconomic status, which, in turn, may limit choices or access to better nursing home facilities.

HISTORY OF PUERTO RICANS IN THE UNITED STATES

THE PIONEERS

The earliest Puerto Ricans traveling to the continental United States arrived before 1898 and represented the intelligentsia, persons with distinguished achievements. Among these pioneers were Ramón Betances and Eugenio María de Hostos, leaders of the Puerto Rican independence movement; Lola Rodriguez, creator of the national anthem (*La Borinqueña*); and Santiago Iglésias, founder of the Socialist Party in Puerto Rico (Fitzpatrick 1987). Like more recent migrants, these settlers moved back and forth, to and from the island.

MIGRATION AFTER 1898

With the signing of the Treaty of Paris on December 10, 1898, Puerto Rico became a colony of the United States, a prize of the Spanish American War. Movement of Puerto Ricans to the United States began to increase soon after, and, by 1910, two thousand Puerto Ricans lived on the mainland, primarily in the northeastern part of the country (Rodriguez, Kolors, & Alers 1996). In 1917, as U.S. corporations were increasing their holdings in the sugar cane industry, an independence movement emerged on the island. When the United States entered World War I, the U.S. Congress voted to assign citizenship status to Puerto Ricans, but the legislation did not grant the population a voice in the U.S. Congress, even though military service became obligatory for all males living on the island. On returning from war, many Puerto Rican draftees settled in the continental U.S., mainly in New York, and citizenship status further served to encourage travel to the U.S. mainland.

Emigration continued to increase throughout the early twentieth century, and by 1930 the number of Puerto Ricans on the mainland had grown to more than forty-five thousand (Rodriguez et. al. 1996). Early arrivals were carpenters, bakers, bricklayers, house painters, and typesetters, but the core consisted of *tabaqueros*, "cigar makers." The *tabaqueros* were educated persons, not in the sense of schooling but in the knowledge they acquired as avid readers and participants in political and labor activity in Puerto Rico. They had formed the backbone and power of the labor movement that had taken root in Puerto Rico by 1915 (Colon 1991). These migrants held menial jobs, mainly in New York City, but also began "colonies" and organizations linked to their home towns that assisted the later Puerto Rican newcomers whose numbers grew exponentially after World War II.

THE FARM LABOR MOVEMENT—SPRINGBOARD TO MIGRATION

Throughout the 1940s, 1950s, and 1960s, the Farm Labor Program also served as a springboard for migration. At the end of the sugar cane cutting season in the island, thousands of Puerto Ricans migrated to the mainland each year to work in farmlands in eastern and central states. Often many remained, forming Puerto Rican communities near farmlands in such areas as Camden and Trenton, New Jersey; Detroit, Michigan; Long Island, New York; and others (Fitzpatrick 1987). Recognizing the needs of the growing Puerto Rican population in the eastern states, the governor of Puerto Rico, Luis Muñoz Marín, in 1948, established the Office of the Commonwealth of Puerto Rico in New York City, which supervised the Farm Labor Program and provided employment and social services, as well as documentation identifying Puerto Ricans as citizens. The agency also represented the general interests of Puerto Ricans in the society (Fitzpatrick 1987).

CURRENT MIGRATION TRENDS

Migration from the island mushroomed through the early fifties, the largest number arriving in 1952, when more than fifty-two thousand people moved to the continental U.S. (Rodriguez et. al. 1996). This pattern began to reverse in the sixties, and by 1969 more Puerto Ricans returned to the island than migrated to the mainland (Rodriguez et. al. 1996). Despite the reversed trend, by 1970 the number of Puerto Ricans in the continental U.S. had grown to approximately 1.4 million. Five years later that number had increased to 1.7 million (U.S. Commission on Civil Rights 1976). Reversed migration has decreased through recent decades so that, although Puerto Ricans continue to move regularly to and from the island, during the 1990s a larger number of people (111,336) left than returned to Puerto Rico (Falcon 2004). Approximately 8 percent of the island population migrated to the mainland in the past decade (Quintanilla 2004). And, as indicated above, under the section "Demographic Characteristics," there are currently almost as many Puerto Ricans on the mainland as in Puerto Rico. Unlike migrants in the 1950s and 1960s, however, current migrants have not concentrated in New York City but have spread throughout the nation.

Those leaving Puerto Rico in recent years are mainly young adults between the ages of fifteen and thirty-nine years of age, whereas people returning to the island are mostly in their fifties or older (Falcon 2004). Unlike the decades of the fifties and sixties, when migrants from Puerto Rico were largely unskilled laborers, recent migrants are largely professionals—doctors, nurses, teachers, or engineers, who leave the island because of low salaries. Many migrate in response to recruiting efforts by stateside institutions (Quintanilla 2004). Unlike migrants of the forties, fifties, and sixties, recent arrivals are more likely to speak English as well as Spanish.

ASSIMILATION VS. INTEGRATION

Most older Puerto Ricans today came to the mainland in the decades of the 1940s through the 1960s, a time when this society was still considered a "melting pot," and all immigrants were expected to relinquish their old customs, language, and traditions, and seek assimilation into the prevailing culture. But these immigrants came with the different dream of "making it" and returning to their island one day. They also resisted the underlying premise of the melting pot theory, feeling it was linked to a value judgment, the assumption that the immigrant's culture was of less worth. This theory also carried the expectation that immigrants would be eager to assume prevailing values, customs, and language in exchange for achieving the "American Dream." In the case of Puerto Ricans, Glazer and Moynihan (1964), who questioned the melting pot theory, concluded, in *Beyond the Melting Pot*, that "something new had been added to the New York scene—an ethnic group that would not assimilate to the same degree as others" (p. 100).

The resistance to assimilation had a price, for it left a psychological imprint on those who struggled to maintain their identity. Puerto Ricans of that period still remember their feelings and reactions to efforts by the prevailing culture to force their assimilation through schools, churches, and other institutions. Tactics used to force them to turn from their native culture involved disdainful, rejecting looks when they spoke Spanish in public, and ridicule of their way of dressing and the foods they ate and their customs and beliefs. Older Puerto Ricans in nursing homes, therefore, may not feel comfortable with people from the general population whose attitudes and behavior may remind them of past experiences.

Social workers must consider migration history in their psychosocial assessments of residents. A Puerto Rican who came to the states in the forties, fifties, and sixties carries memories related to their leaving the island and arriving, unable to speak English, in an alien and not very receptive culture. Later migrants arrived after trails had been set, organizations developed, and a larger Puerto Rican population had made the environment less alien. Current migrants are more likely to speak English as a second language and come to a multicultural society mainly as professionals. They also find children, grandchildren, and great-grandchildren who were born in the states to earlier Puerto Rican migrants and speak English and learned Spanish from their parents or when visiting relatives in Puerto Rico. The earlier arrivals call themselves Puerto Rican and bear the memories of growing up as members of a minority group in the U.S., but they may be more knowledgeable about how to negotiate government systems than their migrant forebears.

SAFEGUARDING NATIVE CULTURE

Many Puerto Ricans migrated to the mainland with a history of resisting U.S. control of the island, including the federal government's efforts to force Puerto Ricans on the island itself to assimilate. The federal government had attempted to change the language of the island by imposing English-only education in the schools. Its effort failed, and although some who migrated to the mainland may have followed the assimilationist trend of previous immigrants, the majority fought to maintain their cultural roots linked to the Spanish-speaking world.

Puerto Ricans' insistence on maintaining their own identity may have also been spurred by the racial prejudice they encountered, for Puerto Ricans are an amalgamation of the Taino Indians, the initial inhabitants of the island; the Europeans, Spaniards who had "conquered" the island; and the Africans whom the Spanish brought to carry on the work Indians had been doing before being almost decimated. Although Puerto Ricans came to the U.S. as citizens, they soon learned that there were different levels of citizenship, with preference for the Anglo Saxon. They had come to a society divided between black and white, with no room at either end for a racially mixed population. The rejection they experienced helped to galvanize their efforts to maintain ethnic identity.

Women, according to Altagracia Ortiz (1991), played the major role of transmitting and ensuring the survival of Puerto Rican culture and identity. In "Puertorriqueñas in New York City," she explained how the culture was maintained and transmitted throughout earlier migration years. She spoke of Lola Rodriguez de Tío's poetry in the 1890s, and of the waltzes of Manuel Tavares and Juan Morel Campos, as well as Luisa Capetillo, a reader in a tobacco factory in 1911 who encouraged workers to organize and oppose capitalistic oppression. She also credits to Pura Belpré, who, during the 1920s and 1930s, was the first Puerto Rican librarian and storyteller to introduce Hispanic culture to children in New York by dramatizing and publishing Puerto Rican folktales and short stories.

Ortiz added Josefina Silva de Cintrón to the roster of women transmitting culture; in the 1930s and 1940s, through her editorials in the journal *Artes y Letras*, the community was informed of cultural and social happenings. Also important to the movement was the first Puerto Rican nun to come to New

York, Sister Carmelita Marrero Zapata, who came in 1925, and from then to the early 1970s helped children and their families navigate their new environment. In the process, she was instrumental in such achievements as the development of Casita María, a settlement house in East Harlem that still provides social and educational services (Ortiz 1991).

By the 1970s, as reported in "Programs of Model Day Care Child Development Centers for Mexican Americans, Native Americans, and Puerto Ricans," Puerto Rican parents, many of whom had been born in the U.S. and spoke English at home, were sending their children to day care programs where a major goal was "to prepare children for the outside world by reinforcing their identity as Puerto Ricans and as individuals" (Cuadrado 1972, p. 30). The programs reinforced cultural pride, encouraged bilingualism, and ensured the transmission of traditions and values. This effort to reinforce values and traditions at an early age was a response to the observation that, in the 1960s and 1970s, many Puerto Rican youth were experiencing an identity crisis.

Preservation of culture and language was also strengthened by such organizations as ASPIRA. In addition to developing school clubs to promote Puerto Rican cultural values and leadership, ASPIRA won a lawsuit to force the New York City Board of Education to implement bilingual education in public schools.

Through decades of efforts by individuals, parents, and community organizations and agencies, the language and culture that the federal government had sought to eliminate in Puerto Rico survived to become a major component of today's sociopolitical panorama in this country. Morris (1995) concluded: "Through centuries of substantive and symbolic conflicts over such issues as language, education and political structure, Puerto Rico's identity has remained distinct, while adapting to the pressure placed upon it. Such resilience demonstrates that identity, while malleable, is also durable. Moreover it suggests that, contrary to commonly held assumptions, external pressures on collective identity may strengthen that identity rather than diminish it" (p. 1).

The historical persistence of native cultural patterns, including the resolution of problems through familial mutual support, suggests that Puerto Ricans will do everything possible to resolve caregiving needs within the family and will not readily arrive at the placement decision. Social workers should realize that the placement decision often comes only after the family has exhausted all financial and emotional resources, and, even then, still causes feelings of guilt and often accusations among family members that an elderly member is being abandoned. These conflicts should be addressed during the admission process and early period of residence in the nursing home. Guilt and disharmony that are not addressed may result in the resident receiving less effective family involvement during his or her stay in the nursing home. By supporting the use of native language and continued family involvement in the care of the nursing home resident, social workers can help decrease the pain of loss and separation.

CURRENT STATUS

As previously indicated, despite decades of living and working in the continental United States, and having arrived as citizens, major indicators show that the overall population remains near the bottom of the socioeconomic ladder, even when compared to other major Hispanic groups in the states.

Barry (1972) believes that the socioeconomic panorama for Puerto Ricans emerged years ago, stating, "By the 1960s, the large mass of Puerto Ricans found themselves trapped at the bottom of the system, their statistics on poverty surpassing even those of their black neighbors" (p. 20). He explains that this is because the community carries a double liability:

> When [these] Spanish speaking newcomers arrived in New York it did not occur to them that American whites would apply the black-white dichotomy to them. Nor did they wish to choose up sides in what seemed to them an inane battle; separation on color lines would not only split the Spanish speaking community; it would even split families. Thus they had the rather innocent belief that they would climb the economic ladder in New York City just as the earlier European immigrants had. Belatedly most discovered that they carried a double jeopardy: both that of being non-English speaking, like the Europeans, and that of color, like the blacks arriving at the same time. (p. 20)

IMPACT OF COLONIAL STATUS

Another issue impacting the status of Puerto Ricans in the United States is that the colonial power leaves a residue in the colonized population of feelings of powerlessness and dependence. This remains strong even though, in its political relationship with the U.S., Puerto Rico is defined as a commonwealth.

The colonial relationship can be better understood through the example of Vieques Island, where, in 1941, the U.S. Congress, through legislation (HR 3325 & HR 5412), took over the western part of this Puerto Rican island for naval use as a practice bombing range (Chronology of the U.S. Naval Base on Vieques 2001). People living in the area were forced to leave their land without compensation, and for sixty years the island continued to be bombed despite many deaths of inhabitants through accidents and environmental destruction. Finally, after decades of lobbying Congress and U.S. presidents, and of organized demonstrations and other efforts to galvanize support, the U.S., on May 1, 2003, acceded and banned the navy from using the island.

This success was due in great part to increased international involvement, which included not only demonstrations but incarceration of key U.S. Anglo and African American figures. That the navy was removed from western Vieques, but the area remains U.S. territory, says much about the power the U.S. holds in relation to Puerto Rico. Instead of returning it to Puerto Rico, the land was transferred to the federal Department of the Interior to be designated as a wilderness area closed to the public (*The New York Times* 2003).

Such control by the colonial power conditions the controlling group to feel superior and powerful while the colonized population is conditioned to see its status as inferior, dependent, and powerless. This concept of the colonized personality, initially advanced by Maldonado-Dennis (1972) in addressing the sociopolitical status of Puerto Ricans, may also help explain the socioeconomic status of the population on the mainland. It is low even in relation to other major Latino groups who arrived later with equal language difficulties and without citizenship status. Those conditioned to feel inferior, when functioning within a society in which they are controlled psychologically by a colonizing power, can be easily subjugated and maintained at the bottom of the socioeconomic ladder.

EPIDEMIOLOGICAL DATA

According to the National Center for Health Statistics, the health of Puerto Ricans is worse than that of other Hispanics (Puerto Ricans' Health Fares Worse Than Other U.S. Hispanics 2000 www.cdc.gov/nchs/releases/00factshispanic.htm). This conclusion was based on interviews conducted from 1992 to 1995, with additional data collected through 1997 for a national study, "Health Outcomes among Hispanic Subgroups." A total of 256,802 people were interviewed, including non-Hispanic whites, non-Hispanic blacks, Mexicans, Cubans, Puerto Ricans, and other Hispanics. Of the sample, 3,128 were Puerto Rican.

The report considered the level of activity limitations, self-reported feelings of health, number of days spent in bed because of illness, number of missed work or school days, number of visits to doctors, and days spent in hospitals. The Puerto Rican group had the highest percentage of persons reporting activity limitations (21 percent) compared to 15 percent of Cubans and Mexicans, and 14 percent of other Hispanics. Although 28 percent of Mexicans and Puerto Ricans reported excellent health, a higher percentage of

Puerto Ricans (18 percent) than other Hispanic groups indicated poor or fair health.

Crawford and Tennstedt (1996) compared late life disability in white, African American, and Puerto Rican older persons in Massachusetts, and they concluded that African Americans and Puerto Ricans are more likely to need long-term health care and social services because of their higher levels of disability. This author's study of residents at a Brooklyn nursing home further suggests that, because of their health status, Puerto Ricans may need nursing home placement at a younger age.

In the Brooklyn study, the most common disabling condition among Puerto Rican residents involved mental functioning. The majority (42 percent) had diagnosed memory and cognitive impairments that stemmed from a variety of causes and sometimes occurred together with other diagnosed conditions. Heart disease was the second most common illness, with 36 percent of the fifty patient charts showing it as the primary diagnosis. Other major illnesses were diabetes (22 percent), cardiovascular accidents (16 percent), and osteoarthritis (also 16 percent). Additional medical problems reported with less frequency were hypertension, cancer, osteomyelitis, asthma, renal failure, and seizures.

Impaired mental functioning (dementia) was the number one disability and leading cause of nursing home placement at the Brooklyn facility, confirming the report by the Alzheimer's Association that this brain disorder is the "looming but unrecognized public health crisis in Hispanic/Latino communities in the United States" (Alzheimer's Association 2004, p. 2). The problem is unrecognized because of two major factors among Hispanics, including Puerto Ricans: first, Hispanics/Latinos with dementia are less likely than non-Hispanics to see a physician and much less likely to use services of other health professionals; second, because of cultural issues, Puerto Ricans believe that diminishing memory and cognitive ability is a normal part of aging and so does not require medical attention. As previously indicated, out of respect for the elderly person and to save him or her from hurt and embarrassment, family members are unlikely to raise the issue with the individual when signs of a problem become apparent. Instead, usually a woman in the family cares for the person at home until emotional and other resources have been exhausted.

As for the ability of residents in the sample of persons residing in the nursing home during the 1980s to manage activities of daily living, 36 percent had a functioning disability index of 12 or higher, with indexes ranging from 6 to 23. Residents with an index of 12 or higher required varying levels of assistance with ambulation, bathing, dressing, and feeding, primarily because of poor mental functioning. These residents remained in the facility for an average of one year and ten months. The major reasons for discharge were hospitalization (44 percent) and death (37 percent). Only 19 percent of the residents were discharged back to the community. With changes in the Medicaid reimbursement formula, where level of payment is linked to level of care required, today's nursing home residents who are admitted for long-term care enter nursing homes in more debilitated conditions, remain for shorter periods, and more expire or require hospitalization soon after admission. By the time this author left the nursing home in 1993, admission was already becoming a revolving door. Between 1987 and 1996 Rhoades and Krauss (1997) found an older resident population and a 15 percent increase in the number of residents needing assistance with three or more activities of daily living.

CULTURAL CHARACTERISTICS IMPACTING THE NURSING HOME EXPERIENCE

This section addresses cultural traits related to expectations of self, family, and social interactions that play a major role in the way Puerto Rican nursing home residents and their families may react emotionally and experience life in a nursing home. These are key traits to consider when assessing and planning interventions with Puerto Rican residents and their families. Authors who have addressed the subject of Puerto Rican cultural values include Fitzpatrick (1987), Mizio (1974), Sanchez-Ayendez (1998)), and Garcia-Preto (2005).

Drawing upon relevant literature, as well as this author's professional and life experiences, it is apparent that Puerto Ricans generally hold dear the inherent value of the individual, and the honor and respect owed each person as demonstrated through *dignidad* (dignity), *personalismo* (developing a warm, caring relationship), *respeto* (respect), the importance of the family, and spirituality—the spiritual realm as more important than the material—related to *fatalismo*, a fatalistic attitude toward grief, and death and dying.

DIGNIDAD

Dignidad is "the belief in the innate worth and inner importance of the individual" (Mizio 1983, p. 218). As with many Puerto Rican cultural values, this belief is based on the Catholic/Christian heritage, which emphasizes that each individual is a child of God and has a spirit bestowed by the Creator that is destined for eternity. Each person, then, regardless of socioeconomic status or circumstance of birth, has immense value and should be measured not by material possessions but by his or her "personal qualities, uniqueness, goodness and integrity" (Mizio 1983, p. 218). When personal qualities are so valued, face to face interaction with free expression of warmth and caring is essential to effective social interaction. For Puerto Ricans, therefore, the degree to which *dignidad* is acknowledged in personal relationships greatly determines the level of comfort they feel in any environment and the degree to which they may be engaged in a helping relationship.

PERSONALISMO

Appreciating the concept of *personalismo* is key to understanding why Puerto Ricans prefer to seek support from informal systems, such as the family, church, friends, or local establishments, and seek assistance from formal sources only as a last resort. It also suggests a strategy that one may use to attract Puerto Ricans to social or health services. Ensuring that there are individuals at the service site that interact with them in a warm caring manner as "friends" will lead them to rate the service highly, consistently use it, and spread word of its excellence.

RESPETO

Because of the innate value of the individual, she or he is to be treated with respect or *respeto*. This not only entails expectations in interactions but also recognizing one's own worth and expressing it through self-development and behavior that earns the respect of others. Accordingly, *respeto* for self calls for the individual to behave with *dignidad,* demonstrating self-control of unacceptable behaviors, such as aggressiveness, and living up to responsibilities to the family as well as keeping ones' word, deferring to others, being cooperative and generous, and showing concern and empathy for the problems and feelings of others.

What is considered respectful behavior differs for females and males, and is hierarchical. A female is expected to show *dignidad* and self-respect by being passive, care-giving, long-suffering, and self-sacrificing. These qualities bar them from expressing emotions and releasing pressures created by problems and conflicts. The male is expected to be assertive, the provider and protector, the *macho* in control of the situation. He is to be shown unchallenged respect, and women's wishes are answered basically through coy approaches. The hierarchical nature of respect calls for the younger to be respectful to the older and everyone to be respectful to those in positions of authority.

Social workers in nursing homes should consider that repressed stress and emotions will be expressed in some way, often indirectly. Puerto Rican females may express feelings of stress and other emotions through psycho-somatic symptoms, complaining of ailments such as headaches, backaches, or stomach aches. Hence assisting Puerto Rican female residents requires staff to be especially alert to body language and to her experiences in the nursing home and with family relationships. Being alert to the residents will better prepare social workers to differentiate biological pain needing medical attention from psychosomatic symptoms that can feel as painful as organic problems but require the actual problem to be identified to bring about more in-depth relief. For example, "I have a stomach ache" could actually mean "the person who is supposed to help feed me is putting food into my mouth so fast and in such an unkindly way that eating has become a dreaded activity; I have a stomach ache."

With Puerto Rican males, social workers need to be aware that, even though throughout life males have been assertive and "macho," not to be challenged, in the nursing home the worker is an authority figure that even men cannot question. Men's dissatisfaction with something said or done to them might not be expressed as a challenge, but with silence and withdrawal. Hence developing a warm, caring relationship (*personalismo*) with residents, male or female, is essential. It is the way to gain trust and encourage residents to express themselves. The same caring respectful interactions should be developed with caregivers and other family members.

PUERTO RICAN NURSING HOME RESIDENTS

Because of the dearth of material about Puerto Ricans in nursing homes, the author developed some descriptive information while analyzing data from fifty case records of Puerto Rican residents discharged from a Brooklyn, New York, nursing home between 1977 and 1985. Residents ranged from forty-nine to eighty-nine years of age, with an average age of seventy-five. Forty-eight percent were widowed, 30 percent were separated, and 9 percent were divorced. There were an equal number of males and females. Only 9 percent were still married, and 4 percent had never married. Only one person in the group had reached a twelfth-grade education; generally their educational level was less than grade 6.

Information indicating length of time in the U.S. was available for only twenty of the residents, and the records indicated that they had been on the mainland from one month to sixty-two years and had an average residency period of thirty-two years. Because these data were based on only 40 percent of the sample, it should not be generalized even to the other 60 percent of the group, but it is offered to indicate how early in the century Puerto Ricans had been present in New York City; the resident who had lived there the longest arrived in 1914.

Regarding their capacity to communicate in English, only 20 percent spoke some English, and 12 percent were able to communicate in both Spanish and English. The great majority of the residents (68 percent) spoke only Spanish. However, even those residents who spoke some English generally communicated in Spanish, and, as their mental functioning deteriorated, they returned to their native language altogether. This tendency was also identified by Kolb (2003) in one of the few studies available including Puerto Rican nursing home residents: "some residents who had learned English as their second language had lost that knowledge because of short-term memory loss resulting from dementia, but their long-term memory retained the knowledge of Spanish learned early in life" (p. 113).

INFLUENCE OF CULTURAL REALITIES IN NURSING HOME SOCIAL WORK PRACTICE

As illustrated in the earlier description of Mrs. Rodriguez's admission, the decision-making process leading to admission and the events on admission day offer insight into cultural realities and family strengths and weaknesses that may affect the resident's life in the facility. This description can also stimulate ideas for interventions that may be required when assisting the resident and family following admission.

CULTURAL DISSONANCE IN CAREGIVING SYSTEMS

Although many facilities have started projects to make "nursing home culture" less depersonalized (culture change), the environment of care-giving institutions, whether hospitals or nursing homes, has generally been impersonal and driven by the constraints of time and tasks, with little attention to individual feelings or the emotional needs or reactions of residents. Social workers should understand that, for persons with a cultural base that emphasizes *dignidad, respeto, personalismo,* and *honor,* the culture of nursing homes usually is antagonistic to the behavior and treatment expected by Puerto Rican elders and their families. For Puerto Ricans entering an institution where there is no time or place for personal interaction or consideration for cultural sensitivities, the result can be severe discomfort, or, in extreme situations, culture shock.

The effect of such cultural dissonance on Puerto Ricans was clearly expressed by an elder participating in the Institute for Puerto Rican/ Hispanic Elderly (IPR/HE) focus groups in New York City (Bosch, Cuadrado, & Meyers 2002). In total shock, a resident described how, when visiting a friend in a hospital, he had passed a room where he saw a male aide washing a female patient. Perhaps if it had been a woman washing a man he would not have felt as shocked, as women are expected to be the caregivers (e.g., nurses, aides, etc.). Understandably for a Puerto Rican, he went on talking about how very disrespectful and shameful it was to have assigned a man to give personal care to a woman.

The Long Term Care Ombudsman Program reports that the major issue that states raised regarding nursing home care is insufficient staff and inadequate training. Both case mix and insufficient staff may impact the volume and types of complaints received by the program. Of the 201,053 complaints received nationwide in 1998, 82 percent were nursing home–related, and "the top five nursing home complaints were in categories involving poor resident care, lack of respect for residents and physical abuse" (Long Term Care Ombudsman Report 1998, p. 2).

Nursing home staff may feel too busy or overburdened to give personal or adequate attention to individual residents (Long Term Care Ombudsman Program Report 1998). In nursing homes that are not required to have staffing based on the ratio of staff to residents, administrators are more likely to focus on holding down costs than on recruiting sufficient, experienced, or culturally competent staff. Therefore, as in the hospital where a male aide was seen giving a female patient personal care, in nursing homes, too, state assignments may often ignore gender-related *verguenza* (shame). Haste and lack of regard for privacy also leads to shaming residents when disrobing, diapering, or bathing. Puerto Rican residents may not express their discomfort as clearly as the elders in the IPR/HE study, but treatment as that described leads them to feel robbed of feelings of self-worth. They also feel belittled and disrespected when shouted at, either when the person is expressing anger or expects that those with limited English ability will understand if one speaks loudly enough.

Residents equally experience the cold impersonal touch when they are fed, assisted with transferring, or helped with any other activities of daily living in a way that suggests they are objects, not persons, or when their calls for assistance are consistently ignored. Although feelings evoked by such treatment may be universal, instead of reacting in self-defense Puerto Ricans are more likely to react to cold impersonal treatment by burying themselves in silence and, ultimately, sinking into depression. Their need to maintain self-control and suppress or repress assertiveness or aggressiveness may also lead them to express emotional stress through psychosomatic symptoms (Garcia-Preto 1996, p. 186).

By understanding cultural sensitivities and nuances, culturally competent social workers help to ensure that nursing home staff, especially those providing direct care, are sensitized and trained to recognize feelings and expectations of Puerto Rican residents and their families. Social workers should use multidisciplinary care meetings, training sessions, and management meetings to add to the discussions of residents' cultural backgrounds relevant to decision making. Social workers should also model the caring, warm, respectful interaction with residents and their families that all staff should exhibit in the facility. And, when required, social workers should be cultural mediators between staff, residents, and their families, ensuring smoother, more effective interactions between them.

Sensitizing facility staff through training that includes role playing also helps them to develop empathy and consider the reality that they, too, may one day be in the same situation as the residents. Social workers additionally must educate and assist residents and their families to express themselves in productive ways when they feel their dignity and rights have been violated. Workers should be present on the floors as the main person in the facility designated by the state to ensure the protection of patients' rights. Such floor rounds should also serve to educate and model culturally sensitive behavior that other staff should emulate.

In addition to suffering when they are mistreated, Puerto Ricans' ingrained sense of compassion toward the misfortunes of others causes residents and their families to also feel deeply any mistreatment of others that they observe. Their emotional distress may be worsened by not feeling free to speak up or defend their rights. The respect they are taught toward authority figures may keep them from approaching supervisory or management staff to complain or advocate on their own behalf. It is important, therefore, for social workers to make the social service office a welcoming space where residents and their relatives feel free to express themselves. Workers should also facilitate communication by having meetings to bring together supervisors, management, and family members to ease, mediate, and encourage communication.

FACILITATING RESIDENTS' INTEGRATION INTO LIFE IN THE NURSING HOME

An individual's reaction to admission and life in a culturally clashing environment depends on various factors. Key among them are the individual's unique historical experiences related to their ethnic heritage, preadmission

and admission experiences, as well as resettlement experiences in the nursing home environment (Drachman and Ryan 1991; Drachman 1992; Kolb
2003).

Accordingly, each person's initial adjustment and experiences living in a
long-term care facility vary as a result of several factors leading to admission.
For the great majority of residents, however, life in the new nursing home
culture is facilitated by a factor related to *personalismo,* the presence of at least
one staff person who takes a personal interest in the newcomer and makes
an effort to make him or her feel at home. Kolb (2003) found this to be true
with Puerto Rican and other Latinas/os residing at Acacia Nursing Home,
and this author had the same experiences with Puerto Rican residents and
their families. Finding staff members to extend a warm, caring hand or word,
and take an interest in the well-being of the newcomer, certainly would make
life in the foreign environment of the facility less painful or lonely for the residents and their families. The social worker is the first person called on to
consciously strive to be the staff member who residents and family see as
their "friend," advocate, and protector.

CAREGIVING AND THE FAMILY AS CENTRAL VALUES

The family is generally the core that forms and supports the individual. In
Puerto Rican communities, families may extend vertically to include several
generations, and horizontally to embrace aunts, uncles, cousins, and even
padrinos or *madrinas* (godparents to the child, *compadres* to the child's parents). The importance of all these relationships in the formation of character
and identity is clearly described by Antonia Pantoja, labeled by Ramos as "a
leading figure in establishing the Puerto Rican community's place in regional
and national policy making" (Pantoja 2002, p. xi). To explain how her background influenced her later life, Pantoja dedicated the first chapter of her
autobiography, *Toward a Clear Identity,* to describing her mother, grandmother, grandfather, aunts, uncles, and godparents, and her relationships with
them and others in the town of her childhood. Clearly the concept advanced
by Hillary Clinton (1996), "It Takes a Village," has traditionally been the norm
in Puerto Rican culture. From this perspective, rearing children is not only a
parent's responsibility, but it is normal for children to be reared by aunts, sisters, or grandmothers when a parent is unable to rear her or his child.

Roles and expectations in Puerto Rican families have traditionally been
clearly delineated and hierarchical in nature. The father holds the central role
in a patriarchal structure where the male is the authority and takes the initiative in the family. As the authority, the male is not to be challenged or questioned by his wife or children; *es una falta de respeto,* it is very disrespectful

to do so. Traditional male roles include being protector and provider for the family, whereas female roles have emphasized caring for the home and maintaining family unity (Garcia-Preto 2005). Mother is the problem-solver, the healer, the peacemaker. The children's role is to be submissive to the parents and to bring pride to the family with their achievements. The oldest daughter, especially, is expected to help with the care of the younger children and with the care of parents in their old age. This has continued in practice, as indicated by a 1998 study of caregivers in Puerto Rico, in which 90 percent of the caregivers were daughters. The common response for providing care was summarized as "taking care of your elderly parents is primarily a woman's responsibility. Women are more reliable; sons do not help as much or in the same way" (Sanchez-Ayendez 1998, p. 78).

The family is the source of security and support for all its members; it is the first place for problem solving. The family, in turn, expects from each member loyalty, honor, and priority over individual wants and outside demands. In this dynamic process of give and take, *mami* serves as the magnet that maintains unity and reinforces love ties, organizing family gatherings and encouraging mutual support among members. She ensures that everyone is kept informed of how the others are doing and, when necessary, serves as the intermediary ensuring that communication is maintained if tensions develop between members. Mothers, as expressed by many participants in the IPR/HE focus groups, continue to worry and look after the needs of their offspring even when they are elderly (Bosch et al. 2002). They suffer their children's problems as their own, often sharing with them their meager incomes or housing, or assuming responsibility for their grandchildren.

Although parents do their best to continue to play central roles until late in life, it is also expected that, as they have loved and cared for their children throughout their life, children will love and care for parents who have become frail and sickly. This expectation of reciprocity remains strong in the Puerto Rican population despite changes forced on the family in recent decades. Families now are spread throughout Puerto Rico and several states on the mainland, and the expected caregivers, women, must now work outside the home because one salary can no longer support a family. Mutual support expectations, therefore, have become increasingly more difficult to meet. Regardless of the circumstances and challenges, however, family members still make a point of keeping in touch through visits, phone calls, letters, and, more recently, the Internet.

Despite limitations and strains of caregiving, Puerto Rican daughters, and, increasingly, sons, continue to provide care to parents for various reasons. One study found emotional attachment to be a key motivating factor. However, sons expressed filial responsibility as the main rationale more than daughters, stating "there was no limit to what they [sons] would do for their parents" (Delgado & Tennstedt 1997, p. 128). A sense of responsibility, taught since childhood, was named as the major motivating factor by women caregivers in Puerto Rico (Sanchez-Ayendez 1998). And comparing a small sample of Latinas, including Puerto Ricans, to African American daughters assisting mothers in a nursing home, Kolb (2000) found Latinas experienced filial responsibility as more linked to duty than did the African American daughters.

The Hernandez-Rivera family provides an example of the sense of responsibility and mutual support of Puerto Rican family members toward one another.

"TÍA"

Tía, a single female who never married lived, in her adult years, with her sister, her sister's husband, and their six children in Puerto Rico. She was an integral member of her sister's family, sharing in the financial and emotional investment of raising the children, a second mother in the household. When the family migrated to the mainland, she chose to stay on the island because her father was elderly and sickly. She felt she needed to stay with him despite her sorrow at losing what had been her core family. She took care of him, as well as her stepmother, until first he died and, years later, her stepmother expired. Tía was left living alone in the house and, with time, she also became elderly but managed well by herself for a long time until becoming very frail.

Tía is still able to walk to church every Sunday. Often a neighbor gives her a lift and another neighbor invites her every Sunday to lunch with his family. One brother brings her cooking products and whatever she needs. He also takes her clothes to wash in his house, makes sure she gets medical attention when she needs it, and generally checks in to make sure she is O.K. Another brother takes her to his house when she is sick and needs bed rest and nursing to recuperate from an illness. And from New York, the children to whom she was a second mother call her at least weekly. The oldest male flies annually to see her, and the oldest female employs a person to clean her house twice a week. It is also understood that when Tía can no longer live by herself she will come to live in New York with the oldest female. Here she will be cared for until she dies and is then buried with her sister.

As expressed by some members of the IPR/HE focus groups, not all elders experienced such support. Their children and other relatives did not seem very involved. These elders may have been able to function more independently, and their need for emotional support may not have been as obvious.

When asked about the support received, many explained that their children loved them but had their own families and work responsibilities. Although excuses offered were preceded by expressions of hurt feelings, these Puerto Rican elders still protected their children. They explained that they understood the complications of their children's lives and could not blame them for not visiting as often as they would like to see them. The excuses they gave for their children suggests that they did not want others to judge their children for what still is, in this culture, considered the sin and shame of ignoring or not sufficiently attending to a parent's emotional and physical needs.

IMPACT OF CULTURE ON THE NURSING HOME ADMISSION PROCESS

As explained by Puerto Rican families coming to the Brooklyn nursing home, the role that hospital discharge planners took in the admission process varied. It ranged from telling the family that the patient would be discharged to the first bed available in the nursing home, to the more professionally conscious planners who discussed the need for long-term care and the possibilities available, among them nursing home placement. Where the latter was considered necessary, the more client-centered discharge planner usually gave the relatives a list of possible nursing homes and suggested they visit before the transfer was processed.

Whether the role assumed by the hospital discharge planner was more directive or just provided information and assistance with the process of decision making, the caregiver could always point to someone else as taking the initiative. It helped to reassure the family and provide a rationale for placement. Thus it facilitated the culturally ingrained behavior of avoiding family confrontations or discussions considered disrespectful and hurtful to another's feelings.

This author's analysis of admission records at the Brooklyn nursing home suggests that caregivers could avoid facing the nursing home candidate and the rest of the family, as 51 percent of admissions were processed directly from hospitals. Although not ideal, discharge planners assumed leadership in explaining the need for institutional long-term care and aggressively processed placement.

There were cases, however, where admission was made directly from the community, and the person admitted was brought to the facility under false pretenses. The social worker then found it necessary to assist the caregiver with explaining to the person being admitted that he or she would be living in the nursing home. Generally that was followed by efforts to help both the person being admitted and the caregiver manage the intense feelings that admission elicits.

Whether admitting from the hospital or the community, following admission the social worker must focus on the resident and family, helping them to adjust to the facility. Given the importance of the family to Puerto Ricans, this may involve working with several people in addition to the main caregiver. Some family members are likely to visit the resident almost every day; some will probably alternate among themselves. In some cases, however, because of guilt or not wanting either to face the person they had placed or see the facility environment, a family member may stay away from the nursing home as long as possible. In any case, encouraging family members to continue their involvement is essential to helping the resident adjust to the facility and the family to make peace with the placement decision.

SPIRITUALITY

Puerto Ricans "emphasize values that pertain to the spirit and soul, as distinguished from physical nature, and are willing to sacrifice material satisfaction for spiritual goals" (Garcia-Preto 1996, p. 185). The concept is based on the Christian belief that the material is ephemeral, but the spiritual is everlasting. It also involves the expectation that completeness of life is achieved only in the spirit. The spiritual realm is also believed to have powerful forces of good and evil which are intrinsically involved in the affairs of the living. This view affects behavior in ways that vary from inspiring self-sacrifice for the good of others, to turning to spiritual methods in seeking relief from illness or misfortunes.

Self-sacrifice is exemplified by the story of a young man who married someone he considered "a nice quiet girl," obviously expecting to lead a happy normal family life. Early in the marriage they had their three children. His life, however, soon became one painful experience after another. As in many cases, during courtship he had not become aware of her mental illness. A few years into the marriage he became aware of her severe depression with psychotic episodes. It brought on aggressive attacks against him, periods of hospitalizations, and frightening events like driving off with the children and threatening an accident. As a result, he basically raised the children by himself while providing custodial care to his wife. Divorce would have been understandable and annulment even possible. However, he insisted on staying the course, explaining that he had made a vow before God "till death do us part" and his happiness awaited him in his eternal life.

The power Puerto Ricans assign to the spiritual realm is also evident in the tendency to seek physical and mental healing from prayer or spiritual healers, sometimes instead of or before going to doctors. Some will blame mental illness or misfortunes on an evil wish or *un trabajo* (a spell) and will seek release or protection through spiritual means.

FATALISMO

Their belief in the intrinsic involvement of the spiritual realm in the affairs of humans leads Puerto Ricans toward attitudes of *fatalismo*, the belief that in this life much of human affairs is beyond the control of the individual and that such affairs follow their own course. Acceptance of what exists, or *Que sera, sera* (Whatever will be, will be) and *Lo que Dios quiera*, (Whatever God wills) follows from this concept. It should be noted, however, that *fatalismo* does not promote closing oneself off from the world, letting the world pass by, or feeling there is nothing one can do. It also involves the belief that the individual comes to earth with a purpose and must develop the self and work toward fulfilling that purpose. Hence the concept *Si Dios quiere* (God willing) is usually accompanied by the adage *A Dios rogando y con el mazo dando* (To God praying and with the hammer pounding) and with *Dios dice ayúdate que Yo te ayudaré* (God helps those who help themselves). That spirit is evident in the dedication of parents often working under very difficult circumstances to ensure that their children get an education, which brings great pride and a sense of achievement.

Accordingly, *fatalismo* does not promote passivity but does encourage acceptance of aging, grief, illness, and death as part of the life cycle. Very often, therefore, the Puerto Rican nursing home resident will not mention that she or he cannot see or hear or does not feel well. Such deterioration is all considered a normal part of the body's process that must be suffered with acceptance and resignation.

The social worker must consider the importance of spirituality for the Puerto Rican nursing home resident in order to develop an accurate biopsychosocial assessment and select interventions that more appropriately address the source of the need or problem. Religious services, prayers, songs, and whatever reminds even the cognitively impaired of their traditional worshiping practices are key factors for maintaining residents' morale and involvement with life around them.

END-OF-LIFE DECISIONS AND BEREAVEMENT RITUALS

The emphasis on spirituality also influences Puerto Ricans' attitudes regarding end-of-life issues. Families may not feel comfortable talking to the resident about health care proxies or living wills, for fear that speaking of the possibility of illness, incapacity, or death might hurt the feelings of the resident or cause these events to materialize. In this author's work at the nursing home, however, when death was imminent, relatives were less likely to select life-prolonging measures, believing that existence in the spiritual realm is peaceful and pain free. After death occurs, the traditional Puerto Rican ritual is to help the soul of the departed in its travel toward God with "*el novenario.*" These are nine evenings following burial when relatives, neighbors, and friends gather to pray and talk about the loved one, and become, quite naturally, a short-term bereavement group. It is also a transitional period to life without the deceased. The practice generally continues on the island, but, given the hectic lives of the younger generation in the states, it has been slowly declining here.

The traditional need to gather following a loss, however, is an important part of healing. The social worker in the nursing home should consider that the death of a resident not only affects the family but also staff and other residents for whom the departed may have been a friend. Gathering all of them together for prayer, a memorial service, or discussion may be helpful.

IMPLICATIONS FOR SOCIAL WORK PRACTICE FROM THE BROOKLYN NURSING HOME STUDY

SOCIAL WORK ROLES

There were no resources defining the role of social workers in nursing homes when this author took the position of director of the Department of Social Services at a Brooklyn nursing home. It quickly became clear that, other than ensuring that beds were filled, admission papers completed, and institutional Medicaid in place, even the administrator and medical and nursing directors were unsure of the roles a social worker should have in the facility.

As a social worker, my primary goals included:

1. Develop an environment that was as warm, homey, and welcoming as a nursing home could be;
2. Empower residents and their families to feel free to express themselves, visit frequently, and have a voice in the affairs of the facility;
3. Develop staff to the point where they would be open to interacting with families in a positive non-defensive manner; and
4. Promote cultural sensitivity in order to ensure that the more common occurrences in the facility would be warm, caring treatment, with efforts at personal connection fitting the *personalismo* interaction pattern expected by Puerto Rican residents and families.

My initial assessment of the nursing home itself showed that some issues needed attention. Most of the residents were Puerto Rican, but most of the direct care providers were African Americans or immigrants from the West Indies. Although, supposedly to be welcoming to Spanish-speaking residents, the facility had been built following the Spanish architectural style, the general ambiance showed no extension of this concept in the interaction of staff with residents and families. It was obvious that the English-speaking staff resented hearing Spanish spoken. Many staff members also resented family members' efforts to be involved in providing care to their own family member or to assist other residents with the most minor tasks. For various reasons, moreover, some residents were not receiving visits from their families as frequently as expected or not at all.

For Spanish-speaking residents and their families, it was imperative that direct care providers welcome the language essential to the residents' identity, history, and, obviously, their ability to communicate. And for people who consider family a central part of their lives, it was essential to maintain family connections if residents and relatives were to experience the nursing home as a continuation of life and not a site for discards.

Some direct care providers stood out as kind, warm, and caring, and, despite the pressures of the job, took time to make personal connections. They also well understood the meaning of treating a person with dignity and respect. Obviously residents and their relatives sought them out even if not assigned to them. There were many workers, however, who urgently needed much sensitivity training.

There are some relatively simple ways of transforming an environment into one more comfortable to a cultural group. These include music through the public-address system, and decorations and food that are culturally appealing. It is also important and easy to ensure that residents' spiritual needs are met in their language and to encourage families to decorate their relatives' rooms with pictures of family, spiritual pictures, or objects residents were used to seeing at home.

Major efforts, however, are required when attempting to transform the *culture* of the environment. This calls for changing behaviors and touching the hearts, feelings, and attitudes of all involved. Social workers in nursing homes can observe and assess the environment, set goals, and develop plans to achieve them. It is a challenge, however, to modify the environment. Functioning under a medical model, as nursing homes have been required to do if they are to receive Medicaid reimbursement, means that social workers have no direct authority >relating to care providers in the facility. Nurses and aides are obviously under the authority of the director of nursing. They also readily respond to medical staff, as they are trained to follow doctors' orders.

Under these circumstances, the basic impediment to the efforts of social workers to transform the nursing home environment is clearly the directors' power to control other disciplines in the facility. Also, some direct care providers distrust social workers, feeling threatened by their presence on the floors. State codes regulating nursing home facilities add further difficulty to the ability of social workers to make changes. Even current regulations may list the provision of social work toward the bottom of the ladder, with less priority than activities staff. This tells administrators and directors in the facility that state regulatory agencies assign little value to social services. The ability of social workers to transform attitudes and thereby the nursing home environment, therefore, calls for strong reliance on the workers' skills, personality, and role-modeling ability. Social workers must earn the respect of administration and directors, as well as the respect and appreciation of direct care providers. Respect from the former involves demonstrating professional expertise and confidence in performing social work functions. Gaining respect and appreciation from direct care providers requires social workers to demonstrate the role they can play in assisting them to carry out their caregiving functions, especially in helping them to relate more smoothly to residents and their relatives. But this is no simple task, regardless of the expertise, confidence, and skills of social workers in cutting through the initial resistance to their active role in the facility.

I needed understanding, confidence, and patience when I set about gaining the respect and acceptance of direct service staff at the Brooklyn nursing home. I learned this early when I first attempted to train nurses and aides on the rights of nursing home residents. The atmosphere in the room was charged and antagonistic, clearly not conducive or receptive to training. The effort was cut short, and as they left I heard someone say, "Now our own aren't going to get any attention." The basis for their antagonism was their belief that this Puerto Rican social worker would only provide caring service to Puerto Rican residents. I was being prejudged from their own standpoint, which was far from my own professional training, cultural base, and personal attitude concerning each person's dignity and value. I determined that, to bring about change, I would need to address the concerns and attitudes of directors and staff, participate actively in the care of residents, organize and strengthen structures to empower residents and their relatives and ensure continuity of change, and establish meeting places to bring together residents, relatives, and staff to encourage friendlier interaction.

INTERVENTIONS

In my approach to bringing about change I dedicated myself to winning the trust of staff and to teaching by demonstrating behavior appropriate for treating and interacting with residents. It was important to spend considerable time on the floors speaking openly with residents and their families in Spanish, and giving kind and caring attention to Puerto Rican as well as non-Puerto Rican residents. This also involved going to randomly selected floors during lunchtime to ensure that those who were unable to feed themselves were receiving needed assistance. It was also important to feed residents with kindness regardless of their ethnic background. This was not only to demonstrate how to assist with feeding in a manner that made the resident happy about eating, but it was also to teach aides that there was nothing degrading about their work. In this area, my goals had been achieved when nursing staff began to take the initiative in calling the social services department when assistance was needed in dealing with a resident or when they felt a resident was not doing well and needed family involvement.

A Family Council, which had not been active, was revived, and with reminder letters and phone calls their meetings were well attended. The council sessions were bilingual, and I regularly spoke Spanish, encouraging relatives to express themselves in the language they felt most comfortable speaking. The major purpose of the council, in addition to educating and informing, was to connect family members to the facility structure, thus giving them a voice. After approximately a year of meeting with only family members, nursing representatives from each unit were invited to participate, and a non-threatening climate was provided where families and nursing staff spoke and listened to each other. Nursing staff would report to their department matters that could be improved or needs requiring attention, and they brought back information on progress made. The culmination of empowerment was when the council requested and gained a seat in the Board of Directors governing the facility.

My participation in the Resident Council and creation of a Resident-Relative Day celebration were also important. Resident-Relative Day was an all-day function conducted in the central atrium and involving every department in the facility. Lunch and entertainment were provided, with the dietary department offering a special ethnic meal, and other departments performing various entertainments based on the theme for the occasion. The first year of the Resident-Relative Day celebration, the Department of Social Services and the Family Council carried the bulk of the work involved, but thereafter everyone wanted to actively participate in organizing the day. It was an event that clearly demonstrated the interdependence of departments in achieving successful outcomes in service delivery. Most important, sending letters and making phone calls to relatives, especially those who were seldom or never seen, always brought about a healthy turnout of families, including children. Families were able to experience an atmosphere that was very different from what they expected in a nursing home, and this helped to lessen guilt feelings so that many continued visiting throughout the year.

Another annual activity was developed, mainly to offer Puerto Rican residents an important part of their culture, but it also further established rapport between social work and nursing staff. A day in the week of Thanksgiving was selected for a home-made meal for residents. The nurses and aides also enjoyed it. The social service department was turned into a buffet setting, and home-cooked Puerto Rican and typical American Thanksgiving food cooked at home by social work staff and others was presented. Puerto Rican residents were thrilled, because, although the kitchen tried to meet cultural tastes, residents recognized the difference between nursing home cooking and a home-cooked meal.

Another important activity as a social worker was to develop and provide training for staff workshops that included sensitivity training on such issues as: the need and significance of communicating in one's own language, the importance of providing care that reinforces the resident's sense of self-worth, treatment with dignity and respect, and appreciation and respect for differences between individuals.

I felt that my goal of developing cultural sensitivity was truly achieved, when, while visiting one of the floors, I observed an African American aide feeding two Spanish-speaking residents—spouses. I learned that she had brought them soup from her home—and not for the first time. This was the same aide who had made the comment in my first training suggesting that because of my ethnic background residents from other groups in the facility would not receive my attention.

In summary, the role of the social worker in providing sensitive, caring, culturally competent treatment to Puerto Rican residents in a nursing home involves not only the social worker's personal way of functioning but calls for ensuring that the overall environment of the facility is welcoming, respectful, and responsive to the needs of all residents and their families. The best way to do this, in my experience, is through the social worker's participation in multidisciplinary meetings, training, demonstrating appropriate behavior, advocating, and connecting all involved staff.

CONCLUSION

This chapter provides a starting point from which to develop an attitude of respect, insight, and appreciation for Puerto Rican history, culture, and diversity. This is important for social workers and other staff working with Puerto Rican elders and their relatives because it can contribute to culturally competent engagement, assessment, and interventions. Although I have provided a general foundation of knowledge, readers will need to add to this in order to improve cultural competence, especially by learning from Puerto Rican residents and their families. The information presented in this chapter should not be used to create generalizations or prejudgments of individuals based on their ethnic or racial identity.

My primary goals in my work in a Brooklyn nursing home, where the residents were primarily Puerto Rican, were to offer key examples of appropriate social work roles and interventions. My clients were the residents, relatives, interdisciplinary staff, and the very institution itself. My social work interventions included developing an environment in the facility that was as warm, homey, and welcoming as a nursing home could be; empowering residents and their families to feel free to express themselves and visit frequently, and have a voice in the affairs of the facility; developing staff so that service providers would be able to interact with families in a positive, non-defensive manner; and promoting cultural sensitivity in order to ensure that the facility provides warm, caring treatment, with efforts at personal connection fitting the *personalismo* interaction pattern expected by Puerto Rican residents and families.

As noted previously, social workers need to use every opportunity at multidisciplinary care meetings, training sessions, and management meetings to have discussion include issues related to residents' cultural backgrounds that should be considered in decision making. Social workers should also model the caring, warm, respectful interaction with residents and their families that all staff should exhibit in the facility. Sensitizing staff through training that includes role playing also helps staff to develop empathy.

When required, social workers should also be cultural mediators between staff, residents, and relatives. To do this and to provide other services in a culturally competent manner, social workers need to understand and respect that many Puerto Ricans hold dear the inherent value of the individual and the honor and respect owed each person, as demonstrated through *dignidad, respeto, personalismo,* the importance of the family, and spirituality, including the attitude of *fatalismo.*

Culturally competent service providers also need to understand the differences between Puerto Rican residents who migrated to the states in different periods of history, and the experiences of Puerto Ricans with the racial realities in the U.S. It is important to remember that historical resistance to discarding native cultural patterns, traditions that include resolving issues through familial mutual support, suggests that, generally, Puerto Ricans will attempt all possible options to resolve caregiving needs within the family and will not readily come to the placement decision. In reality, this decision is usually made with profound guilt and a feeling of failure and disappointment at not having met the expectations of the care recipient, the family, and the community. This family reaction calls for empathy among social workers and other staff, who need to recognize and understand the guilt and disappointment many family members experience and their wish to keep their loved one close as long as possible, as well as their fear of hurting the older person's feelings.

REFERENCES

Abacci Atlas (2004). Demographics of Puerto Rico. http://www.abacci.com/atlas/demography.asp?countryID=302.

Administration on Aging (2001). *Achieving cultural competence: A guidebook for providers of services to older Americans and their families.* U.S. Department of Health and Human Services: Washington D.C. www.aoa.dhhs.gov/minorityaccess/guidebook2001/into.html.

Babin, M. T. (1971). *The Puerto Ricans' spirit: Their history, life and culture.* New York: Macmillan.

Barry, D. (1972). *Urban poverty and New York City Mission Society.* New York: New York City Mission Society Report.

Bosch, I. (2001). Using transformative learning with diverse populations: Understanding the challenge of black Latinas. New York: Unpublished manuscript.

Bosch, I., Cuadrado, M., & Myer, S. (2002). The Hispanic elderly: Problems, support systems, experience with formal services, and factors in service settings they find appealing. New York: Institute for Puerto Rican/Hispanic Elderly. Unpublished manuscript.

Chronology of the U.S. Naval Base on Vieques (2001). www.xln-arts.com/Vieques/Chronology.html.

Clinton, H. (1996). *It takes a village.* New York: Simon & Schuster.

Colon, J. (1982). *A Puerto Rican in New York and other sketches.* New York: International.

Congress, E. (1994) The use of culturagrams to assess and empower culturally diverse families. *Families in Society: The Journal of Contemporary Human Services,* CEU Article No. 46, pp. 531–538.

Congress, E., & Johns, M. (1994). Cultural diversity and practice with older people. In I. Gutheil (Ed.), *Social work with older people,* pp. 65–84. New York: Fordham University Press.

Cuadrado, M. (1972). Bilingual early childhood services in the Puerto Rican community. In *Programs of model day care child development centers for Mexican Americans, Native Americans, and Puerto* Ricans, chap. 3. Washington, D.C.: Interstate Research Associates.

Cuadrado, M. (1998) Characteristics of Puerto Rican nursing home residents in Brooklyn nursing home. Unpublished manuscript.

Delgado, M. (1998). Puerto Rican elders and merchant establishments: Natural care-giving systems of simple businesses. In M. Delgado (Ed.), *Latino elders and the twenty-first century issues and challenges for culturally competent research and practice.* New York: Haworth.

Delgado, M., & Tennstedt, S. (1997). Puerto Rican sons as primary caregivers of elderly parents. *Social Work* 42 (2), 125–134.

Drachman, D. (1992). A stage of migration framework for service to immigrant populations. *Social Work* 37 (1), 68–72.

Falcon, A. (2004). *Puerto Ricans stateside 2000: A demographic overview.* New York: Puerto Rican Legal Defense and Education Fund.

Fitzpatrick, J. (1987). *Puerto Rican Americans: The meaning of migration to the mainland.* Englewood Cliffs, N.J.: Prentice Hall.

Fitzpatrick, J. (1996). *The stranger is our own*. Kansas City: Sheed & Ward.

Garcia-Preto, N. (1996). Puerto Rican families. In M. McGoldrick, J. Giordano, & J. Pearce (Eds.), *Ethnicity and family therapy*, pp. 183–199. New York: Guilford.

Garcia-Preto, N. (2005). Puerto Rican families. In M. McGoldrick, J. Giordano, & N. Garcia-Preto (Eds.), *Ethnicity and family therapy*, pp. 242–255. New York: Guilford.

Glazer, N., & Moynihan, D. (1964). *Beyond the melting pot*. Cambridge, Mass.: M.I.T. Press.

Harrington, C. (2001) Nursing facilities, staffing, residents and facility deficiencies, 1995 through 2001, University of California San Francisco, Department of Behavioral Sciences. Downloadable from National Citizens Coalition for Nursing Home Reform, www.nccnhr.org.

Karuza, J., et al. (1992). Oral status and resident well-being in a skilled nursing facility population. *The Gerontologist* 32 (1), 104–112.

Kolb, P. (1999). A stage of migration approach to understanding nursing home placement in Latino families. *Journal of Multicultural Social Work* 7 (3/4), 95–112.

Kolb, P. (2000). Continuing to care: Black and Latina daughters' assistance to their mothers in nursing homes, *Affilia* 15 (4), 502–525.

Kolb, P. (2003). *Caring for our elders: Multicultural experiences with nursing home placement*. New York: Columbia University Press.

Koss-Chioino, J. (1999) Depression among Puerto Rican women: Culture, etiology and diagnosis. *Hispanic Journal of Behavioral Sciences* 21 (3), 330–350.

Long Term Care Ombudsman Report (1998). With comparisons of national data for FY 1996–98. www.aoa.dhhs.gov/ltcombudsaman/98report/98finalreport.html.

Maldonado-Dennis, M. (1972). *Puerto Rico: A socio-historic interpretation*. New York: Random House.

Maldonado-Dennis, M. (1976). *The emigration dialectic: Puerto Rico and the USA*. New York: International.

Mann, E., & Salvo, J. (1984). Characteristics of new Hispanic immigrants to New York City: A comparison of Puerto Rican and non-Puerto Rican Hispanics. Presentation by the director and senior demographer of the NYC Department of City Planning to the Annual Meeting of the Population Association of America, Minneapolis, Minnesota.

Marino, J. (2004). The coming milestone in U.S. Puerto Rican relations. *Puerto Rico Herald*, February 20, 2006. Retrieved 8/9/2004 from www.puertorico-herald.org/isssues/2004/vol/ 8no808- en.shtml.

Mizio, E. (1983).The impact of macro systems on Puerto Rican families. In G. J. Powell (Ed.), *Psychosocial development of minority group children*, pp. 216–236. New York: Taylor & Francis.

Morris, N. (1995). *Puerto Rico: Culture, politics and identity*. Westport, Conn.: Praeger.

National Association of Social Workers—Massachusetts Chapter (2001). Nursing Home Social Work Practice Standards. Retrieved 9/5/2003 from www.naswma.org.

National Association of Social Workers (2001). *Standards for cultural competence in social work practice*. Washington D.C.: NASW.

National Association of Social Workers (2004). *Standards for palliative and end of life care*. Washington D.C.: NASW.

New York State Department of Health (1996). *New York State Health Rules and Regulations, Title 10, Nursing Homes Minimum Standards*. http://w3.health.state.ny.us/NYCR.

New York Times (2003). "Navy Leaves a Battered Island and Puerto Ricans Cheer," May 1, p. 1.

Ortiz, A. (1991). Puertorriqueñas in New York City. Comité de Noviembre Journal. New York: Institute for Puerto Rican Hispanic Elderly.

Pantoja, A. (2002). *Memoir of a visionary.* Houston: Arte Publico.

Puerto Rican Legal Defense and Education Fund (2004). Puerto Rican poverty rate still highest among Latinos nationally: Census data comparing US Puerto Ricans with Puerto Rico. New York, May 19, 2004, Press Release.

Puerto Rican Legal Defense and Education Fund [PRLDEF] (2004). Latinos in the United States and Puerto Rico. *Latino Datanota,* no.1 (May 2004).

Quintanilla, R. (2004) Puerto Rican migration to mainland nears milestone, *Batallion News* online. Retrieved 8/8/2004, from www.thebatt.com/news/2004/02/11/News.

Rhoades, J., & Krauss, N. MEPS Chartbook No. 3. Retrieved 10/10/2000, from www.meps.ahrq.gov/papers/chartbk3a.htm.

Rodriguez, C., Sanchez-Korrol, V., & Alers, J. (1996). The Puerto Rican struggle to survive in the United States. In C. Rodriguez & V. Sanchez-Korrol (Eds.)., *Historical perspectives on Puerto Rican survival in the United States,* pp. 1–10. Princeton, N.J.: Marcus Wiener.

Sanchez-Ayendez, M. (1991). Puerto Rican elderly women, shared meanings and informal supportive networks. In M. Hutter (Ed.), *The family experience: A reader in cultural diversity.* New York: Macmillan.

Sanchez-Ayendez, M. (1998). Middle-aged Puerto Rican women as primary caregivers to the elderly: A qualitative analysis. In M. Delgado (Ed.), *Latino elders and the twenty-first century: Issues and challenges for culturally competent research and practice,* pp. 75–97. New York: Haworth.

Tirrito, T., & Nathanson, I. (1994). Ethnic differences in caregiving: Adult daughters and elderly mothers. *Affilia* 9 (1), 71–84.

Tucker, K., et al. (2000). Self-reported prevalence and health correlates of functional limitation among Massachusetts elderly Puerto Rican, Dominicans and non-Hispanic White neighborhood comparison group. *Journals of Gerontology* 55A (2), m90–m97.

U.S. Civil Rights Commission (1976). *Puerto Ricans in the continental United States: An uncertain future.* Washington, D.C.: Office of Management-Publications Management Division.

Valle, R., Levkof, S. E., & Reynoso, H. (2000). Dementia, culture, and literacy: Different factors demand differential assessment. *Accord Newsletter* 6 (2), 1.

Vourlekis, B., Gelfand, D., & Greene, R. (1992). Psychosocial needs and care in nursing homes: Comparison of views of social workers and home administrators. *The Gerontologist* 32 (1), 113–119.

Zalaquett, C. P. (2004). Hoy demographics, who are we: Spanish/Hispanic/Latino? Census 2000, Retrieved 4/4/2004, from www.coedu.usf.edu/zalaquett/hoy/demographics.html.

RESOURCES

Organizations and Websites

Centro de Estudios Puertorriqueños. Hunter College, New York. www.centropr.org.
Friends & Relatives of Institutionalized Elderly (FRIA). www.fria.org.
Institute for Puerto Rican/Hispanic Elderly. e-mail: iprhe@aol.com.
NYC Department for the Aging Alzheimer's and Long Term Care Unit. www.nyc.gov/aging.

Conclusion

TOWARD CULTURALLY COMPETENT SOCIAL WORK PRACTICE

Patricia J. Kolb

The contributors to this book have provided information that is honest, important, sometimes disturbing, and always useful in advancing the dialogue about race, ethnicity, and social work practice. The information is consistent with the bio-psycho-social-spiritual orientation of social work and is supported by the interdisciplinary nature of gerontology.

Important themes that run throughout the book affect many older adults in all the groups. Families and individuals confronting the potential need for admission to a nursing home share the need for information and support. Social workers in hospitals, community agencies, nursing homes, and other settings are often called upon to help older adults and their relatives in need of these services. Furthermore, it is essential that older adults and their relatives in all groups are shown respect as individuals and effectively communicated with, perhaps through a translator or interpreter.

Important responsibilities are assumed by family members in all the groups discussed in this book, and the challenging and rewarding aspects of assisting older family members must be validated and supported by culturally competent service providers. However, along with shared experiences, the authors of these chapters have clearly identified differences in the experiences of people belonging to the various ethnic and racial groups discussed, and these include:

- Intergenerational relationships and traditional role expectations for each member of a family, including expectations related to care giving, age and gender, and intergenerational conflict
- Food, music, and recreational activities that residents were accustomed to prior to admission

- Immigration and migration histories
- Experiences related to prejudice and discrimination
- Attitudes toward formal services and institutional systems
- Cohort experiences, values, and beliefs
- Meanings associated with institutionalization
- Diversity of spiritual and religious beliefs and attitudes regarding religious institutions
- Attitudes regarding time
- Beliefs regarding mental and physical health and illnesses, particularly dementia, and treatment approaches
- Ways in which symptoms of illnesses are expressed
- Ethnic identity
- Attitudes regarding nursing homes and the meanings given to placement
- Morbidity and life expectancy
- Attitudes related to advance directives and end-of-life planning
- Cultural expectations related to personal care, including bathing, especially in relation to the gender of the person providing assistance
- Meanings related to nonverbal communication
- Relative emphasis on collectivistic versus individualistic orientations
- Socioeconomic status
- Educational backgrounds
- Emotional responses to placement
- Language proficiency

The social work profession is engaged in a process of researching, conceptualizing, and creating approaches for achieving cultural competence, ethnic sensitivity, and cultural sensitivity in our work. This field has made significant progress in these areas, but many obstacles still need to be overcome. For example, these terms are ambiguous; they mean different things to different people. Other obstacles involve the reluctance of many social workers to pay more than superficial attention to prejudice and discrimination and the ways these realities affect the lives of so many social work clients. The historic realities of prejudice and discrimination toward members of ethnic and racial groups in the United States are discussed in every chapter. Issues pertaining to race and ethnicity in the U.S. remain emotionally charged, and many people avoid open discussions regarding racial and ethnic relations and realities precisely because of the emotions that surface. Although it is understandable that one might wish to avoid the topic, doing so prevents us from becoming the best practitioners, teachers, or researchers that we can be. Because gerontological social workers need to understand individuals' experiences through all stages of their lives, we have excellent opportunities to learn about the multifaceted realities throughout life of people from diverse backgrounds and to share our knowledge of human behavior and our practice experiences.

Specific approaches for culturally competent practice with older adults and their families, and for work with administrative and interdisciplinary staff, have been discussed in relation to specific groups, but each approach, as noted, has wider applicability, and I recommend their use as interventions to be implemented in social work practice with older adults and their relatives in diverse racial and ethnic groups. These approaches include:

- Working with support groups of residents and relatives and educating participants about their rights in the nursing home
- Facilitating discussion and activity groups incorporating culturally significant activities, for example, traditional foods and music
- Organizing outings to ethnic restaurants or having food brought in that reflects residents' cultural backgrounds
- Collaborating with residents and relatives to improve the cultural sensitivity of interdisciplinary staff
- Facilitating participation of residents and relatives in care planning meetings, family councils, and resident councils
- Conducting multidisciplinary staff training to increase understanding of residents' cultural backgrounds so that staff is educated regarding interactions that may be supportive or may be contrary to a resident's cultural background
- Working with administrative and interdisciplinary staff, residents, and relatives to promote residents' autonomy and self-determination
- Working with administration and staff, residents, and relatives to develop "culture change" in nursing homes that addresses residents' needs and desires related to their racial or ethnic background, such as participation of relatives in care giving
- Acting as a "culture mediator" between residents and their relatives and interdisciplinary staff
- Recognizing the resilience and strengths of residents and relatives, and providing opportunities for residents to talk about their lives and express what will assist their adjustment to the nursing home and promote good quality of life

Index